EXPLORING ETHNIC DIVERSITY IN BURMA

D1717610

NIAS STUDIES IN ASIAN TOPICS

EXPLORING ETHNIC DIVERSITY IN BURMA

edited by Mikael Gravers

NIAS Studies in Asian Topics Series, 39
First published in 2007
by NIAS Press
NIAS – Nordic Institute of Asian Studies
Leifsgade 33, DK-2300 Copenhagen S, Denmark
tel (+45) 3532 9501 • fax (+45) 3532 9549
email: books@nias.ku.dk • website: www.nias.press.dk

British Library Cataloguing in Publication Data

Exploring ethnic diversity in Burma. - (NIAS studies in
Asian topics ; 39)
1.Ethnicity - Burma 2.Ethnicity - Burma - Religious aspects
3.Minorities - Burma
I.Gravers, Mikael
305.8'009591

ISBN-10: 87-91114-96-9
ISBN-13: 978-87-91114-96-0

Typeset by NIAS Press
Produced by SRM Production Services Sdn Bhd
Printed in Malaysia

Publication of this work was supported by a generous grant from
the Danish Research Council for Humanities.

CONTENTS

MAPS

FIGURES

PREFACE

Today, issues of ethnicity and ethnic identity are of global concern. This is especially so with regard to the nation-state, which in recent years has come under increased pressure – both from globalizing and from localizing processes. In Burma as in other countries there has been discussion about the role of ethnicity either as a source of conflicts (and constituting a threat to the nation-state) or as an essential element in democratic development. This is not a simple conundrum to resolve. However, it is the aim of this volume to take the analysis beyond such generalizations and probe into the complexity, the multiple voices and the historical dimensions of ethnic classification and identification in Burma.

It has not been possible to cover all ethnic groups or aspects of ethnicity in Burma/Myanmar in this volume. More than one third of Burma's population, estimated at about fifty million, belongs to ethnic minorities or, more precisely, to non-Burman ethnic groups; at least 100 different languages and dialects are spoken in the country. Moreover, this volume focuses on the major ethnic (minority) groups and their respective situations and representations, whereas the Burman angle is underrepresented. This, however, is not done out of disrespect but in part because scholarship is subjected to a division of labour that sometimes may inhibit a more holistic perspective and partly because it is impossible to cover all aspects of the complex ethnic situation in Burma within the covers of a single volume.

Paradoxically, the armed forces (*Tatmadaw*) and its ruling body, the State Peace and Development Council (SPDC), regard political claims based on ethnicity as a major problem for the stability of the state; in contrast, the non-Burman ethnic groups, particularly their elites, consider the lack of ethnic rights and democracy to be the main problem. In this contradiction, then, there is a basic agreement that ethnicity matters. However, while the political conflict in Burma has ethnic dimensions it is not caused by ethnicity and diversity as such. The multiple roots of the conflict are located in the complex historical development of Burma. In part this involved the politicized role of ethnicity (combined with nationalism) in the building of the post-colonial state.

Hence, the ongoing national constitutional convention, organized and controlled by the SPDC, is designed to maintain a unitary nation-state with a so-called 'disciplined democracy' under absolute military rule. The Constitutional Drafting National Convention has 1,074 delegates of whom 633 are from the non-Burman ethnic groups and those ethnic organizations that have entered into a ceasefire with the regime. Delegates are not allowed to discuss proposals other than those approved by the regime. Whereas the *Tatmadaw* considers ethnic federalism to be a relict from the colonial past or even a neocolonialist ploy aimed at fragmenting the Union of Burma, the opposition in exile has agreed upon a federal constitution based on the present states and divisions in order to secure both democracy and ethnic rights. As a crucial part of this proposal, the opposition alliance has agreed that local secession should not be an option in any new constitution.

Recently, the SPCD has changed the basis of their much-heralded ceasefire agreement with about 17 armed ethnic organizations, probably in order to strengthen control of the border areas. In mid-2005 two battalions of the Democratic Buddhist Karen Army (DKBA) were escorted to their headquarters in the Myaing Gyi Ngu monastery. Here, the DKBA's founder, the monk U Thuzana, told them that they were no longer soldiers, hence could not continue their practice of demanding supplies from Karen villagers. *Tatmadaw* donated 90 million Kyats to the DKBA, probably as compensation, whilst Burmese army units replaced DKBA troops in the area. Interestingly, U Thuzana has announced that he is no longer the leader of the DKBA. It is not unlikely that some in the DKBA will now cooperate with the Christian-dominated Karen National Union (KNU) – from which they split in 1994 – or stay neutral in the future. Much depends on the negotiations of a ceasefire between the SPDC and the KNU. But these negotiations seem to have halted after the removal of Khin Nyunt, the former Prime minister and head of military intelligence now under house arrest. He was the architect of the ceasefires.

Meanwhile, SPDC has moved to control a number of other ceasefire groups such as the New Mon State Party (NMSP) in southern Burma; its activities in Moulmein are now being investigated. The NMSP is discussing a withdrawal from the national convention, which could end their ceasefire.

Figure 0.1. Education is an urgent need in the refugee camps. Karen children
in a music school, Mae La Refugee Camp, Thailand. (Photo: M. Gravers)

In early 2005 the regime arrested ten prominent Shan leaders; among
these was Hkhun Htun Oo, chairman of the Shan Nationalities League
for Democracy. These leaders are now serving long prison sentences in
remote jails. In May 2005 the Shan State National Army broke the ceasefire
and joined forces with the Shan State Army South in response to forcible
disarmament. The situation in Kachin state is also precarious after a coup
and counter-coup within one of the two armed Kachin organizations, the
New Democratic Army – Kachin (NDA-K). Members of the NDA-K have
been ordered to disarm. Internal rifts caused by struggles to control the
natural resources of Kachin State also mar the main Kachin organization,
the Kachin Independence Organization. Likewise, the Kayah (Karenni) State
has recently seen fights between groups supported by the SPDC and the still
insurgent Kayan New Land Party, who were forced out of their territory.
The oldest Kayah organization, the Karenni National Progressive Party,
broke their ceasefire after a few months, while the third organization, the
Karenni National Peoples Liberation Front has maintained its ceasefire and
financed its activities from logging and tin mining. The political divisions

and uneven control of resources within Kayah state illustrate the problems faced with implementation of any new constitution. All ceasefire groups seem more or less frustrated with the constitutional convention as well as with the increased control by the *Tatmadaw*. The SPDC will not allow other armed organizations than the *Tatmadaw* in the new constitution. This complex situation, very briefly outlined above, could develop into a renewed and serious armed conflict.

A major problem that this volume does not cover is the drug trade, which has become an important part of Burma's declining economy. Burma produces and estimated 2,000 tons opium per annum and is a major producer of amphetamines as well. Money earned from the trade in heroin and amphetamines is laundered in hotels and businesses run by the military and their relatives. In 1989, the Communist Party of Burma (CPB) lost it support from China and after an internal conflict the movement fragmented into four ethnic armies. About 80 per cent of the CPB soldiers were from the Wa ethnic group and formed The United Wa State Army of the Wa ethnic group, the largest ceasefire army, is deeply involved in the drug trade of amphetamines and heroin.

The humanitarian situation in the minority areas is deteriorating. In eastern Burma there are between 600,000 and one million internally displaced persons plus some two million Burmese refugees and migrant workers in Thailand. Livelihood, health and human rights are nearly non-existent for too many. It is not surprising, then that the present times are seen as the *kala yuga* – 'the dark age' as defined in Hindu and Buddhist cosmology – by many both within Burma and in exile.

Religion is an important dimension of the conflicts in Burma. According to the journal *Irrawaddy* (12 September 2005), the SPDC has closed several Christian churches after they had received many Buddhist converts; Burmese troops continue to demolish Christian crosses in Chin State. Muslims also encounter widespread discrimination and violence. Mosques have been attacked and burned by mobs led by bogus monks and Muslims are at the bottom of the social hierarchy. The Muslim Rohingya in Arakan State are not recognized as an ethnic group by the SPDC and but rather are labelled as 'illegal immigrants'. Muslims who have been living in Karen State classify themselves as 'Karen Muslims' – many speak Karen – in order to delineate an ethnic boundary that signifies an alliance and asserts a non-Burman identity.

Figure 0.2. 'Karen Muslims' in front of the EU office in Mae La. (Photo: M. Gravers)

Religion is thus developing into an important ingredient of collective identification. However, this does not mean that ethnicity and ethnic boundaries will disappear or be subsumed under a single Myanmar identity (as is imagined by the SPCD and its supporters); rather they will change and become encompassed within larger ethnic and/or religious communities. That said, ethnic or religious identification does not mean that there is little or no identification with a common country and state of Burma/Myanmar. On the contrary, this identification seems to be widening as the concerns increase about the country's future and despite disagreements on what political course is to be followed.

In the refuge camps in Thailand there exists a mixture of hope and despair amongst the estimated 150,000 refugees. A general fear of eviction by the Thai authorities is an ever-present reality. Those who have spent a lifetime in camps are becoming impatient and want to see fundamental changes. Moreover, there are also serious worries about loss of culture and language. On the other hand, some young refugees are obtaining globalized knowledge in the form of English and IT skills and are often better informed about the international situation than some of their cousins remaining relatively isolated inside Burma. There have been confrontations in the exile communities between 'hardliners' and those wanting a drastic change of the current political strategy; the latter want to see an immediate end to the long conflict. Meanwhile, the Burmese diasporas are rapidly growing and dispersing beyond the immediate region. They have also reached as far as Denmark where recently I spotted the flag of the Karen National Union in a peaceful demonstration staged by immigrants.

Control of the media and flows of information is total in Burma; this is a major mechanism used by the SPDC to stay in power, namely, a strategy of isolation. However, this strategy has wider repercussions because both regime and the population are equally deprived of reflexive discussion and interpretation of information from the international community. This is could be a serious obstacle to democratization, not least because the social space becomes inundated by rumours including negative views of ethnic claims.

As this book goes to print, the Burmese army is engaged in a major ethnic cleansing in the northern and western Karen State. More than 10,000 Karen have been driven from their villages and are now arriving in camps in Thailand. Villages and fields are burnt. The operation is believed to be related to the security around the new capital Pyinmana, the new strong hole of the army and SPDC.

Ethnicity is increasingly developing into new hybrid forms influenced by diaspora communities. Globalization of ethnic classifications and identity also has an impact inside Burma despite the relative isolation. The distinction between ethnic organizations as liberation and democratic forces versus terrorist groups has been narrowed and blurred since 9/11. Ethnic identity and space are constantly being contested, redefined and reorganized in the political landscape. Thus, it is important to relay the diversity of ethnicity and its profound changes in Burma. Hopefully, this volume may contribute to the debate on these crucial issues.

ACKNOWLEDGEMENTS

The publication of this volume was made possible by a generous grant from the Danish Research Council for Humanities. Five of the chapters in this volume are revised versions of papers originally presented at the International Burma Studies Conference in Gothenburg, Sweden, in September 2002. Some of these were read at the ethnicity panel in the conference. Unfortunately, two other participants in the panel who contributed with valuable papers did not have time to work on their papers for the inclusion in this volume. The conference became an extremely important and memorable occasion for Burma scholars courtesy of the meticulous preparations by Gustaaf Houtman in cooperation with Per Lindberg and the staff from the Department of Anthropology, Gothenburg University. They provided the perfect and friendly environment for the conference. The contributors to this volume owe their warm thanks to the organizers. The conference revealed that a new generation of talented scholars is gradually taking over from the pioneering generation and that the amount of field research undertaken in Burma has increased over the past decade despite the difficult circumstances.

We are most grateful for the detailed and valuable comments, critique and suggestions provided by the two anonymous readers who reviewed the manuscript for NIAS Press. The editor of the volume would like to thank Gerald Jackson, Editor in Chief of NIAS Press, for his unwavering confidence in the project, and Senior Editor Leena Höskuldsson, also of NIAS Press, for her active and professional engagement in the production phase. My thanks, too, go to Martin Demant Frederiksen who meticulously standardized the contributors' manuscripts and Hanne Elsnab who keyed in the copy-editor's corrections with skill. And last but not least, I am grateful to the contributors for their efforts, patience and advice, and in particular to Sandra Dudley and F.K.L. Chit Hlaing for joining the project at such very short notice. Due to these efforts, the book has developed into a being relatively diverse yet coherent volume.

Mikael Gravers

CONTRIBUTORS

F. K. L. Chit Hlaing (F. K. Lehman) is a Professor of Anthropology, Linguistics and Cognitive Science at the University of Illinois, USA. He was brought up in Burma near the China border, in a gem-trading family. He came to United States in 1941 and after World War II entered university for a degree in mathematics and physics. He took his Ph.D. in anthropology and linguistics at Columbia University in 1959, with a thesis on Indian civilization. Since then, he has done ethnographic and linguistic fieldwork in Burma, Thailand, India and China, among the Chin and Mizo peoples, the Kayah, the Shan, the Wa and the Burmans. Most recently, in 2003, he conducted field research on the multi-ethnic China-Burma cross border trade. He has published many papers on these matters as well as two monographs (on the Chin and on the Kayah). He was the first President of the Burma Studies Foundation

Karin Dean's academic interest and background are borderland studies in political geography. Her Ph.D. research for the Department of Geography at the National University of Singapore focused on the spatialization of the Kachin nation into Burma, China and India. Based in Bangkok, she currently reports and writes on the various issues relating to the Sino-Burmese, Indian-Burmese and Thai-Burmese boundaries and the ethnic nationalities of Burma.

Sandra Dudley is a social anthropologist who has conducted long-term field research with and taught English to Karenni refugees in Thailand, for part of this period acting as cultural consultant to the International Rescue Committee during the large-scale influx of Kayah refugees from the Shadaw area of Karenni (Kayah) State. She completed her PhD on the Karenni at the University of Oxford in 2000. She has interests in and has written on ethnicity, nationalism, exile, culture and material culture, and museums. Recent publications include Dell, E. & Dudley, S. (eds) 2003, *Textiles from Burma*, Philip Wilson Publishers.

Contributors

Sandra Dudley has worked at the University of Oxford's Queen Elizabeth House and for many years at Oxford's Pitt Rivers Museum, and is currently Lecturer in Interpretive Studies in the Department of Museum Studies, University of Leicester.

Mikael Gravers is an Associate Professor in the Department of Anthropology & Ethnography, Aarhus University, Denmark. He has studied the Karen in Thailand and Burma since 1970 and written on subjects such as nationalism, ethnicity, religion, environmental strategies, and religious movements. 1999–2001 he was head of the anthropological section of the Thai-Danish interdisciplinary research project Forest and People in Thailand and conducted research in villages near Doi Inthanon. In 1994, 1997 he worked in Vietnam among the ethnic minorities in the Central Highland. From 1999 to 2001 he was a member of the Danish Research Council for Development Studies. In 1996 he received a grant from HRH Crown Price Frederik's fund. He has published *Nationalism as Political Paranoia in Burma. An Essay on the Historical Practice of Power. Curzon.1999. (Second edition, revised and enlarged).*

Mandy Sadan studied History at Lincoln College, Oxford University and Art and Archaeology at SOAS, London University. In 2005 she completed her doctorate in history at SOAS, in which she considers the impact of the colonial and post-colonial state on ethnic category formation in Burma. Her doctoral work was funded by the Arts & Humanities Research Board, UK. She has research interests in the way that visual and material cultures contribute to the formation of complex ethnic categories in state systems and the impact of national histories on minority representations. In 1993–94 she worked as Research Fellow on a project considering aspects of cultural change in Arunachal Pradesh at SOAS and is presently working on an AHRB funded project which considers the construction of historical visual representations of Tibet, based in the Photograph Collections at the Pitt Rivers Museum, Oxford University. She lived in Burma from 1996–99, where she initially worked for the British Council but subsequently spent most time working on archive digitisation and documentation projects with local Kachin community groups in collaboration with the Green Centre for World Art at Brighton Museum, UK. Her primary research focus is on Kachin identity formation and to pursue this she has engaged in extensive archival studies in the UK as well as making a detailed study of Jinghpaw ritual language in Kachin State.

Lian H. Sakhong is General Secretary of the Chin National League for Democracy (Exile) and General Secretary of the United Nationalities League for Democracy (Liberated Areas), an umbrella political organization for all the non-Burman ethnic nationalities in Burma. He was a post-graduate student at Rangoon University when the student-led democracy movement erupted in 1988. He quickly joined the movement, and was arrested and interrogated on three separate occasions between 1988 and 1990. In 1991, he was forced to flee from his homeland and finally resettled in Sweden as a political refugee. While in exile, he persued his further study and earned his Ph.D. from Uppsala University in 2000. He has published extensively on Chin history and traditions and onpolitics in Burma, including his book *In Search of Chin Identity: A Study in Religion, Politics and Ethnic Identity in Burma* (Copenhagen: Nordic Institute of Asian Studies, 2003). Since 1999, he has edited a series of ten books on Minority Issues and Ethnic Politics in Burma under the title of *Peaceful Coexistence: Towards a Federal Union of Burma.*

Ashley South is an independent writer and consultant, specialising in ethnic politics and civil society, displacement, and humanitarian issues in Burma. Recent consultancies include updating the Global IDP Database *Burma Profile*, and co-writing a report on *Foreign Aid and Post-Ceasefire Reconstruction in Myanmar/ Burma* for the International Crisis Group. He is the author of a political history of lower Burma: *Mon Nationalism and Civil War in Burma: The Golden Sheldrake* (RoutledgeCurzon 2003). After an MSc in Asian Politics at SOAS in 2001, he returned to Thailand to run a major border-based relief operation and has visited Burma about 70 times since 1991. He lived and worked along the Thailand–Burma border in 1991–97, first as a teacher, and later as a field coordinator for a consortium of international aid agencies and was – from 1994 to 1997 – responsible for providing humanitarian assistance to several Mon and Karen refugee camps along the border.

In 2003–2004, he and his wife Bellay conducted independent research on displacement in Burma, with a Writing and Research Grant from the John D. and Catherine T. MacArthur Foundation. Some of their findings will be included in a forthcoming report for Human Rights Watch. He is the author of *The Golden Sheldrake: Mon Nationalism and Civil War in Burma* (Curzon 2002) and has published August 2004 issue of 'Contemporary South-East Asia' (ISEAS Singapore University), and various other journal articles.

Takatani Michio is Professor at the Graduate School of Integrated Arts and Sciences, Faculty of Integrated Arts and Sciences, Hiroshima University. His field of specialization is social and cultural anthropology. He is a Master of Arts in Sociology (University of Tokyo). He has conducted field work in Myanmar (Burma), continually from 1983 to the present, and was a Visiting Scholar at Universities' Historical Research Centre, Myanmar (1996–1997). He is presently focusing on ethnological studies on Shan cultural area and anthropological studies of inter-ethnic relationships between the Bamar (Burman)and the Shan. He is the author of 'An Anthropological Analysis of Burmanization of the Shan' (1998), *Anthropological Study of Tourism in Myanmar* (in Japanese) 1999, 'Spirit Worship in Northern Shan State' (1999), 'Shan Construction of Knowledge' (2003).

ABBREVIATIONS

AFPFL	Anti-Facist People's Freedom League
ARMA	All Ramanya Mon Association
BIA	Burma Independence Army
BKNA	Burma Karen National Association
BLC	Burma Lawyers Council
BMM	The Baptist Missionary Magazine
BSPP	Burma Socialist Programme Party
CCOC	Chin for Christ in One Century
CHBA	Chin Hills Baptist Association
CPB	Communist Party of Burma
DKBA	Democratic Buddhist Karen Army
DKBO	Democratic Buddhist Karen Organization
ENSCC	Ethnic Nationalities Solidarity and Cooperation Committee (now Ethnic Nationalities Council, ENC)
FAA	Frontier Area Administration
FACE	Frontier Area Commission Enquiries
GUBSS	Gazetteers of Upper Burma and Shan States
HMYD	Hmannan Maha Yazawin Daw
HRFM	Human Right Foundation of Monland
HRP	Hongsawatoi restoration Party
IDP	Internally Displaced Persons
INGO	International Non-Governmental Organization
IRC	International Rescue Committee
KBC	Kachin Baptist Convention

KCO	Karen Central Organization
KIA	Kachin Independence Army
KIO	Kachin Independence Organization
KNA	Karen National Association
KNDO	Karen National Defense Organization
KNL	Karen National League
KNLA	Karen National Liberation Army
KNPLF	Karenni National Peoples Liberation Front
KNPP	Karenni National Peoples Party
KNRA	Karenni National Resistance Army
KNU	Karen National Union
KRNRC	Karenni Resistant National Development Council
KTC	Kachin Theological College
KYO	Karen Youth Organization
MLCC	Mon Literature and Culture Committee
MNDF	Mon National Democratic Front
MWO	Mon Women Organization
MYO	Mon Youth Organization
NDA-K	New Democratic Army – Kachin
NLD	National League for Democracy
NMSP	New Mon State Party
OIOC	Oriental and India Office Collections
PVO	People Volunteer Organization
SLORC	State Law and Order Council
SPDC	State Peace and Development Council
UKL	United Karen League
UKO	Union Karen organization
UNLD	United National League for Democracy
USDA	Union Solidarity Development Association
YMCA	Young Men's Christian Association

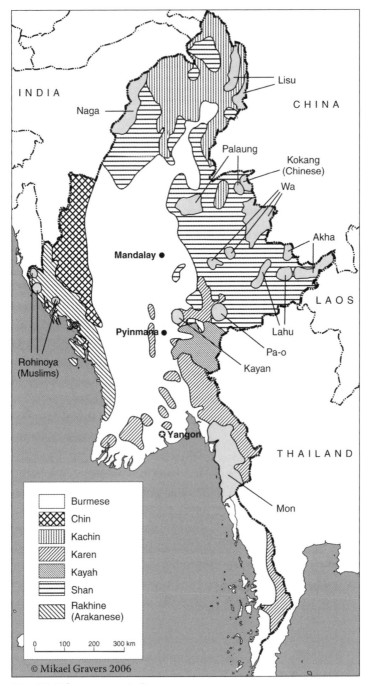

Map 0.1. Ethnic groups in Burma

Chapter 1

INTRODUCTION:
ETHNICITY AGAINST STATE – STATE
AGAINST ETHNIC DIVERSITY?

Mikael Gravers

THEORETICAL PRELUDE

Ethnicity is one of the main ingredients and sources of cultural and political identification in the present world order. Ethnicity in its present forms is closely related to the modern development of nation states. However, it is also considered a source of conflicts and violence and one could often wish that ethnicity would altogether disappear from the political agenda, for example in Burma/Myanmar, a country long mired in ethno-nationalism and related conflicts and violence. Perhaps we should let ethnicity rest and concentrate on the development of democracy in Burma? Will the phenomenon of ethnicity perhaps disappear, as Eric Hobsbawn (1990: 183) predicted of nationalism, citing Hegel: 'The owl of Minerva which brings wisdom, flies out at dusk. It is a good sign that it is now circling round nations and nationalism.' However, such evolution is a distant utopia and hardly realistic in the near future because ethnicity, nationalism and democracy are deeply intertwined in the present global order and in the history of Burma as well. Ethnicity has been ingrained as a criterion of identification and of political legitimacy in modern societies for too long to vanish completely. Whereas ethnicity is often imagined and presented in primordialist terms and can claim a long history, it is also a high modern designation and imagination of how a nation state is identified or resisted and dissolved. Basically, ethnic modernity is involved in a struggle between representations of identity and rights (cultural, territorial, civil).

Moreover, ethnicity is not merely a political mode of identification, locally and globally, but an essential part of the way people imagine their place in the world and the way they reflect upon and sense their position. Ethnic belonging is existentially important in national and trans-national contexts. It is, in many instances, made synonymous with a nation and refers to the same criteria: a named population, historic territory, myths, culture and historical memory.[1] Recently, the term 'ethnic nationality' has been adopted by ethnic organizations from Burma in exile. National identity has become 'ethnified' – and vice versa – in a global process. However, ethnic identity often involves visions of being embodied, bounded and rooted in a different and deeper way than a more abstractly conceived national identity. Ethnicity is thus an important source of self-identification, solidarity and empowerment in terms of belonging to a community and to a common culture and history – a source reinforced by migration and displacement. It involves our feelings of certainty (or the givens) versus alien and unpredictable environments. In other words, ethnicity is also of high emotional significance to the populations and individuals concerned – a dimension that is difficult to assess fully because the political dimension, its discourse and simplifying rhetoric often determine identity and its representations. It is, I suggest, part of a modernist cosmology, which can encompass both the past and the present, primordial as well as utopian imaginations. This property accounts for its global prevalence – yet it does not explain why ethnicity becomes engulfed in violent conflicts in some but not all states. In order to analyse this we need detailed and empirically well-founded studies, which will take us beyond universalistic explanations of ethnic and nationalist violence.[2]

The contributors to this volume aim at striking the difficult balance of being sensitive to the subjective as well as to the objective sides of the process while critically reflecting upon both sides. However, any study of ethnicity will inevitably become part of the struggle of representations, its modes and classifications, which are also part of our study.[3] In particular, the role of ethnic classification whether by missionaries, officials or scientists, is important to assess historically. In doing so we must also reflect upon the scientific naming of our concepts and notions and their influence on the historical process. All parties have contributed to the process of classification and to the ubiquity of the phenomenon naming 'races', 'hill tribes', 'frontier peoples', 'minorities', and more recently 'ethnic groups'; after all, ethnicity is a modern designation and the term appeared in the dictionaries only in the 1950s and 1960s (cf. Barth 1969). Today, representatives from ethnic groups in former colonies, including Burma, will scrutinize old ethnographies, and perhaps our texts, in search of identity and difference (Sakhong, chapter 8 in this volume). Some will agree while others may react furiously when their vision appears to be deconstructed and annulled by powerful or insensitive others. In our research, we are encouraged to the probe into ethnic diversity in all its shades and shapes, while they desperately search for a primordial ethnic essence in order to uphold a legitimate representation of their cultural and political claims. To write about ethnicity is to enter the political field of ethnic difference at its core where it is formed and articulated. Thus, sensitivity and responsibility must follow engagement in this subject (Herzfeld 2001: 10–13) because it is about the making or the unmaking of some of the most persuasive cosmological models of the world we live and act in. Such representations of identity tend to appear as a sacred ontological substance – like a soul: if it leaves the body it is as if we shall perish. Therefore, ethnicity and nationalism dominate modern cosmological models of states such as Burma because they integrate individual and collective narrations and identities and organize the social and geographical space. What is defined as ethnic or national encompasses notions of community, locality, culture, and time and space, in which the mechanism of exclusion dominates (Gupta and Ferguson 1997). It is important to investigate the process of how such models are cognized, and how they become sources of imaginary and guide actions including the contradictions, ambiguity and diversity.

ETHNIC DIVERSITY, A FUTILE EXERCISE?

In his classical anthropological study of the Kachin, Edmund Leach dismissed the ordinary ethnographic conventions as to what constitutes a tribe or a culture as hopelessly inappropriate (1964: 281): 'I suggested that it is futile to attempt to record all the stereotyped ethnographic variations for they are almost numberless' (ibid.191). Replacing 'tribe' with ethnic group does not mean that we escape the tropes of these conventions. Nevertheless, the historical process of making stereotyped ethnic variations is important to study in changing political contexts – and a seemingly futile numbering and naming are crucial parts of the process. Chit Hlaing (F.K.Lehman, chapter 4 in this volume) in his contribution to this volume, demonstrates how history, politics, language, culture and religion form a complex fulcrum of common beliefs on which ethnic identity and relations are based. This volume aims at analysing the complex mechanisms in the formation of ethnic diversity in Burma.

The State Law and Order Restoration Council (SLORC), as the ruling military body was named in 1988, gave ethnicity a new dimension when it defined the '135 national races of Myanmar' as a basis for its nationalism and cultural 'Myanmarization'. It was launched as a direct critique and dismissal of the eight 'big races' – the Burman, the Mon, the Shan, the Karen, the Kayah (Karenni) the Kachin, the Chin, the Rakhine (Arkanese) – the major ethnic categories used during the colonial rule. Maintains that these categories were part of the colonial divide and rule policy the military thus have a point in including the minor groups. However, the criteria, as well as the number 135, remain obscure (see Takatani, chapter 7 in this volume). The number 135 may have been adopted from the British census of 1931 indicating languages. However, the SLORC seems to have calculated the different groups in every state, added them together and in this way sometimes counting the same group more than once. Furthermore, in every state 'Bamar' (ethnic Burmans) are counted, while the Kayin (Karen) are only counted in the Kayin State, despite the fact that they live in Irrawaddy, Pegu and Rangoon divisions. In the Chin State the official classification numbers 53 groups. Lian Sakhong (2003) counts 63 Chin tribal sub-groups and the number of dialects among the Chin is about 42. Thus, the State Peace and Development Council (SPDC) is probably counting the Chin sub-groups as separate ethnic groups.[4] This is interesting, because the Chin now emphasize a common ethnic, national and religious (Christian) identity above the traditional segmented tribal society (Sakhong, chapter 8 in this volume).

Whereas the text of the 1974 constitution uses the term *tuin ran sa* [son of the country] to signify 'ethnic group', the recent official classification uses *taingyitha lu myo* [national race][5] and the '135 national races' make up the Myanmar nation. Myanmar is thus the overarching category signifying the national identity and subsuming the various national races. The idea behind the classification of 135 national races seems to be decentralization within a national unity, i.e. to undermine the political power of the seven non-Burman ethnic categories and to maintain centralized control by the army (Steinberg 1992: 227). Local autonomy is given to ethnic groups while the military is to secure the national unity; this division also implies a rejection of a federal state based on the eight ethnic categories.

The army emphasizes that its organization has emerged from all the national races of Myanmar: 'Tatmadaw [the army] is born of the offspring of Kachin, Kayah, Kayin, Chin and Bamar, Mon, Rakhine and Shan', in the words of the newspaper the New Light of Myanmar describing the preparations for the Armed Forces Day.[6] Paradoxically, the eight 'big races' are mentioned in this context, not the 135 'national races'. The colonial army had relatively few Burmans but whole regiments of Karen, Kachin and Chin as part of the colonial 'politics of difference'.

In fact, the ethnic diversity of Burma is more complex than the major ethnic categories indicate and many minor groups have been overlooked in its political history. The enhanced focus on ethnicity and ethnic rights by international organizations, journalists and academics may have brought the minor groups to the fore[7] – but it also accentuates the problems of classification either by subjectively ascribed ethnonym or by external (bureaucratic) classification: for example the Karen related group, the Padaung, who now use the term Kayan – or the Kokangs, who are ethnic Chinese living in the Kokang area in the northern Shan State on the border with China. These groups clearly use the new names as representations of differences in order to establish a legitimate political existence. Ethnic classification is indeed a crucial part of the political struggle in what Bourdieu (1992: 234) has termed 'labour of representation'. The ethnic groups in Burma and the military are participating in a struggle to impose their own visions of the world as well as the appropriate distinction to confirm their identity and their cultural legacy. However, this struggle to represent an authentic vision of each ethnic group and its position in Burma is based on a dialectic exchange across ethnic boundaries, i.e. by a confrontation between internal and external classifications – between group identification and a social categorization made by, often powerful, others (Jenkins 2000), such as the list of 135 'national races'. In this process, the participants are forced to reduce ethnicity to a few very general characteristics, often stereotyped and essentialized, in order to signify differences as if these have had their origin in a natural order. Ethnic names are thus important instruments in a struggle for political legitimacy.

Ethnic classification involves several other contested notions of culture, religion, history, territory and, last but not least, of a nation. All these notions are often subsumed under ethnic identity signifying sameness and community as well as differences and enmity. Such notions can become synonymous with the basic ontological foundation of existence. This factor is crucial because ethnicity can become a source of fear and anxiety, of loss and deprivation at a collective level as well as for the individual (Bauman 2001), possible explaining why fear and a sense of betrayal of identity are easily interpellated and used to activate violence even against neighbours (Appadurai 1996: 153). We should therefore not underestimate the existential (and emotional) dimension of ethnicity when it is used to mobilize people in violent conflicts. The discourse of ethnicity connects the individual, the group and the state in an existential struggle of representations. It is, however, very important to emphasize that ethnicity in itself does not generate violence.[8]

The process of ethnic violence, and the high degree of organization behind the presumed spontaneous eruptions of ethnic violence, have been researched and documented by anthropologists.[9] Ethnic identification generates symbolic boundaries of identification and of inclusive/exclusive membership used in violent conflicts. Violence in the name of ethnic identity, rights and survival is an extension of nationalism and of political *ethnicism*, in this context a process in which ethnic classification and identity provide a dominant rationale in terms of fundamental rights to resist, or to defend the group and attack adversary groups in order to survive. This extreme ethnic rationale often legitimates ethnic cleansing as well as the definition of an ethnic core of a nation. In the process, ethnic boundaries thus come to signify potential enmity and violence. Identity is very often attached to a territory, and conflicts are about territories as much as about symbolic boundaries. Displacement from the land of origin invigorates the discourse on the lost homeland. Dudley (chapter 3, this volume) shows how global influences affect ethnic identity, nationalism and political aspirations change among Karenni in refugee camps. At the same time, a historical narrative of political betrayal by the British - of victimhood, bereavement, and prosecution – becomes a crucial ingredient in maintaining a collective identity. The camps with their gated spaces, excluded from Burma and marginal to the international community, symbolizes a contradictory mixture of future aspirations and the sufferings of the past. As a consequence, a discourse on the historical legitimization on the use of violence unfortunately often becomes the main element of identification, transmitted through the social memory of those who suffered from the violence of earlier struggles. Or it is manipulated in political myths and rituals, carried by rumour and misinformation. In other words, *ethnic violence is politically generated and organized in the process of ethnicism – and not a property of the ethnicity as such.* The problem is that violence of the past is ingrained in the social memory of the present actors, and often presented as part of an ontological charter of primordial cultural values seen as the foundatiion of ethnicity. If this charter is not protected, then ethnic identity is believed to be in danger. At this point, all acts of the adverse group are potential acts of symbolic or potential physical violence. In a post-violence scenario identification tends to focus on the relation between victims and perpetrators. Basically, this labour of representation (Bourdieu 1992) becomes a struggle among claims to the real victim-hood and therefore sometimes a prelude legitimizing revenge. This is why a process of reconciliation involves the very difficult task detaching ethnic identification from previous violence.

Let me give a brief example from Burma to illustrate how violence becomes ingrained into the social and individual identity and worldview. First a quotation from a paper on the Karen history published by the Karen National Union (KNU) in 1998: '[T]he Karen suffered untold miseries at the hands of their Burman lords … culturally they [the Burmans] have attempted to absorb and dissolve our language, literature, traditions, and customs. We have been denied all political rights and militarily, our people have all along been systematically exterminated as part of the annihilation, absorption, and assimilation programme of the Burman.'[10] In this way the collective memory and history are mobilized in order to explain why the KNU uses violence in defence of ethnic identity. On the individual level a 13-year old soldier in the Karen National Liberation Army explained to a journalist that he is a soldier because his parents were killed by the Burmese army ; he has been easily recruited in the hope that he can shoot some Burmese soldiers.[11] Recall the dialectic mechanism of internal-external ethnic classification wherein external categories are often internalized, as in the example where 'Karen-ness' is defined by a vision of Burman acts in the past, the present and possible acts in the future. To be a Karen is to be a victim of violence. However, the Burman side can produce an identical vision: for example a boy is forced into the army at the age of 11 and learns that the Karen will torture him if he ever fell into their hands.[12] Both boys are victims of the conflict although the Karen may actually have witnessed the violence against his family. And on the collective side, the Karen, and especially the KNU, figure as a threat to the Burmese nation and state among those who support the military regime. A recent report from the Karen Women's Organization (2004) describes the systematic use of rape by officers and soldiers in Karen villages in acts of ethnic cleansing. Rape is a mutilation of body and identity and generates humiliation, shame, hate and fear. Thus, violence is ingrained in the ethnic identity at an organizational level as well as on an individual level, and the longer the conflict the deeper the cognitive imprint and the more it appears as natural and inevitable and the stronger the interpellation.[13]

To reiterate, ethnicity is not merely synonymous with violence and ethnicity is often a screen used to conceal very different political interests as well as ambiguous interpretations of its cultural content (Chit Hlaing chapter 4 this volumes). Ethnicity is basically relational and historically founded in its subjective as well as objective modes. Although it is not a static mode of identification, it is often constructed as a primordial cultural substance inherited from a mythical past. This process of ethnic reification, however, can only be explained by probing into the historical development and the political practices. Remember, that ethnicity is a modern concept used to define groups as communities based on social and cultural distinctions and boundaries and, furthermore, a bureaucratic designation used in mapping political differences. Perhaps what is really primordial is the very marking of differences and naming of a cultural substance (Comaroff and Comaroff 1992: 51) which is how in post-colonial societies defined ethnicity, but not the substance itself. If these premises are taken into consideration, the analysis of ethnicity may be able to penetrate the blur of political and idiosyncratic definitions to reveal the historical agencies behind the concepts and its use.

Why did ethnicity acquire such an important role in Burma and Burmese post-colonial politics? And why has violence encompassed ethnic identification in such persistent and intransigent ways? This volume aims at probing into this complex process, although it does not pretend to give exhaustive answers to these questions. Basically, the conflict in Burma is not an inter-ethnic conflict but a protracted post-colonial conflict between the state represented by the military with its vision of a unitary nation state and ethnic groups struggling to obtain territorial and cultural autonomy as legitimate national entities. Ethnicity in Burma has become part of a political strategy of ethnic differences developed during colonial era and further escalated in the turbulent post-colonial time. By 1947–48, ethnicity was deeply ingrained in the discourse on nation, state, territorial space and identity and erupted in violent conflicts. As of 2005, the memories and narrations of these conflicts were still a vivid part of the political discourse. Although we cannot explain every event in the present by the past, we must address the way history is used now and how it has entered the recent discourse. There is a growing interest in the historical events in 1946–47 leading to independence as seen in publications and the important proposal of a new Panglong Conference as a prologue to reconciliation.[14] All parties seem to agree that Panglong has had a decisive influence on history. In order to understand the significance of this proposal we have to look briefly into the historical background.

ETHNICITY IN THE PRE-COLONIAL BURMA

In order to explain the influence of ethnicity in the present political situation we face the question of its role in the pre-colonial kingdom(s) of Burma. Are we able to discover a pre-colonial mode of ethnic identification, that is fundamentally different from the colonial and the post- colonial eras?

It is impossible to fully reconstruct the ethnicity of the past and projecting the present conceptions back in time will not account for the previous forms of ethnicity.[15] However, we can make a useful theoretical comparison by considering ethnicity of the past as part of a multiethnic model, an inclusive political strategy of crossing ethnic boundaries, in contrast to the model of a unitary state, which mainly applies ethnicism as a strategy of difference and exclusion. Post-colonial rebellions, except the Communist, have emphasized the ethnic dimension of identity and difference. In pre-colonial times ethnicity had a different place. For example, a *mìn laùng*, a 'pretender' and 'rebel', had to disguise his identity and social status in order to mobilize followers across ethnic boundaries. The last Mon king, Hs'Min Dhaw ('Dhammaraja'), 1740–47, was a *mìn laùng* and he was said to be a Mon brought up in a Karen community, or a Pa-o, or a Shan – or was he? We will probably never know, because the identity of a *mìn laùng* had to be blurred in order to ensure that the most important aspect of his identity would not be questioned, i.e. his pretended royal origin. Hs'Min Dhaw was supported by Mon, Karen, Pa-o, Shan and Burman forces. Significantly, three thousand Pa-o (and/or Karen?) came to his support from the eastern hills. From the

Karen and Pa-o in these hills originated a line of *mìn laùng*. The first, to whom later *mìn laùng* referred to, was Saw Quai (Gwae) Ran who lived in the eighteenth century.[16] Other Karen, Burman and Mon opposed Hs'Min Dhaw and contributed to his downfall. His power depended more on his religious status as a Buddhist, a righteous king (*Dhammaraja*) with high *kamma* manifest in his symbolic power of *hpòn* [glory], than on ethnicity. However, it would be wrong to dismiss ethnicity as a factor. When the Burman king-to-be, Alaunghpaya, subdued the Pegu kingdom in 1757, he appealed to the local Burmans to side with him against the Mon and the Karen (but not the Shan). In the years after, thousands of Mon and Karen took refuge in Siam. Yet he had many Mon among his officials (Lieberman 1984: 236). The Karen call this period 'the Alaunghpaya hunger' referring to the widespread famine after the devastation by the king's army. Ethnicity was incorporated in the form of the state by different parameters of power than we recognize today.

Here we can only make a brief outline of these features, or rather of a systemic model of the state. Power rested on a *horizontal or spatial inclusion* by alliances as well as on a *vertical or social integration of classes* in a social hierarchy (for concepts on space, see Dean, chapter 5 in this volume). The horizontal inclusion radiated from the royal centre and its main cities and towns into the distant villages in the forests and was based on a system of vertical flow of manpower, services, money, products and tributes from the distant allied chiefs in exchange for patronage and protection. The zones near the centre delivered royal services and tax, and from the outer zones came tributes in form of silver and symbolic obeisance. The peasants and the chiefs owed services or products in exchange for royal protection and relative prosperity.[17] The royal realm of Burma (*Myanma Naing Ngan*) was thus constructed on both spatial and social criteria intertwined on a horizontal and a vertical axis.[18] In principle, the model did not have borders or boundaries to define power but lines of relations and spheres or domains of influence. The horizontal extension and the vertical integration thus depended on lines of personal relations and debts. Kinship, affinal relations and patron-client relations related the individuals in a complex social hierarchy. The king, nobility and local chiefs married cross-cousins in order to preserve control at the centre and took minor wives from tributary chiefs or clients in order to uphold alliances. Local princes or officials who inherited their positions often ruled larger towns. The same was the case in tributary areas whose chiefs were called *sawbwa* [prince] (from Tai *chaofa* or *saopha*; (see Takatani, chapter 7 and Sadan, chapter 2 in this volume).[19] At the bottom of the hierarchy were the debt slaves, redeemable but bonded to their patrons, and the prisoners of war often donated to monasteries and unredeemable. Thousands of captives were moved to powerful centres in wars and raids and other thousands became refugees. Protective power was thus important both to the centre and to individual welfare.

Religion and religious merit were an important source of symbolic capital and power manifested in the royal pagodas and their spires, *hti*, a symbol of *kamma* and the power of the king who was the upholder of Buddhism and the monastic system providing his subjects with opportunities for merit making. Buddhism integrated horizontally as well as vertically, while the local spirits (local lords), or *nat* in Burmese, had to be respected both as part of the local power hierarchy of ancestor spirits as well as integrated in a royal system of *nats* – the 37 *nats*, with Thagyia Min (king Indra) at the apex.[20] Thus, the king would also use the title of 'lord of water and land' – a term often used for local spirits – as well as 'universal ruler' (*cakkavatti*) thus signifying total control of the realm and its forces. Interestingly, the Burmans borrowed the nat cult from the Mon. The kings of Pegu initiated a cult of offerings to 36 'stream-winning gods' (*dewatau sotapan*) to protect the kingdom. These spirits residing near pagodas in trees, i.e. local lords, were related to the Earth Goddess (Visundahri) and the ancestral spirits (*kalok*) by symbolic kinship. The Buddhist Pwo Karen emulated this model.[21] These practices demonstrates that religious cosmology played a major role in connecting the space and hierarchy of the two axis, building on the same structural principles – and yet with different ethnic symbols.

In his important article 'Frontiers of "Burma"', Leach (1960) rightly dismissed the modern concepts of 'border' and 'frontier' as suitable concepts for pre-colonial Burma. His hill and valley continuum was defined as two distinct, yet connected, ecological, social and symbolic systems. James C. Scott has initiated an important rethinking of the hill-valley dimension of the Burman kingdom as a political continuum: 'the hills as a position is constituted by the state and yet not firmly within it' (Scott 2002: 9). However, the most important distinction was probably not between hill and valley as a ecological and political spaces but between people living in or near cities/towns and those dwelling in the forest. Townspeople had wealth, *hpón* and power and were close to the centres and the apex of power. In other words, they had more knowledge (of power) and more powerful patronage. People living in the forest, on the other hand, possessed a different kind of power.

They were experienced in how to cope with wild animals, had knowledge of valuable forest products and protective medicine as well as of the necessary protective magic. The people of the forest also had ritual contracts with powerful local spirits of streams and mountains and knew the dangerous and taboo areas.[22] The political landscape thus was not so much defined by ecological differences but by contrasting forms of knowledge and power as distributed both spatially and within the social hierarchy. Seen from the centre, the forest dwellers were mobile, distant and not easy to control, but not isolated or outside the system.

Whenever the king had spent his *kamma*, that is when prosperity declined and taxes increased, royal pretenders and rebels (*mìn laùng*) gathered their forces in the forests, as for example when Hs'Min Dhaw constructed a fortress in the forests north of Pegu. Here he probably obtained his magic to make him and his supporters invulnerable. Thus, pretenders to royal power and subversive religious merit would emerge from the forest, including followers from various ethnic groups. Likewise, cities and towns consisted of ethnic conglomerates, according to Thant Myint-U (2001: 27, 30). Later rebellions were also multi-ethnic, as in 1866 when rebellious sons of King Mindon mobilized some Karen while other Karen defended the king (Ibid. 131). In 1878 the Shan *saopha*s [princes] headed a rebellion against King Thibaw, who did not take minor wives from the Shan princes. In the north the Jingphaw of the Kachin were often in rebellion against the centre and one broke out in 1884. Thus, the forested, non-Burman ethnic spaces were potential zones of rebellion – not because they were ethnically different but because they contained a different power, a rebellious zone of power. Centres of power expanded or contracted depending on the resources and symbolic power they were capable of mobilizing people. If one of the axes collapsed the whole construction imploded and new centres would arise, unlike the modern state with a more fixed centre and space.

Symbolic power and an economy comprising material and symbolic debts and religious merit formed a moral system, a community of exchange comprising the king with his ten royal duties at the apex and the debt slave at the bottom of the hierarchy.[23] It mobilized people to the centres – but not for the defence of a whole culture or to conquer entire ethnic groups. In daily communication however, place of origin or religion were as important as means of identification as ethnic origin. Reference to a town or a village, a monastery or a pagoda, a mountain or a river as well as to a local chief and kinship relations were instrumental in placing a person on the social map.

Connected with place were alliances (or 'contracts') with the local guardian spirits to which new settlers had to pay respect. No one would dare to settle in a place without paying respect to the local lord.

Ethnicity thus was not part of the pre-colonial power model as a decisive mechanism of difference and as an instrument of vertical or horizontal inclusion/exclusion! On the other hand, ethnicity was a very important part of individual identification and thus of personal relations. If a person wanted to settle and marry in another ethnic group he would need relatives or well-established friendships and religious affiliation – yet he would often remain a stranger and be classified by his ethnic origin and named after his native place. This was the practice among the Pwo Karen, as explained to me in the 1970s by elder Karen in Thailand. Men would travel far and visit Karen villages and monasteries in Thailand and Burma and establish relations, thus connecting ethnic enclaves into an ethnic space (Dean, chapter 5 in this volume). Likewise, the culturally different groups in the Kachin category would know each others place in the *mayu-dama* affinal system; if not, they would include a person in the system! The major difference between the pre-colonial period and the present is that ethnicity as a dominant exclusive/exclusive political mechanism has become manifest as well as mapped in the modern nation state. Ethnic boundaries were maintained within the orbit of state centres, but not as part of modern state territorialization.

COLONIAL ETHNICISM

The 'ethnification' of power and status is a process initiated by a colonial power and included the response from the ethnic groups. It is important to emphasize that the various groups and their agency must be part of the investigation in order not to reduce everything to the results of colonial practice – there is no hegemony without counteractions.

The colonial practice used ethnic (racial) classification emphasizing *cultural differences, boundaries and places on a map* (Dean, Chapter 5 and Sadan, Chapter 2 in this volume) more than the existing relations across ethnic boundaries. Ethnic differences became territorialized in an absolute sense when the British began mapping Burma in 1826. Criteria of 'civilized/primitive' entered ethnic classification and the British excluded the primitive tribal groups from the Burmese kingdom arguing, that the kingdom had never extended effectual political control over these areas, which thus became 'excluded' or 'scheduled' areas in colonial terminology. Thus, from a modern state concept pre-colonial Burma's actual control of the excluded areas could always be questioned. And this argument was repeated by some representatives of ethnic groups during the negotiations for independence. Another criterion of difference was Christian versus Buddhist as synonymous with 'White Westerner' vs. Burman (*kala pyu/bamar*). Individuals from the minorities who converted where considered *kala* by the Burmese king and his officials (Gravers, Chapter 9 in this volume), and Burmese kings often complained that the Christian missionaries totally 'converted' the ethnic identities of their followers.[24] Thus, a double exclusion took place as a result of this policy of difference: the Christian from the Buddhist and the ethnic minorities from the majority. This process and its mechanisms are crucial, I suggest, in understanding why ethnicity became highly politicized – and polarized – in Burma.

One of the first scholars who realized the importance of this process was J.S. Furnivall (1956: 304) who termed Burma a plural society – 'a medley, for they mix but they do not combine'. It was an asymmetric incorporation into a single political economy (Comaroff and Comaroff 1992: 53) The ethnic groups were bound together by the market economy and by the colonial administration which applied ethnic criteria to recruit individuals for specific jobs, but they were never integrated in a community, culturally or socially, as the foundation for a nation state according to Furnivall. In the colonial times, culture and ethnicity became reified and bounded, based on absolute differences in race, religion and mentality. The model of difference and exclusion is symbolically condensed and illustrated by the functions of the clubs in the colonial era as depicted in Orwell's *Burmese days*. Even educated, Westernized Burmans were not admitted.[25]

Ethnic classification during the colonial period implied that diversity was based on natural and primordial differences. In the modernist version of a state Furnivall foresaw, almost as a self fulfilling prophecy, that unless the independent state of Burma was kept together by a universal nationalist ideology it would relapse into chaos because ethnicity had gradually become a criterion for an autonomous area, or even a state, by having been excluded or scheduled from Ministerial Burma under British rule. Thus, Kayah, classified as a native a state(s), was considered having been beyond the control of the Burmese kingdom. In an agreement between Burma and Britain in 1875 Western Kayah was declared independent. However,

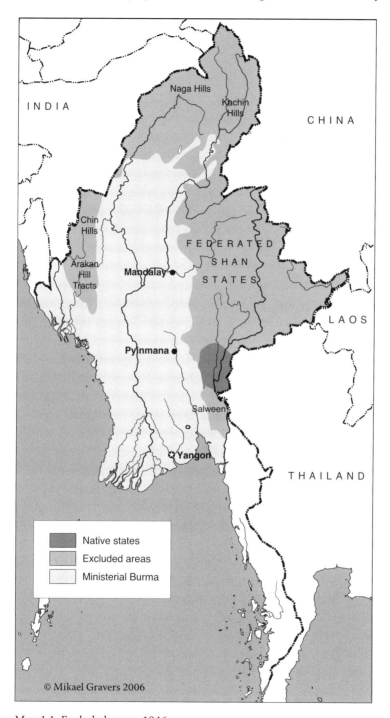

Map 1.1. Excluded areas, 1946

15

the Burman king considered Eastern Kayah to be a tributary state under Burman protection and the *sawbwa*, Sawlawpaw, sent tribute to Mandalay in 1880. After 'pacification' of Kayah in the 1880s these principalities came under *de facto* British control.[26] Shan States, Kachin Hills, Naga Hills and Chin Hills became excluded areas – in all 47 per cent of the total area and 16 per cent of the total population directly under the control of the British governor in the Constitution from 1922 (see Map 1.1 on previous page).

At this time the colonial administration defined a Burman as a person from any minority group and a Burmese as a person from the ethnic majority, thus creating a confusing categorization, which has been emphatically rejected. Today, all groups and parties also reject the term 'minority', which has a derogatory political connotation as not qualifying as a nation or for a state. The process of exclusion began in the 1890s after the annexation of Upper Burma when travel to the Chin and Kachin hills was regulated and restricted, and the areas were delineated on maps. This regulation prohibited Shans from moving into the Kachin Hills, which for a long time has had a considerable Shan population. It probably also kept many Burmans out of the frontier areas. In 1935, the frontier areas were further classified as Part I, 'backward areas' including Kachin, Chin the Kayah and Karen in upper Salween district, and as Part II the 'advanced areas' including part of Shan States and Karen areas closer to Ministerial Burma. Part II was eventually to be included in Ministerial Burma after being developed, while the first part would remain excluded and under direct British control. Moreover, the colonial administration established special 'communal' constituencies for the legislative council: for example 12 seats for the Karen, eight for Indians. Yet, the scheduling process divided the groups, in particular the Karen, and signalled the problems which came to the fore in 1947. In Toungoo a Karen National Association (KNA) mass meeting stated that this centre of the Karen should be excluded and joined with Salween district. The KNA said that 'Toungoo was the cradle of their tradition and the seat of Karen chiefs, and from this centre they migrated throughout the length and breath of Burma'. Migration had accelerated after 1852 and thousands of Karen came down from Toungoo, Arakan Hills and Pegu Yoma and obtained land in the lowlands, thus deepening the contradictions between an expanding social space and a bounded ethnic territory. Interestingly, the KNA Salween wanted their own delegate for the round table conference, dissatisfied with being represented by Karen from the plains. Their council of elders claimed the area had always been independent from Burma under their own chiefs (*sakaw or sawkai*) as well as neglected by the British administration. They demanded to have the district declared as a Karen Free State in a memorial from February 1935.[27] Thus, at this time the politics of difference and ethnicism had made its impact.

The army and military police were recruited from Karen, Kachin and Chin with only a few Burmans, and the battalions were classified as 'Karen Rifles', 'Chin Rifles' and so forth.[28] The Burmans considered these measures to be a deliberate divide and rule policy and not a preparation for future autonomy. Thus, five of the main eight ethnic categories, Shan, Karen, Kachin, Kayah, and Chin, could claim a territory, a state and representation by referring to the colonial classification of excluded or frontier areas which were all defined by ethnic differences, while the Burmans could only consider the ethnic mapping exercise as a quartering of the geo-body of their nation (Tongchai 1994).[29] During the colonial period notions such as 'hill tracts', 'native states' and 'frontier area' signified a backward/primitive and contested, unruly zone, i.e. partially excluded by negative criteria. This is crucial because the classification and its meaning have become deeply ingrained into present cognition and modelling of the political landscape in Burma.

The British Frontier Area Administration (FAA) in exile in India during the Japanese occupation planned elections of village and regional councils, eliminating hereditary princes *(saopha or sawbwa)*, chiefs and headmen. The director of FAA, H.N.C. Stevenson, even planned to make the frontier areas into one big federation of principalities (the previously mentioned excluded areas) and as a self-governing state under the Empire. Stevenson launched his plan in 1945 and published it in the anthropological journal *Man* (vol. XLV, no.2). His idea was to create a system of councils from village to state in the Frontiers Areas. These councils were to be united in a Grand Federal Council placed under the British governor. Thus, he wanted to replace the traditional chiefs with a democratic system, though under British control until it had reached a stage in development and education when it could be amalgamated with Ministerial Burma. Stevenson believed that colonial rule had made the Frontier Areas more autocratic. He wanted a more cohesive whole in order to federate it with Ministerial Burma. However his federative idea was based on 'racial groups'. Interestingly, some of his critical thoughts on autocracy (feudalism) and development were close to the AFPFL policy. But his grand scheme was too expensive, politically sensitive to London and offensive to the AFPFL.[30] The Burmans regarded his plan as a colonial scheme for splitting Burma and maintaining a British colony. However, Stevenson emphasized that the Frontier Areas would be federated with Ministerial Burma – 'knitting the democratised administration into that of Ministerial Burma in a coherent whole' (OIOC file M/4/2832).

The ethnic groups in the frontier areas had reason to believe that the British would secure some form of autonomy after 1935. These expectations were the background for the two Panglong conferences in 1946 and 1947. Shan *saophas* and Stevenson, who had studied anthropology under Bronislaw Malinowski, arranged the first conference. It was organized as a traditional Shan cultural and Buddhist festival (*Tabaung*) at full moon March 1946 in the small town of Panglong, Laihke State. The idea was to promote his construction of a frontier state within the Commonwealth or directly under British rule. Burman nationalists could only see this as an attempt to split Burma and the ethnic groups. Thus, to the dismay of Stevenson U Nu, in his speech, criticised the British for splitting the ethnic groups and for keeping the hill peoples at a low level of development. Stevenson mobilized the traditional leaders against the Anti-Fascist Peoples Freedom League (AFPFL), General Aung San's Party, and resisted an immediate inclusion of the hill peoples in a union as agreed between Aung San and the British government in January. He distrusted Aung San due to the atrocities of the Burma Independent Army during the war, but, as viewed from London, he acted too independently. It was probably Aung San's distrust of Stevenson that led to the latter's forced retirement. Stevenson seems to have inhibited AFPFL's political contacts and mobilization in the frontier areas. He thus became a liability and was retired before the second conference in February 1947. Although described as a parody of a 007 agent by Leach, he was a hero among those who resisted the union with Burma. His insistence on ethnic diversity and federalism has had a considerable impact upon the political role of ethnicity since 1945.

The participants in the second conference in 1947 were Shan, Kachin and Chin leaders. Kayah only sent observers since they maintained their status as an independent (or native) state, and the Frontier Administration supported them in this claim. The Karen also had four observers, who came late with no mandate to join the frontier federation from the Karen National Union. The Karen majority were not included in the 1935 Schedule Act. However, the Salween Karen, who were in Part I 'backward area', did not have representatives. The Karen observers did not participate in the debate and still expected that the British would give them a state. The Shan *saopha*s and the Kachin *duwa*s [chiefs] demanded democratic rights, equal representation and rights to secession. After an initial hesitation, Aung San promised to secure these rights for the frontier peoples and to provide financial aid from Rangoon. The Kachin State would have its borders delineated, resulting in the inclusion of Bhamo and Myitkyina towns formerly in Ministerial Burma, but they did not obtain right to secession. All parties left the conference in good spirits after the initial disagreements. The Shan rulers, in particular, were viewed by the AFPFL as a feudal relic and as allied with the Frontier Area Administration. The good spirit owed much to Aung San, who later confirmed and guaranteed the cultural autonomy as well as national and democratic rights of all groups (Silverstein 1993: 69). Further, in the constitution of 1947 (Ch. X) the right to secession after ten years was secured for the ShanState and the Kayah State whereas the Chin opted to stay in the union when they were promised economic aid.[31]

Despite the spirit of mutual trust generated at Panglong, the conference left many problems unsolved: the minor groups of the Frontier Areas such as the Naga, Wa, Palaung, Padaung, as well as the Salween Karen in Part I, were not represented. The Mon, the Rakhine and the Karen were outside the FA and thus excluded. The Karen National Union still believe they were deliberately excluded (Gravers 1996a). Many Burmans feared that the Union would dissolve – a fear that gave rise to support for the military interventions in 1958 and 1962. The problems all relate to the 1922 and 1935 Acts and the British insisting on maintaining these laws as a basis for any future independence agreement. Thus, the problems during and after Panglong were partly due to the colonial ethnic categorization being used as fundament for the political agreement and partly to the confusion created among the participants by the ambiguous use of the terms 'federation', 'union', 'state' and 'nation'. The Shan *saopha*s had been forced into a federation of the Shan principalities (*möng*) in 1922. This was the model for Stevenson, but large parts of the Frontier Areas did not form clearly delineated political units, principalities or states, which could be used as a basis for a federative political process. Moreover, the Shan federation was considered a feudal arrangement by the Burman side. The Shan are in the majority (approximately 60 per cent); the other groups in the Shan states are Kachin, Pa-o, Palaung, Wa, Padaung, Lahu, Akha, Danu as well as other groups (Takatani, Chapter 7 this volume). Likewise, in Kayah State the ethnic landscape is varied and complex. Besides the majority of

Kayah we find Kayan (Padaung), Brè, Manö, Yangtalai, Pakü (Sgaw), Geba (Bwe), Pa-o – all Karen related groups formerly in three principalities ruled by Kayah *saophas* – principalities modelled after the Shan. During colonial rule Eastern Kayah resisted the British fiercely and were only 'pacified' in 1889. In the years after independence, the Kayah government was eager to dissociate from the Karen and their insurgency – in which they were involved – claiming to be 'no sort of Karen at all' (Lehman 1967a: 14), while the majority actually see themselves as a particular kind of Karen (ibid. 7). This is an example of how the political layer tried to erase an ethnic relationship still existing in cultural terms. The Kayah and some of the minor groups have been organized in different political and armed groups (M. Smith 1994); (on the Kayah see further F.K.L Chit Hlaing, Chapter 4, and Dudley, Chapter 3 in this volume).

As well as defining states into a federation, there was also a problem of ethnic representation before and after Panglong. Moreover, the exact meaning of the important concepts of a 'federation' and 'union' were never developed in a detailed sustainable form before the constitution was written. A precise specification of the power sharing and delegation of authority between the central state and the federate state never materialized. The term 'union' came to be used more and more to mean a unitary state (as used at present by the State Peace and Development Council) of mixed ethnic origin but as one nation. The Chin representatives, for example, did not understand the difference between 'federation' and 'union', according to Lian Sakhong (2003: 215).[32] The conflicting statements by the Karen in Salween during the Frontier Areas Commission Enquiries (FACE) following Panglong is another example of the confusion. The Salween Karen did not want to be represented by Delta Karen who had never visited their district (Gravers chapter 9 in this vol.). Internally they were divided: those who experienced the Japanese and BIA atrocities, mainly members of Force 136 and Christians, wanted an independent state federated with Kayah or a Frontier Area state; those who had not experienced such sufferings preferred to join Ministerial Burma. However, to most of the Salween Karen the difference between federation and union was unclear and they frankly admitted this.[33] Further, the division between the two types of excluded areas (Part I and II) confused most representatives. The Frontier Area Commission Enquiry was meant to clarify matters after Panglong and secure all opinions, but it only added to the confusion. For example, FACE included Kayah in the projected federation with Burma although according to the 1935 constitution, it was formally not part of Burma. All the ethnic representatives to FACE were elected at hastily called mass meetings and had little time to be given their terms of reference from their people. A lot of disagreements never surfaced, but after Panglong Kachin leaders aired their disagreement in the media. About half of the Kachin delegates at the Panglong conference came from the Shan States thus adding to the skewed representation. Chin representatives admitted they had not understood all that was decided and now wanted to be an independent state. Reading through the documents from 1945–47 reveals a multi-vocal diversity but where only a few voices were actually heard. All the minorities, however, expected autonomy. This is perhaps the most important lesson for the future: high expectations stumble against confused realities. When the spirit of Panglong had evaporated after the assassination of Aung San, the peoples of Burma returned to the ethnicism and nationalism of pre-independence struggles. The British government also had difficulties in switchingg from seeing Burma as a plural society of ethnic divisions to seeing it as a modern multi-ethnic nation state under one governmental administration but with local autonomy. They were trapped in their ethnic conceptions and the rhetoric of one racial/ethnic category being equal to one ethnic community and one united political representation, especially in the case of the Karen, who British officials said lacked a sense of community.

The mixture of ethnic categorization, confused political concepts and geographical notions is perhaps the crucial factor for the ensuing conflicts – and all parties have failed to enter an alternative mode of political construction. Although it is not helpful to maintain a picture of Burma as a perpetual victim of colonization and its categories, it is precisely this model which has to be dismantled and replaced.

Since the coup in 1962 the military has used a cultural corporative and unitary model of the Burman state, replacing local administration and reviving the model of the British Frontier Area Administration but as an integrative instrument of the central government. The military intervened in the Shan States and pressured the *saophas* to surrender their power. The Burman nation turned into a hegemonic nation state ruled by Ne Win's Revolutionary Council and the Burma Socialist Programme Party (BSPP). Although non-Burman culture and language were officially protected, Burman became the national language and all citizens are supposed to share a common identity.[34] In 1982 the regime limited the access to citizenship to descendants of ethnic groups living in the country before 1823. Where the colonial administration divided and subdivided, the military has tried to erase differences and homogenize into a state model of a singular spatial representation. Fighting an endless number of insurgencies has continuously legitimated military rule and violent suppression of differences.[35] Today it seems as if the State Peace and Development Council (SPDC) refuses a tripartite dialogue with the National League for Democracy (NLD) and the ethnic groups and their organizations. They stick to their 135 'national races' and deal only with those organizations, which have signed cease-fire agreements. The military also maintain that Burma must not copy Western democracy but needs 'a disciplined and durable democratic system which will be the most compatible with the desires of all nationalities'.[36] The regime has granted local autonomy to those ethnic organizations and smaller groups who have signed cease-fire agreements and the Ministry for Progress of Border Areas and National Races has plans for economical development in the 'backward areas'. A spokesman for the SPDC explains that there is a consensus developing in relation to a future constitution – 'by this consensus method the military believes that although the "national races" may be smaller in number, they shall have a louder voice in a parliament'. The old system, he argues, created anger and frustration ending in insurgency.[37] The regime has had some success with its policy in some of the areas that have suffered from decades of war. This development has forced a rethinking of the situation among the main ethnic organizations. But the model used is still the unitary and cultural corporate one. The military has re-mythologized Burma's history by using archaeology and religion to establish an early Burman ethnic origin and identity.[38] Culture used in this way is seen by the nationalist ruling body as the best defence against chaos and as offering protection to the geo-body from both internal dissent and external neo-colonization. The regime protects identity and state territory as if they also constituted their own body.[39] It will take more than Minerva's owl to dismantle this model because it links nation, state and military in a life-and-death vision. At the same time, history and myths are crucial to the minority ethnic groups as a defence of their identity and unity, for example among the Chin and the Karen (Sakhong chapter 8 in this volume; Gravers 1996a). In the process, ethnicity and the state collide in various political models.

THE NEW PANGLONG INITIATIVE

In 2001 ethnic leaders, most of them living outside Burma, met to discuss the political future in the wake of the brief release of Daw Aung San Suu Kyi in order to prepare for the tripartite dialogue that had been proposed by the UN in 1994. They formed the Ethnic Nationalities Solidarity and Cooperation Committee (ENSCC, 2002; now Ethnic Nationalities Council) to promote the new Panglong initiative. It is not a political party or organization, but is described as 'a reconciliation task force'. Its members are leading figures from the United National League for Democracy (liberated areas), non-cease-fire groups, the Kayah National Progressive Party and the Karen National Union.[40] The importance of this initiative is that the ethnic claims to independent territories seem finally to have been abandoned. A discourse of democracy and federalism is gradually replacing exclusive ethnic rights. However, the initiative would base a future federation on the main ethnic categories forming the states of the union. This immediately invites the question: what about the minor groups, the Pa-o, the Palaung, the Wa, the Naga, the 16–20 subgroups under the category Karen, as well as many other groups? Ethnicity as the dominant criterion could lead to new conflicts and, to paraphrase Leach's, could end in yet another futile exercise of 'which-term-used-by-whom' would be applied. Importantly, the ENSCC is aware of the problem of boundary making and agree 'to refrain from attempting to subdivide or change boundaries or names of the current states and divisions' (ibid. 9). Renouncing the right to secession removes one stumbling block, but will it prevent endless discussion of which ethnic criteria should be the used – such as 135 'national races'? The Panglong initiative suggests 'a proportional representation for all electoral processes in order to enable smaller groupings to participate fully in the political process' (ibid. 17). This is positive, but ethnic proportions are not necessarily natural and based on clearly objective criteria. As we have seen, ethnic classification and identification depend on the positions of those who define and those who are defined. Easy solutions cannot be expected for the simple reason that ethnicity is not a substance which can be moulded to conform with the constitutional objectives without inviting conflicts on internal/external classifications. The crucial thing is to clarify 'federalism' and 'federation', i.e. which segments are to be federated and how is power going to be shared between the central government and the federated states? It is proposed that the federation will consist of eight ethnic states: Kachin, Kayah, Karen, Chin, Rahkine, Mon, Shan and Myanmar and have a parliament with an upper and lower house. The states would have 'legislative assemblies' (ibid. 120). Local domains for smaller groups, partly autonomous in the administration of culture and religion, would not have to be federated states or to split the present states and divisions. It is important to notice that the new Panglong initiative defines the ethnic groups as *ethnic nationalities,* not ethnic minorities, thus equalizing all groups (see Chao Tzang Yawnghwe 2004: 38). This is a crucial distinction since 'ethnic nationality' signifies a historic continuity, a primordial genealogy, and at the same time a modern national entity, although the publications cited above are not always consistent in their use of the distinctions. If the main criteria of a new constitution thus remain contested ethnic identities and categorizations, including historical memories of sufferings and disappointment, the process is probably not going to be successful.[41]

Other questions arise: are the cease fire groups going to participate in a dialogue and an agreement?[42] And what will happen to organizations such as the Democratic Karen Buddhist Organization? Will the military insist they are invited and will the KNU then walk out? The best outcome would possible be to invite all the organizations in order to make as many stakeholders as possible responsible. As other criterion for representation could be locality. A long process of dialogue and open exploration would have to take place before a coalition and a constitution could be formulated. What the Panglong conference promised were equal rights, and a new Panglong agreement must formulate basic and general democratic rules including human rights and not merely the specific ethnic rights. However, the SPDC will probably maintain its idea of a union, i.e. a unitary state, in their definition and reject a federation as a cover for ethnic separatism.

Meanwhile, the SPDC reconvened the constitution drafting National Convention in 2004 without the participation of NLD and Daw Aung San Suu Kyi. The 13 ethnic organizations who have signed cease fire agreements with the SPDC are among the 1,076 delegates although their situation changed dramatically and seems more uncertain after their patron, Khin Nyunt, was ousted and jailed in October 2004. Federalism was absolutely not on the agenda at the reopened convention in 2005 and proposals from the ethnic cease fire groups on rights for ethnic nationalities were rejected. Strongman Snr. General Than Shwe seems determined to finalize the drafting of a new constitution securing full military control as soon

Figures 1.1. and 1.2. Karen children rehearsing a dance in Mae La refugee camp, Thailand. (Photos: M. Gravers)

as possible. Negotiation of a cease fire agreement with the KNU had not been completed as of March 2005. The KNU is in a precarious position between the tiger and the crocodile: securing its supporters inside Burma is extremely difficult while the Thai government may force the return of refugees. Meanwhile many of those exiled, discouraged by the recent developments, are giving up the struggle and seeking asylum in the USA and other Western countries. The frontier zone is now a highly insecure space.[43]

A new frontier problem has developed since 1949: a transnational zone in Thailand of exiled persons from several ethnic groups, a major part (an estimated 120,000) being Karen, and groups living in Western countries supporting the various opposition organizations. Bangladesh still hosts some 200,000 Muslim Rohingya refugees, some of whom may be recruited by international Muslim organizations and terrorist groups.[44] This transnational zone is a political space it is very much influenced by the ethnic spatiality inside Burma, yet it is very different and contains other identities. As well as this fragmented space there are those who are neither inside nor outside: the estimated one million internally displaced persons. These populations, inside and outside Burma, also contain a generational gap in experience between those who left before and after 1988, as well as differences in education, religious orientation and in relative suffering. These differences will inevitably influence their views and the struggle for representation. This problem has to be addressed openly in debates in order to be reconciled. New subjectivities have developed inside Burma, within ethnic groups and between neighbouring groups. However, we cannot expect that the ethnic organizations always endorse such variations in experience and opinion. The new Panglong initiative is well aware of these problems and can definitely contribute to their reconciliation. On the other hand, if ethnicity is still promoted as the determining political principle of the various national states in the federation, it will be necessary but difficult to secure minority representation within the states as well as to prevent new ethnically inspired rebellions.[45] Moreover, although the NLD has endorsed tripartite negotiations, we are still waiting for more concrete proposals on how Daw Aung San Suu Kyi and the Burman part of NLD envisage a federal constitution. Finally, the military has always justified its rule by claiming an identity of primary guardians of a unitary state and will probably not even discuss federalism. The basis for a dialogue however is flexibility and willingness to discuss all proposals with all parties involved;

this prerequisite for progress is badly missing. Nationalism and ethnicism have evolved into a political paranoia under which every move has become suspicious.

It is beyond the scope of this introduction to scrutinize fully the question of reconciliation (see South, chapter 6 in this vol.) And it is difficult to assess if a truth commission, as in South Africa, is an appropriate instrument. Is an international human right tribunal feasible – or is it better to use the method of social forgetting and thus silence the sufferings and grievances? These complicated questions were addressed during a seminar in May 2004.[46] It is important that the process of reconciliation is discussed during the tripartite dialogue and becomes a part of a political settlement. Before grievances are aired in such forums, a community of trust must be created and those who suffered must have an experience of relief and security.[47] If this is not the case, narrations of suffering quickly turn into accusations, revive distrust and become invitations to new violence.[48] Moreover, what has become apparent from the historical experience briefly outlined above is that a continuation of closed ethnic boundaries mixed with ethnicized victim-hood and exclusively constructed claims, runs the risk of emulating colonial ethnicism and thus inhibiting any reconciliation. Ethnic rights in terms of language, traditions and religion must be secured constitutionally, without necessarily being the foundation of the electoral and administrative systems of the federal states, as a universal right of all citizens, in this way maintaining the ethnic diversity as part of civil society while creating a new unity. Some factions of ethnic organizations, formerly involved in armed conflict, seem now to be adapting to a new function as part of an emerging civil society (South, chapter 6 in this volume; South 2003). Assisted by outside mediation such organizations may replace violence and fear with relative trust. Civil society, however, is rarely as sharply separated from the state as often described and imagined in Western societies, but a grey and contested zone (Ferguson and Gupta 2002) In Burma the ethnic organizations belong to this zone and have perhaps gained a little more space for manoeuvring than they had previously. However, there are no common rules and security, only meticulous state surveillance in this space – a situation that makes these organizations vulnerable – and it is a space of potential violence. A substantial and general demilitarization is necessary for civil organizations to develop. This is another important subject which needs detailed proposals to be taken up in a dialogue.

The preamble to the reconciliation process should take as its cue the fact that *all* ethnic groups have suffered and that *all* have been excluded from a peaceful existence and mainstream international development. A new narrative has to integrate ethnic diversity, state unity, and democracy as a counter narrative to colonial divide-and-rule, and to post-colonial nationalism and ethnicism. Reconciliation only begins when the labour of representation initiates a critical reflection upon the old ethnicism. It means that all parties have to reassess – not reiterate – the old positions. In order to facilitate such critical reflections, a thorough research of ethnic diversity, its history and ethnography, could be an important tool. The present volume is conceived – and hopefully received – in this spirit.

RECURRENT THEMES OF THE BOOK

The following chapters provide different aspects of the dynamics of ethnicity and the formation of ethnic identity as well as a discussion of concepts related to ethnicity. All contributors refer to the historical background and narratives as well as to recent events and developments in Burma. Several chapters include discussion of prominent literature on ethnic groups in Burma, such as the work of Edmund Leach, F.K Lehman and others. Chit Hlaing (F.K.Lehman) in his discussion of ethnicity (Chapter 4) above and adds important details to the complex process of identity formation and observes that political change and new labels do not necessarily mean a change of identity. Dean (Chapter 5) provides the reader with a discussion of important concepts of social and ethnic space in relation to boundaries and territorial place exemplified in Kachin State. The impact of colonialism is analysed in Sadan (Chapter 2 Kachin), Sakhong (Chapter 8 Chin) and Gravers (Chapter 9 Karen). Sadan examines the construction of the ethnic category Kachin and its political implications. Sakhong and Gravers focus on the history of Christian conversion and the conflicts it created. The Chin and the Kachin have almost completely converted to Christianity, whereas the Karen are divided between Buddhism and Christianity. In both cases religion and nationalism are crucial in changing ethnic identification. Takatani (Chapter 7) analyse the role of culture, religion and language in the formation of modern Shan identity and the construction of the modern Shan state as a parallel but dialectic relationship with 'burmanization' and the formation of modern Burman identity. Dudley (Chapter 4) probes into the political construction of Kayah identity between modernity and tradition in the refugee camps in Thailand as viewed differently by the elders and the young generation. South (Chapter 6) looks at the ethnic situation after the cease fire agreements between the SPDC and 13 ethnic organizations and discusses an emergent ethnic civil network and the possibilities of a new civil society versus a unitary state.

NOTES

[1] See A. Smith (1991) who has indexed the properties and the ethnic basis of a nation.

[2] See, for example, Appadurai (1996) for a critique of the thesis of primordialism in explaining ethic violence, and Friedman (2002) on ethnicity and violence as a result of a global fragmentation process. These general theoretical discussions are important, but they rarely focus on the actual agency involved in ethnic conflicts.

[3] Political engagement and academic work is a difficult mixture and needs a delicate balance in order to generate engaged, but not biased scholarship. however, it is impossible to disconnect the two.

[4] See *The New Light of Myanmar* 8–9 March 2000 'Call us Myanmar', www.myanmar.com/nlm/arti/mar8.html (and mar9). Likewise, the military regime considers the name Burma as a British colonial construction and part of the 'divide and rule' because it excluded the other ethnic groups.

[5] *Lu myo* is translated as 'race'; the original meaning is 'kind of man' according to Taylor (1982: 8). *Taingyitha lu myo* is translated as 'national races' and is used by the SPDC; the term *lu myo zu*, 'ethnic nationalities', is preferred by the opposition (See Yawnghwe 2004: 38).

[6] www.myanmar.com/nlm/art/mar14.html (as of 14 March 2000

[7] See for example, M. Smith (1994).

[8] An ethnic dimension of violence has been a integral part of life in Burma for decades and documented in numerous publications by various organizations such as Amnesty International (1988,1990), *United Nations Commission on Human Rights Special Briefing on Women in Burma* (1998), and recently by the Shan Human Right Foundation (2002) in *Licence to Rape*.

[9] See Tambiah (1996). He demonstrates how ethnic and religious violence is a part of the democratic process in India; Kapferer (1988) has shown how a mythological past becomes a primordial ontological essence in the present political Sinhalese nationalism and the rationale of violence. Cognition, myths and symbols are all important ingredients; however, without political organization and mobilization ethnicity does not generate violence on a larger

social scale. See also Schmidt and Schröder (2001) on the anthropology of violence.

[10] KNU (1998), www.karen.org/knu/KNU_His.html The origin of Karen victimhood dates back to the first missionary publications and has been reiterated in numerous publications since. The Karen lost influence and were suppressed after the kingdom of Pegu was subdued by the Burman king of Ava in 1757.Later rebellions and conversion to Christianity added further sufferings and their victim-hood has been narrated in missionary literature. (See Gravers 2001c and Ch. 9 in this volume).

[11] *Times Online*, 3 January 2003 *www.karen.org/news/wwwboard//messages/ 1866,html*

[12] *Sunday Times* 5 January, 2003 *www.karen org/wwwboard//messages71914. html*

[13] See *Images of Asia* (1996). An estimated 40–50,000 children are soldiers in the Tatmadaw or ethnic armies. The *Irrawaddy* (vol.12, 7: 23) gives the figure 70,000 plus 6–7,000 in ethnic armies, an amazing figure. The Karen twins, Luther and Johnny were exposed in the international media recently, Gravers 2001b.

[14] See the interesting and detailed analysis by the Universities Historical Research Centre, Yangon (1999) and Chao Tzang Yawnghwe and Lian Sakhong (eds) (2004). The first title gives a critical view of the colonial regime and its role in dividing the ethnic groups as seen from inside Myanmar today. The second represents all ethnic organizations in exile and discusses reconciliation of the ethnic division. Interestingly, despite different positions both view the Panglong conference as crucial for understanding Burma's history as well as for writing a new constitution.

[15] For a discussion of ethnicity in Burma, see Lehman (1967a), Lieberman (1978), and Taylor (1982).

[16] See Lieberman (1978) on Hs'Min Dhaw and the so-called Gwè Karen. Hs'Min Dhaw used *Gwè or Gwei* as part of his title. If it is a Pwo Karen word, it could refer to Gwae Gabaung (Zwei Kabin), a mountain near Pa-an. This mountain is still the main symbol of the Pwo Karen core land. The Karen who were moved to Northern Thailand around 1802 were named after this mountain and called *Yang Suai Kabin* ("Karen from Suai Kabin = Gwae Gabaung) in the Kham Muang language. Saw Quai (pronounced *gwae*) Ran could well have been S'Min Dhaw! However, the whole point of *gwè/gwae* is that it not an ethnic classifier, but could be a local name. Phayre's account (1959: 198) mentions 'gwè Karen' and 'gwè Shan'. On the Karen rebellions see Gravers (2001c).

[17] The peasants doing royal service (corvée) were included in the *ahmudan* system; peasants paying tax in the *athi* system; lowest in the hierarchy were the slaves (*kyun*). See Lieberman (1984) for details, and Thant Myint-U (2001) for a valuable analysis of royal power, administration and ethnicity.

[18] See Taylor (1987: 1) on the term '*naing ngan*'.

[19] See Than Myint-U (2001: 76). Sons of *sawbwas* were often educated as pages at the Burman kings'court.

[20] The 37 *nat*s are related by kinship, a replica of the social system with sibling relations as a symbol of the unity of Burma. See Brac de la Perrier (2003) on the *nat* cult.

[21] See Shorto (1967) on the Mon cult and Gravers (2001c) on the Karen cosmology.

[22] The forest is a relatively undomesticated space with uncontrolled forces, but not synonymous with the modern conception of 'wild' versus 'civilized'. See Gravers (2001a) for a discussion of Karen notions of landscape and environment.

[23] The ten duties of a righteous king included almsgiving, liberality, avoidance of the use of violence. See Michael Aung-Thwin (1983: 54).

[24] The term '*kala*' was first used as a broad categorization for foreigners from South Asia and countries west of Burma and came to include the Europeans and Americans.

[25] The sahib club culture is portrayed in Noel Singer (1995: 190 ff). See also Taylor (1987) on class and ethnicity. Migrants from India constitute about half of Rangoon's population.

[26] See file L/Pj/6/264, p.10 in the Oriental and India Office Collections (OIOC), the British Library,

[27] See the file M/1/33 in the OIOC. Exclusion of Toungoo would have made the special 12 seats for the Karen difficult to maintain. The document demonstrates how the Karen were trapped in the contradictions of being one culture, one nation and yet appear as divided in religious communities and in ethno-geographical sub-groups. In the Salween district with a mainly Sgaw Karen population, most were Buddhist or Animists, but those writing the memorial from the National Karen Association in Papun were probably Christians.

[28] Taylor (1987: 100). The Karen soldiers numbered 1,448 in 1939 and 2,797 in 1941; the Burmans only 472 in 1939 and 1,893 in 1941.

[29] The Mon and Arakanese or Rakhine could point to their important historical kingdoms. On the process of exclusion see Cady (1958); Silverstein (1980).

[30] See File M/4/2811 in the OIOC, British Library. Stevenson's federation was to be based on thorough anthropological investigations. Edmund Leach, however, was reluctant to return and do fieldwork in 1947. He found the situation 'increasingly lively', i.e. political unstable (M/4/2832)

[31] See Maung Maung (1989) for a Burman view of Panglong. Silverstein (1987, 1997) analyses ethnic politics and describes the Panglong events. More research, though, is needed on these significant events.

[32] For a discussion of the differences between a federation and a union, see Svensson (2004).

[33] OIOC file M/4/2854. The Karen were confused, said the British. 'It suited the British that we were confused', according to Saw Tha Din, KNU president in 1947, interviewed by the author in 1971. Then the British could remain silent and avoid replies to the Karen demands for a state in the so-called memorial forwarded to London.

[34] See Silverstein (1997). The Burma Socialist Programme Party (1963: 49) used Aung San's definition of a nation, 'a collective term applied to a people irrespective of their ethnic origin'. This definition is used to emphasize the solidarity and unity between 'indigenous racial groups', and thus erasing the differences.

[35] See M. Smith (1991). The KNU-led rebellion is the longest lasting (from 1948). Some Pa-o joined the KNU rebellion in 1949 and again rebelled in 1951 followed by Kachin in 1962 as well as Kayah, Mon and other groups. The picture ,however, is complicated by various armies: some are probably drug traders and advocate more a kind of warlordism than of ethno-nationalism. See M. Smith 2002: 34 for a more recent listing of 38 ethnic organizations and parties

[36] Genral Khin Nyunt, Secretary-1, SPDC, in a speech January 2001 (*www.karen. org/news/wwwboard/messages/868.html*).

[37] See Pigou (2001: 21).

[38] See Houtman (1999b) for an interesting discussion of fossils used in what is termed the process 'Myanmarfication'. The Karen National Union also use a re-mythologization of their origin making the year 739 the factual date of their arrival in Burma, having migrated from China (see Karen History in the KNU Narrative *www.karen.org/history*).

[39] For a discussion of nationalism in Burma see Gravers (1999).

[40] The UNLD groups active inside Burma who formed the United Nationalities Alliance seem not to be in the task force.

[41] Alan Smith (1997: 243) warns against an enthusiasm for the rationality of federal formulas that overshadow the difficulties. See Svensson (2004) on the difference between a federation and a unitary state and discussion of the concepts amongst representatives of the democratic opposition. A union is normally defined as looser than a federation.

[42] See the list in M. Smith (2001: 34).

[43] See South (2004) on the National Convention; and Kyaw Zwa Moe (2005) on the 'liberated area'.

[44] The Rakhine (Arakan) state has some 600,000 Muslims out of a 2,38 million population. There have been several violent anti-Muslim incidents in recent years in Burma, includingthe burning of a mosque in Toungoo. The perpetrators were said to be Buddhist monks – or perhaps soldiers in monks' robes?

[45] See Lian Sakhong (2001: 27); Steinberg (2001: 33) argues that the ethnic groups also have to address the army's real concerns for maintaining national unity – Balkanization will not gain international support.

[46] See Gravers (2004b) for a discussion of reconciliation and its main concepts. A majority of representatives endorsed the idea of a reconciliation commission.

[47] Actually, we have obtained multi-vocal and heartbreaking narratives from traumatized persons and groups; to repeat the common description 'silence of sufferings' would be a cliché.

[48] See Kleinman et al (1997).

Chapter 2

CONSTRUCTING AND CONTESTING THE CATEGORY 'KACHIN' IN THE COLONIAL AND POST-COLONIAL BURMESE STATE

Mandy Sadan

INTRODUCTION

The issue that this paper seeks to address is how the ethnic category 'Kachin' relates to the collection of communities and sub-groups that it represents within the Burmese state. In Burma today Kachin nationalist rhetoric determines that the category Kachin is comprised of six principal lineages, all of which are deemed to be descended from a common ancestor. These communities are the Jinghpaw, Lawngwaw (Maru, Lhaovo, Lhaovar), Zaiwa (Atsi, Atzi), Nung-Rawang, Lisu and Lachik (La:cid, Lashi). Inevitably, all of these communities are themselves complex entities and their affiliations to the category Kachin have historically been contested, reconfigured and renegotiated at both local and national levels. One of the main concerns of this chapter, however, will be an exploration of some of the historical contexts that have problematized the notion of the ethnic category 'Kachin', and in particular the implications of these for local discourses on multi-group identity.

A sense of trepidation arises in undertaking this task, however, because any deconstruction of the reifying rhetoric of Burma's modern ethnic categories such as this may lead to considerable unease among the political elites of the communities concerned. While it is conventional to talk of the manipulation of ethnic category by the political centre, seen both now and in the past, some regional elites are rightly apprehensive that the nationalist manipulation of ethnic category will equally well be revealed by such analysis. The details of post-independence conflicts often demonstrate that the activities of regional elites themselves, with their prescriptive notions of ethnic affiliation, served to homogenize the cultural and social experience of difference among the peoples that they claimed to be representing at a sub-category level.

However, underlying this sensitivity towards research that probes the realities of diversity at a local level is usually to be found a pressing concern that the Burmese military regime will exacerbate any divisions revealed to promote a policy of 'divide and rule'. This concern is especially acute at this time, when political discourse with the Burmese centre remains principally at the level of ceasefire agreements and when the role that ethnicity may have in any future restructuring of the Burmese state is being highly contested. As Mikael Gravers outlined in the introduction to this book, any researcher whose work is based on substantive relationships with members of 'minority' or 'nationality' communities must surely be obliged to take such concerns seriously. However, in some cases this concern not to aggravate the internal tensions of particular groups has produced a tacit agreement on the part of researchers that certain issues relating to ethnic diversity are best kept out of the public domain. A desire not to complicate the rhetoric of negotiation that regional elites employ with the central regime leads to a perpetuation of the essentializing, reductionist usage of terms such as 'Kachin', 'Chin', 'Karen', etc. These perpetuate the historical notion that ethnic categories are essentially unproblematic in the present and reflect coherent ethnic entities in the past. Nonetheless, for discussions of ethnicity and ethnic diversity in Burma to be able to transcend these limiting discourses, more nuanced understandings of these terms need to be developed. This chapter is an attempt to engage with this issue by outlining some of the historical contexts that have engendered this situation and will do so by problematizing use of the term 'Kachin' within the Burmese state.

Of course, the idea that one of the major ethnic categories that we have become so used to utilizing in our discourses on Burma should conceal a host of inconsistencies and complications at a sub-category or group level is hardly a novel insight. Two decades ago Robert Taylor highlighted the difficulties that this kind of intellectual mapping of the Burmese state can create:

This ascriptive conceptual mode for intellectually mapping the structure of Burma has been so widely accepted by Burma's political elite that they, like the Europeans who created it, have tended to accept the broad ethnic categories as embodying living social formations with political prerogatives. ... In this century, ethnic categories have taken on a life of their own, shaping the political thought and behaviour of central and regional elites. It is now impossible to avoid the use of broad ethnic labels even while attempting to demystify them.[1]

This chapter does in fact attempt to illustrate two of the difficulties outlined in Taylor's hypothesis. These are the problems that can arise from an over-reliance on the use of categories to underwrite an analytical ethno-political model of the Burmese state, and the impact that the British colonial period had in engendering this situation.

Yet not all would agree with the conclusions that Taylor originally drew in his paper that 'a false problem has been posed in the practice and study of Burma's politics' and that certain desirable aspects of pre-colonial relations could and should be restored such that 'it is possible under the present constitutional and political structures of Burma, that ethnicity might once more become the subordinate and generally unobtrusive political factor that it was before the colonial period'.[2] That colonialism and forces of modernism and globalization have transformed the historical boundaries of group identities seems without dispute. However, we are yet to explore satisfactorily what the precise nature of those historical transformations might be, and the diversity of experiences and responses that these transformative processes encountered. This chapter, therefore, will also explore the question of how, and if, our understanding of ethnic diversity in Burma can somehow become 'decolonized': whether or not we can begin to discover the psychological saliency of labels of group identity according to models that to some extent stand outside the structures of the colonial and post-colonial state systems. The need to 'decolonize' ethnic categories in Burma is thus not only a historical challenge but also a significant epistemological difficulty.

The statement that we may need to 'decolonize' our understanding of ethnic category in Burma is, however, directed towards issues of colonialism other than just those outlined by Taylor. Linda Tuhiwai Smith challenges the very fundamentals of western research models by which we may approach communities such as 'The Kachin'.[3] She considers these models to be methodologically bounded by colonial contexts even in a post-colonial world and rejects the assumption in the academia that there is an innate integrity to 'pure' research: that it essentially helps to illuminate a greater good, no matter what specific local difficulties might ensue as a result. Smith ultimately reserves the right to define the usefulness of any research agenda to the community that the research has made its subject (or object). Whilst not conceding the correctness of this stance completely, we should take note when Smith, a 'Maori' researcher, states:

> At a common sense level research was talked about [by Maori people] both in terms of its absolute worthlessness to us … and its absolute usefulness to those who wielded it as an instrument. It told us things already known, suggested things that would not work, and made careers for people who already had jobs.[4]

This leads us again to the issue of sensitivity to present concerns if engaging in politically 'difficult' research of one kind or another. One direction that can be taken is the tendency merely to privilege 'indigenous knowledge' as a sop to the challenge of attaining local authentication of one's research. At its worst, this approach leads to a quite uncritical authority being attached to the statements of key local representatives who have taken on the role of spokesperson for their communities, no matter how partial their interpretations or their own frame of understanding. Anyone who has taken the time to acquaint themselves with minority languages of Burma to engage more fully with peripheral historical or cultural discourses will readily appreciate the fallacy of this approach. The multifaceted concerns that underpin elite statements of 'indigenized' ethnographic fact as made by select 'informants' from peripheral communities reflect complex histories and often-intransigent present difficulties. Yet as Mikael Gravers outlined in his introduction, there can hopefully be a renegotiation of the boundaries of both sensitivity and academic objectivity, but this can only be effected by the nature of our engagement with these issues.

The methodology suggested in this chapter is intended to be a development of local research models relating to the interpretation of Kachin ethnicity, not just an uncritical account of them. It is intended to be a constructive engagement with contemporary local discourses relating to the ethnic category Kachin, and ultimately to indicate a strategy by which the term may be understood as something other than as it is defined presently by its own rhetorical limitations. It thus seeks to engage with issues with which even Kachin elites and local researchers are having difficulty negotiating at a sub-category level at the present time. However, it will do so by using materials and sources that they themselves have gathered together as being psychologically salient to the difficulty they seek to address.[5] This chapter will attempt to elucidate a methodology, using oral tradition and associated rituals as significant forms of data, to illuminate that a socio-ritual system and a coherent cognitive model of space/place (see Dean, this volume) existed in a domain that came to be known as 'Kachin'; that it had a geographical, social, cultural, political and economic coherence; and that the complexity of this formulation renders the demand that the term 'ethnic' must be used to privilege it even seem somewhat crude. Furthermore, it may be possible to demonstrate the cognitive boundaries of this system in some detail, to explore its psychological saliency and how it functioned as a cogent cosmological model (see Gravers, Chapter 9 in this volume)].[6] This is a radically different viewpoint from the conventional national model of these communities – that they lack the ability to 'prove' substantively their historical relationships in ways that are informed by serious academic approaches. In understanding diversity in Burma past and present, it may indeed be necessary to abandon our attachment to the prescriptive trope of primordialist 'ethnicities', as Taylor has suggested. However, this does not necessitate the abandonment of the historic claims to distinctiveness of certain communities from the Burmese polity, or the assertion that 'ethnicity' by any name is nothing more than a historical fallacy.

THE PREDICAMENT OF COLONIAL ETHNIC CATEGORIES IN BURMA AND SYMBOLIC DISCOURSES ON HISTORICAL DIVERSITY

The contention that Burma's modern ethnic categories were constructed as a result of British colonialism, and that 'ethnicity', if it could be said to exist at all, existed in a significantly different form prior to this, is, 20 years on from Taylor's article, something of a given for much theoretical analysis of ethnicity in Burma. Indeed, such analyses of inter-ethnic relations have had an important place as a public model to which the political centre of modern Burma has claimed to aspire for at least half a century – notably from 1953 onwards when the Panglong Agreement was morphed officially into a more abstract concept known as the Panglong Spirit.[7] This Spirit is supposed to embody innately harmonic inter-community relations, which it is contested existed prior to the intervention of the British colonial machine in Burma.

However, while the contention that the experience of British colonialism effected significant cognitive as well as political changes to 'ethnic' relations in Burma does not seem to be too controversial a proposition, any statement beyond this, such as that of Taylor's cited previously, does in fact postulate a historical model that has yet to be proven as substantively accurate across the broad geographical and historical landscape to which the modern Burmese state lays claim.

While some research has been conducted on pre-colonial relations between the Burman polity and lowland dwelling groups labelled Mon, Karen and Arakanese, the same cannot be said of historical relations with communities such as the 'Kachin' peoples.[8] One reason for this is the relative dearth of historical text arising from 'the Kachin' peoples and other communities lacking longstanding literary traditions.[9] Despite the fact that orality in its various forms constitutes significant religious, political, social, cultural and historical domains in Burma both past and present, without text-based historical documentation in their own languages by which they can present their own model of the past, locating the identity 'Kachin' historically and determining its relations with a Burman centre has, therefore, traditionally been to a great extent dependent upon the documentation of 'Other'. We can 'find' Kachin only by its illumination through Burmese (or Chinese or Shan etc.) texts.

Kachin elites thus face two principal dilemmas when they try to contest the kind of historical model of pre-colonial (or a-colonial) ethnic relations that reconfigures the category 'Kachin' as a colonial construct. First, establishing the nature of Kachin–Burman relations through the historical record of 'Other' is deemed to emphasize unduly the historical integrity of the greater Burmese state by relying upon Burmese sources to validate and legitimate a 'Kachin' historical presence. Second, and conversely, by highlighting the relative lack of data concerning the category Kachin, support will be given to the contention that this category is merely an invention of the British colonial period, a political and geographical construct, and that it otherwise has no historical validity. Both interpretations are considered highly damaging to political claims for the autonomy of this ethnic category in the present that are based on the idea that it did in fact function as a discrete political, economic, social, cultural and geographic entity over an extended historical period.

While there is a considerable amount of unpublished colonial-period documentation relating to the structuring of ethnic categories that could be utilized in this discourse, local researchers presently lack access to it as well as training in the academic strategies by which it may be critically deconstructed.[10] In the absence of substantive own-language documentation, therefore, the strategies by which both the Burmese centre and the Kachin elites interpret their historical relationships have become highly symbolic and focus on contested interpretations of colonial contact. A specific example of this symbolic discourse may be given.[11] A small room upstairs in Myitkyina Museum is dedicated to 'Notables from Kachin State'. In 1998 its display, consisting mainly of photographs of state leaders from the Socialist era onwards, was evidently designed to illustrate a broad historical vision of Kachin relations with the Burmese state. At the far end of the room was a painting of General Aung San, copied from a well known photograph taken at the Panglong Conference, and standing adjacent to this was the near life-sized, gold-painted statue of a Kachin chief, dressed in the costume of a Burmese General.[12] This statue is of the Daifar Duwa (Duffa Gam in colonial archives), a Kachin chief from the Hukawng Valley who had joined forces with Mahabandula prior to and during the first Anglo-Burmese war (1824–26) to invade Upper Assam.[13] This statue was the only figuration of a historic, pre-Socialist era, named 'Kachin' personality in the museum, and the institution thus perpetuated the sense of historical wilderness by which even Kachin peoples themselves construct their accounts of secular history. However, the juxtaposition of this Kachin chief in Burmese battle dress (figured thus as a prototype Kachin Burmese nationalist hero), the implicit figure of Mahabandula, and the painting of General Aung San, symbolized a linear relationship between the period of the first Anglo-Burmese war, the struggle for independence from the British and Panglong as an expression of the innate desire of the Kachin peoples to be a part of a greater Burma. The whole symbolized the natural historic order that should have pertained were it not for the perversion wrought by the colonial experience. The Kachin should 'yearn after their mother and not their aunt'.[14]

The lack of access to documentation by which the above model could be contested challenges Kachin researchers to develop alternative strategies of historical discourse. For example, a large statue of a Kachin chief who resisted the expansion of British control in Upper Burma at the end of the nineteenth century has been placed at the entrance to the large community festival or *manau* ground in Myitkyina. The biography of this individual clearly reflects a dual or ambiguous discourse in relation to local and national historical narratives of Kachin historical affiliation.

State officials may construct it as an anti-colonial symbol, local people as a historic affirmation of independence from both Burmese state and colonial interventions. Another symbolic strategy relates to that of etymologies. The use of constructed folk etymologies as an alternative form of historical evidence reflects a very common strategy employed by communities lacking substantive own-language historical written records. These etymologies lay claim to being products of an indigenous intelligence that would traditionally be expressed orally. However, highly metalinguistically framed discourse to explain the etymology of terms is frequently seen to be derived from a different cognitive framework to that of 'traditional' knowledge. Scribner and Cole, for example, suggest that such cognitive structuring may have been influenced by the experience of schooling and literacy.[15] The significance of folk etymologies as a form of historical discourse and the attestations towards historical 'proof' that are made on their behalf is, therefore, more nuanced than it might at first appear in relation to text and documentation and the ability to authenticate identities by the assumption of a literate, educated stance in the absence of other text-based sources.

One Jinghpaw researcher has constructed an oppositional symbolic discourse based on an alternative folk etymology of the name *Bandula*.[16] In this local symbolic discourse 'Bandu', it is argued, was derived from the Kachin family name *Dumdu* – a segment of the Jinghpaw Maran clan lineage. *La* is the conventional terminology for the third born son in Jinghpaw. The historical construction promoted by the museum is thus turned on its head – Mahabandula 'becomes' Kachin and the Daifar Duwa by implication joined with him as an expression of Kachin brotherhood. When this model of historical relations between the Kachin and the Burmese centre is used to interpret the museum display described above, the juxtaposition with the figure of Aung San could emphasize the *de facto* failure of the Panglong Agreement and brings into question a supposed notion of an innate *Spirit.* This symbolic reinterpretation accords with local discourses on this subject that otherwise cannot enter the public domain.

FOLK ETYMOLOGIES OF 'KACHIN' AND THE FAILURE TO INDIGENIZE THE DEEP MEANINGS OF THE TERM

Symbolic etymological proofs such as this are very often found at the crux of local discourses on the origins of ethnic labels, and these proofs are often clearly intended to be interventions against the official national histories developed at the political centre. The ability to explain the origins of names – ethnonyms, place names, family names – implies the ownership of these terms, which then become symbols of the cognitive possession of place, the indigenization of identities, as well as ownership of the deep meaning of these features historically. They help to assist the primordial claims of ethnic categories to be considered meaningful and historically grounded entities within or independent of the Burmese state.

Sakhong's analysis of Chin (this volume) demonstrates such a strategy by which an ethnonym can be indigenized (primordialized) and thus 'authenticated' using research strategies that blend 'indigenous knowledge' with Western research methods. However, while Sakhong has used oral tradition to authenticate use of the term 'Chin' as a self-referent, the opposite can be shown to be true for the term 'Kachin'. What distinguishes the term 'Kachin' in this respect is that it has so singularly failed to attain status as an indigenous form by the creation of convincing folk etymological explanations. In traditional Jinghpaw oral culture, when proper nouns, especially names, carry a narrative weight, they are constructed in ways that are culturally embedded and require no further explanation for the audience.[17] Typically this is done by the combination of syllables that already carry separate meanings and can be understood in combination as embodying qualities or representing types that are culturally already pellucid. This is strategy that could be employed to deconstruct the bi-syllabic term 'Kachin' and to create an indigenous etymology for it. Significantly, this has not been achieved convincingly to reclaim the origins of this term for local peoples.

'Kachin' people themselves have contested over an extended historical period that 'Kachin' is not an indigenous term of self-reference. Although various folk etymologies of the term have been constructed and promoted, their explanations typically resolve on the fact of some linguistic or social misinterpretation by 'Other', hinting at their possible origin in the complex auto-ethnography of Kachin peoples when in discourse with non-Kachin people, and in contexts in which their own explanatory idioms did not predominate.[18] For example, Kachin nationalists today sometimes emphasize that usage of the term arose as a result of miscommunication with Eugenio Kincaid, the first Baptist Christian missionary to have direct contact with the Kachin in the 1830s. This states that when Kincaid asked local people who they were (through the medium of Shan translators), they

Figure 2.1. Kachin cultural symbol, the *manau* posts in Putao. (Photo: K. Dean)

misunderstood his question and replied that they were from Gahkyen – a local village.[19] There have also been attempts to interpret Gahkyen as Ga Hkyeng, meaning 'red earth'. This has been interpreted as referring to the land sometimes called 'The Triangle' in colonial archives that lies between the Mali and N'mai rivers and is considered by many to be the heartland of traditional Kachin (Jinghpaw) culture.[20] Some Kachin people will tell you that 'red earth' relates to the lowland areas close to the Irrawaddy River (the locale of Gahkyen village) where there was much bloodshed in conflict with Burmese and Shan authorities. They choose to interpret 'red earth' as relating to the blood of defeated Burmese or Shan forcesthat stained the soil. The Burmese government has also constructed its own etymology for 'Kachin', which overlays a Burmese translation upon the Burmese transcription. The term then comes to mean 'people who love to dance'. This interpretation accords well with the touristic representation of the Kachin peoples as a 'colourful' nationality minority in modern Burma/Myanmar, their culture(s) essentialized upon the community dance of the *manau*.[21] All of these etymologies have their own political and cultural implications depending upon who is giving the explanation and in what circumstances.

Despite this, it might indeed be possible for someone so inclined to construct an indigenous etymology for the term 'Kachin' following much the same model as that employed by Sakhong. Indeed almost identical linguistic (lexical) strategies could be used, which would also focus on the same syllable and its plethora of transcriptions: jien – cheyn – chin – kaiyn.[22] This could be a useful strategy for some Kachin nationalists who wish to establish a link between Ka*chin* and *Jing*hpaw, the largest of the Kachin sub-groups who were first referred to as 'Kachin' in British colonial archives (see below). If dissociated from a phonological or tonal context (which is what has happened as these terms have been recorded historically), the constructed etymology of this syllable could even be extended to hypothesize a broader landscape of intersecting ritual and oral tradition encompassing both 'Chin' and 'Kachin' groups.

However, at some point this kind of pseudo-linguistic analysis starts to contravene the sensibilities of local communities and, in fact, does little to unravel the historical processes by which these terms have emerged. It is in fact very difficult to avoid drawing the conclusion from the historical record that the term 'Kachin' has long been a problematic of local self-reference, and that its cognitive associations have been difficult to 'indigenize' or positively to transform even by the communities which it represents.

It is also possible to demonstrate this by studying corpora of oral traditions, albeit in a different way to that employed by Sakhong. Rather than utilize extrapolated and dissociated fragments of oral tradition as evidence, use of the term 'Kachin' can be analysed using the quantitative computational analysis of an extensive corpus of Jinghpaw ritual language in context.[23] Even when a corpus of more than a quarter of a million lexical items is examined, the term 'Kachin' is found not to appear at all. This more than anything else must support the view that 'Kachin' was not a traditional, indigenous form of group reference, Significantly, it also suggests that the extent to which traditional ritual discourses have been able to transform the term 'Kachin' successfully into an indigenously preferred term of self-identification appears to have been extremely limited, even at a time of heightened Kachin nationalism.

THE EMERGENCE OF KACHIN AS AN ETHNOGRAPHIC CATEGORY IN COLONIAL BURMA

As stated, it is possible to trace objections by 'Kachin' people over an extended historical period to the use of the term 'Kachin' as a group or self-identifier: from the 1830s with the first substantive direct contact with these groups, right up to the eve of independence in 1948 when Kachin elders at the Frontier Areas Committee of Enquiry objected to its usage for the new state.

The term 'Kachin' was not a colonial invention and seems to have been well-established in both Burmese and Shan political circles by the time the British military and colonial administrations established themselves in Burma from 1824 onwards.[24] Burmese and Shan translators seem to have used the term to denote to colonial officials a somewhat vaguely defined hill-dwelling community and mountain region, which had a sometimes difficult relationship with the plains.[25] The associations of *Kajien, Kakiayn* or *Kakhyen* in the derived model seem to accord well with the Tai (Shan) 'Kha – Pa' social classification that was used to distinguish many hill-dwelling groups from their lowland Tai neighbours, and this could explain the origins of the prefix of the term.[26] Certainly for Kachin peoples the derogatory connotations of the term could have been derived from an embedded awareness of this context.

However, it was not long before the colonial archive recorded accounts from local 'Kachin' elites in which they contested the use of the term. The term that they most commonly sought to privilege instead was *Singpho*, a variant pronunciation of Jinghpaw (usually transcribed during the colonial period as *Chingpaw* or *Chinghpaw*). The term 'Jinghpaw' – and historically that of 'Singpho' – relates to the largest of the modern Kachin subgroups, and is deemed to constitute a nexus of lineages which together form affinal kinship relationships.[27] It also describes the dominant linguistic and cultural space of the Kachin region (see Dean, this volume).[28] The origins of the term are uncertain, but, in contrast to the term Kachin, the view that there is an authentic folk etymology of Jinghpaw derived from oral tradition can be traced at least to the early nineteenth century.[29] In what has become the dominant version of this tradition, human beings were believed to have emerged from a drum, *chyingtawt*. This would (or could) be linked euphonically in the traditional system of prosody with the couplet *chyinghpaw*, meaning 'to open' (*hpaw ai*). Thus Jinghpaw is deemed to refer to the people who emerged from the drum. There are variations to the explanation described above, but the key point is that it is possible to construct an etymology for the term 'Jinghpaw' which is deemed to be indigenously meaningful and which is considered to be culturally embedded.[30] This has helped to distinguish it as a local referent in ways that have not been achieved convincingly with the term 'Kachin'. The principal difficulty in a modern context, however, is that *Chyinghpaw/Jinghpaw* as an extrapolated and isolated ethnonym may in some contexts be interpreted either as a generic, global term for 'man' or as a specific nexus of lineages descended from these ancestors.[31] This ambiguity is politically problematic between Kachin groups today in relation to preferred labels of multi-group identity and the concerns that non-Jinghpaw groups have in relation to Jinghpaw dominance of the Kachin category.

Initially there was a tendency to conflate the terms '*Kahkyen*' and '*Singpho*' in the colonial archive but it is also clear that distinctions were made between these as they were transferred to the colonial domain. The 1830s were times of considerable Jinghpaw inter-community rivalry and 'Singpho' chiefs, residing from Mogaung westwards to the trans-border region with Assam, utilized the term '*Kakhyen*' as a label of alterity in reference to their more easterly kin when in discussion with colonial officials. They apparently assimilated to the intellectual construction of the term 'Kachin' as 'Other', seemingly aware of and indeed supporting the somewhat derogatory connotations of that term in relation to their more easterly kin to their own advantage.[32] This was a political tactic to advance their claims to status as the political structure of the North East Frontier was being delineated.[33]

Over the course of the next 40 years, the dramatic development of the Assamese tea industry led to the geo-political separation of those groups labelled 'Singpho', who came to be considered a minority within India, and those labelled 'Kachin', a term which was understood solely as a Burma-oriented ethnographic trope. Only by the 1880s, when the separation between the Singpho of Assam and the Kachin of Burma had become an administrative reality for an entire generation of colonial officials, was close enough direct contact established again with Kachin communities in the east and south of the Kachin hills region for them again to proffer their preferred terms of self-reference. However, developments in transcription systems now led to a new orthography for the term previously known as 'Singpho' – *Chingpaw* – so that the Singpho of Assam and the Chingpaw of Burma appeared in the colonial archives as relating to two different ethnicities with supposedly 'different' names. What had commenced as a linguistic and administrative confusion had become consolidated as a political, geographic and ethnographic fact.

As the British colonial administration established itself in skeleton form in this region, the term 'Kachin' remained as a functioning general administrative category, but it came to have far wider connotations than the Jinghpaw communities to whom it had originally been applied, as more hill-dwelling communities were brought within its administrative orbit. Greater contact, however, merely led to the emergence of a series of ethnic appendages to the label 'Kachin', and the development of a series of sub-groups based on an ethnographic distinction of hill dwelling as opposed to lowland dwelling communities.

Sub-categories of Kachin began to be formalized after 1895, following the 'pacification' of the Kachin Hills and the implementation of the Kachin Hills Regulation. Some sub-categories were framed linguistically and were consolidated by the need to develop criteria for the categorization of communities in the official census.[34] Language was interpreted in this context as a signifier of the primordial ethnic origins of peoples that was then transposed to an ethnographic present of 'race'. This classificatory strategy reconfigured the social and historical significance of polyglotism in this region and underestimated its anthropological value.

The military also developed generalized categories of ethnic groups, defined by stereotypes of social 'ethos' and physical characteristics which were used to delineate suitable recruiting fields and to classify recruits entering the Indian Army. The need to expand recruiting fields from the 'traditional' Kachin-designated domain in the environs of Bhamo meant that the first regular Kachin recruits included Jinghpaw, Lisu, Zaiwa and Nung soldiers. Significantly some of these, such as the Nung soldiers, lived beyond the boundaries of the Kachin Hills Regulation and were not, therefore, affiliated to the term 'Kachin' in any other official capacity.

There were, however, some significant ambiguities in this development of Kachin sub-groups: some groups included under the Kachin umbrella by the army or by the administration were separated from it in linguistic classifications. In particular this affected the classification of speakers of other branches of Tibeto-Burman language than Jinghpaw, such as Nung, Maru, and Lisu peoples. Not classified as Kachin by linguistic descent, and thus by implication neither by ethnicity (or 'race' as this was interpreted in the colonial state), but called 'Kachin' by the administration and in the army, and thus deemed to possess a certain ethnic 'ethos' that was deemed racially grounded, a tension developed in the various applications of the term – whether it referred to one community and one language, many communities but one language, to a geographical place or space, and so on. These inconsistencies still have ramifications today because contradictory colonial constructions are used as 'evidence' to undermine the multi-group identity Kachin as being no more than a political model.[35]

THE IMPACT OF MARTIAL AND MISSIONARY CONSTRUCTIONS OF THE KACHIN ETHNIC CATEGORY AND DISCOURSES ON SOCIAL STEREOTYPES

The colonial period also engendered cognitive as well as classificatory ambiguities in relation to the understanding of the term 'Kachin'. In some contexts, the modern identity 'Kachin' was deemed by some communities to have clear, identifiably positive connotations. Young Kachin men began to enter the martial apparatus of empire in 1898 when the first Kachin recruits entered the Burma Military Police.[36] In 1916 some Kachin Military Policemen received training with the 10th Gurkha Regiment in Maymyo and subsequently 'formed an indigenous wing in the 85th Burma Rifles when it was raised on the 15th July 1917'.[37] By the end of the First World War, there were sufficient numbers of Kachin recruits, and they were of sufficiently high regard following their wartime activities especially in Mesopotamia, that a Kachin Battalion was soon founded.[38] In the military sphere, 'Kachin' was considered as a multi-group category with positive connotations. Kachin soldiers became symbols of community progress that could be assimilated to notions of literate and technical education, modernity and social development.

Figure 2.2. Shatapru Baptist Church in Myitkyina. (Photo: K. Dean)

The other main sphere to define new connotations for the term was that of the Christian churches. Eugenio Kincaid of the American Baptist Mission was reputed to have been the first missionary to have had a direct, albeit brief, encounter with Kachin communities in the region near Bhamo in the 1830s. However, it was only after the Second Anglo-Burmese War of 1852 and the later suppression of the Panthay Rebellion in 1868 that more extended contact was possible, with French Catholic missionaries and those of the American Baptist Mission travelling and staying in the Kachin Hills near the Chinese border during the 1870s. By 1890, the decision had been made by the Baptist missionary Dr Ola Hanson to transcribe the Jinghpaw language using roman rather than Burmese script and this was subsequently approved by the government. The Catholic and Baptist churches utilized the term 'Kachin' in their local missions and transformed its associations: modernity was increasingly interpreted by Christian converts as being in opposition to 'traditional' Kachin society, which was predominantly animist.

There was a complex relationship between the spread of Christianity(ies), the development of an ethnic army and the emergence of ethnic nationalist communities, and we should be very wary of presenting these problematic developments as if they were either uniform or completed colonial facts. By the 1920s, the military and the missions were at the forefront of defining new cognitive boundaries for the term 'Kachin' and its implications for local communities. By this time also, Christian soldiers, who themselves embodied these new understandings of the term 'Kachin', seem to have emerged as a recognizable and influential socio-political constituency. As clear associations were made between joining the army and educational advancement in many communities, certain attitudes expressed by these soldiers increasingly seem to have acquired status as an educated stance. There also developed a Jinghpaw-language discursive public sphere in which their viewpoints could be disseminated. This was the first Jinghpaw-language newspaper, *Jinghpaw Shi Laika*. First published in August 1914 as a bimonthly and then as a monthly newspaper, it had been initiated by the American Baptist Mission. However, as so many of the contributors were soldiers, at times it almost had the appearance of being a military magazine. Many of the soldiers' published letters aspired towards a multi-group Kachin nationalist identity that could be positively associated with literate education and Christian modernist notions of development. They also promoted the commodification of ethnicity by encouraging the development of local vocational education projects which they hoped would transform traditional crafts, such as weaving, into marketable resources, which could enter national markets.[39]

Both the army and the missions used a set of social tropes in their discourses about ethnic or racial groups, similar in nature to those described by Dean (this volume).[40] These tropes came to be used as rhetorical devices by administrators, officers, missionaries and the new Kachin elites in expository discourses about the ethnic category Kachin. These discourses were often intended (and still are) to motivate people to engage in certain types of political or social action.[41] Binary categories such as highland/lowland, slavery/social morality, hard work/laziness, licentiousness/sobriety, all came to have political as well as social meanings for the category 'Kachin' in the newly emerging state and in the lead up to independence.

Some of the classificatory tropes employed were embedded in the model of the term from pre-colonial times.[42] However, there was an important difference in the way that they functioned in the imperial state compared to the negative connotations of the term 'Kachin' in Burman or Shan models. These latter stereotypes, for example which emphasized notions of 'lesser civilisation,'[43] existed primarily as an oral domain; they were part of a social discourse which was open to transformation and reinterpretation in differing contexts.[44] This posited a very different cognitive transcultural relationship than that which developed during the colonial period. Of importance in this process was the proliferation of colonial texts which sought to demarcate the social and cultural boundaries of the term.

Texts which defined ethnic categories, including the ethnographic musings of missionaries and military officers, as well as an increasing number of published reports arising from the political centre that delineated the political implications of the category 'Kachin' within the new Burmese state, arose from a literate sphere that appeared both to encapsulate the essence of its object, as well as to fix it as a timeless 'Other'. The textual domain of ethnic categorization was very difficult to transform, especially as those who were in a position to do so were closely associated with the institutions from which these texts arose – the military, the administration and the missions.

This textual domain which sought to concretize the social tropes and 'tribal ethos' of the category 'Kachin' also intersected in a powerful way with the principal Jinghpaw-language public sphere which discussed notions of modernity and development as a 'Kachin' issue – the Christian sermon.

CHRISTIANITY, SERMONS AND THE KACHIN ETHNIC CATEGORY

As previously stated, there has been a complex relationship between the spread of Christianity and the emergence of Kachin nationalist identity (see Gravers, Chapter 9 in this volume, for discussion of the complexities of this process in relation to Karen identity). These historical discussions are frequently confused, however, when rather simplistic relationships are posited between these multifaceted experiences, often with the implication that conversion to Christianity and the assumption of a nationalist identity were a linear process or locally uncontested. The real impact of Christian missions on emergent Kachin nationalism therefore requires much more rigorous analysis to improve our hitherto rather unsophisticated representations of this complex process. There are today, and were significantly so during the colonial period, communities of Kachin people who resisted the spread of the missions and conversion to Christianity. Indeed, the cognate Singpho communities of Arunachal Pradesh are today considered a predominantly Buddhist Scheduled minority in India (a fact which may prove a thorny predicament for 'Burmese' Kachin nationalists should the time come for greater social contact to be facilitated across borders) – which demonstrates the limitations of a prescriptive account of 'the Kachin' as 'Christian'.

Immediately following independence in 1948, the religious orientation of the Kachin nationalist movement was still contested. There were committed animist elders, such as Htingnan Kumja from the Hkahku-dominated region of the Mali-N'Mai 'Triangle' region, who felt that traditional Kachin animist practices were the only true expression of the Kachin spirit; there were animist-Buddhists such as Sinwa Naw, the first political leader of Kachin State, and others who had been raised in the complex anthropological environment of lowland areas; and there were the Christian educated youth leaders and soldiers who expressed a different kind of vision of Kachin modernity and socio-political development. However, as stated, it was the Church and the Christian military organizations that dominated the public sphere of Jinghpaw identity through their ability to organize, proselytize and connect their oral domain to the high status and elite context of modern print technology. What the textual domain of the colonial era confined to the page, the oral sphere of the Jinghpaw-language sermon supported and reiterated in relation to understandings of the Kachin ethnic category in its public sermons.

Christian sermons, therefore, especially those in the largest Kachin Christian constituency, the Baptist Church, have had a significant impact on the construction of a coherent nationalist Kachin identity. This is also a result because of the progressive narrowing during decades of military and political conflict of secular print and text domains in which issues of identity and nationalism could be discussed. Following independence, this narrowing occurred as a result of official central censorship by the state as well as the *de facto* censorship of militarized Kachin nationalist organizations, who were predominantly led by Christian soldiers. Before the ceasefire of 1994, the Jinghpaw-language public sphere was almost entirely the preserve of the Kachin Jinghpaw-language churches and their nationalist sermons and publications, as religious texts were one genre that lay outside the remit of the official censor. As this sphere perpetuated much of the ethnographic rhetoric of the colonial period and continued to employ its texts in its discourse by privileging ethnographic works by missionaries such as Ola Hanson, Father Gilhodes and Christian officers such as C. M. Enriquez ('Theophilus'), it has been very hard to challenge, refute, renegotiate or decolonize the constructions of traditional Kachin morality and society that are perpetuated by the Kachin institutional churches. Furthermore, the representation of a uniform Kachin history arising from the church has long been an entirely historicist exercise in exalting the success of religious conversion. This rhetoric dominates representations of Kachin history in most discourses and through its lack of subtlety does little to dispute the claims of the Burmese centre that the Kachin have been misled by colonial officials and foreign missions in their interpretation of their historical relationship to the Burmese State. Today, some even within the religious establishment itself recognize the difficulties engendered by this representation of the past and bemoan the fact that the Kachin people lack an adequately researched secular history. However, their inability to find other means of representing the Kachin ethnic category historically, for reasons outlined earlier, dissuade many from a revisionist approach.

CONTESTING STEREOTYPES OF HIGHLAND AND LOWLAND FOR THE KACHIN ETHNIC CATEGORY DURING THE COLONIAL PERIOD

Clearly there have always been internal debates as to what constitutes Kachin identity, how the category should represent itself culturally, socially and politically within the state, how its various and varied communities should be encouraged to relate to the boundaries of identity that were established by Kachin Christian nationalists in times of conflict, and how these communities should respond to the representations of them by 'Other'. One of the ways in which this debate has been expressed has been through the creation of a local term deemed an indigenous equivalent of 'Kachin'.

One term which is often cited as being an indigenized equivalent of 'Kachin' is *Jinghpaw amyu ni*.[45] This may be translated as 'roots and branches' of the Jinghpaw. It evokes the concept of the multiplicity of clans

53

and lineage segments that intersect across the Kachin region and that are deemed to be of the Jinghpaw lineage. However, in the 'open system' of ritual identity formation that Edmund Leach first attempted to describe, in which diversity was homogenized at an ideal level by the prevalence of a dominant ritual idiom, which was Jinghpaw, it would also be possible to extend this classification to non-Jinghpaw lineages. However, the ambivalence of the term 'Jinghpaw' described previously, in which it may be used to refer either to a specific lineage or a generic term for 'man' has problematized usage of this term in the present. Today, connotations of reified ethnic status have made many non-Jinghpaw groups distrustful of any attempt to privilege the term 'Jinghpaw' as a multi-group referent.

In recent years the term 'Wunpawng' has been preferred and this is commonly presented today as if this had a primordial status as a local self-referent. In fact the usage of the term as an ethnonym is a relatively recent innovation, although it is derived from a nationalist interpretation of archaic oral tradition, as will be shown. The emergence of this term, however, reveals much about the way in which nationalists have felt it necessary to redefine the cognitive associations of these various terms over time in a reflexive response to the term 'Kachin': a desire to repossess the primary group category identity from the negative connotations with which it is still associated. The term 'Wunpawng' as an ethnonym emerged from a number of variants used by local development, cultural and political organizations from the 1920s onwards. These organizations sought to address issues of category stereotyping that were being promoted at the national centre. The first of these organizations, and the one which perhaps most clearly reveals the relationship of the indigenized term 'Wunpawng' to the term 'Kachin' is that founded by Jinghpaw Gam in the late 1920s and it is that which will now be considered.

There was never a time when the civil and military officers in the Kachin hills or missionaries felt that their work was uniformly accepted by local Kachin people. However progressively throughout the 1920s and 1930s the ability to conceal significant undercurrents of discontent towards the military, the missions and the administration was becoming harder. Most worryingly for the colonial administration, by the late 1930s, the group that the administration intended to be the newly honed Kachin elite – the regular soldiers discharged into civilian life – were proving to be a potentially disruptive political force.

Although there was considerable variation in the experience of empire among the Kachin soldiers, one thing that they shared was a degree of awareness as to how the identity 'Kachin' was related in various colonial spheres, as well as how it was figured in the complex ethno-political structuring of the Burmese state that was taking place. Some soldiers, such as the first regular Kachin recruit, Subedar Major Jinghpaw Gam, questioned the political implications of the ethnographic social tropes that were used to describe the category 'Kachin'. Jinghpaw Gam was particularly suspicious of the way in which the binary category of highland/lowland was being utilized in the political structuring of the country. His judgement was astute. In 1937 this classification was used to debar the Kachin from participation at the political centre of the Burmese state by the designation of the Kachin Hills as an Excluded Area. In 1948 the new Constitution delineated a political constituency, 'The Kachin' (upland), as being distinct from other constituencies, 'The Non-Kachin' (lowland), all of whom resided in a mixed geo-political region, 'Kachin State' (upland and lowland). This latter fact both supported and confused the ethnic specificity of the term within the new state model.

Although apparently premised on local models of ethnic relations, the colonial model of upland–lowland was significantly different from them. The Shan construct of 'Kachin' as an upland group, for example, related primarily to hierarchical social categories.[46] However, the colonial interpretation employed very different intellectual models, incorporating different ideas on the relationship between land-ownership and political rights, language, migration and race, and various notions of 'primitivism'. Highland and lowland were interpreted in this context as static, environmentally naturalized political categories: characteristics that, apparently, could not even be transcended by the newly emerging political structures, only recognized and upheld by them. Insofar as it related to a people, the status of the term 'Kachin' as an upland ethnographic fact, which was to be permanently distinguished from the lowlands, was now something that Kachin society was expected to internalize as being 'true' anthropologically, socially, politically, even biologically. In 1937, for example, the health discourse of the Kachin Regeneration Campaign related the immutability of the Kachin highland ethnic category as being due to physiology: Kachin people became unwell, it stated, if they should attempt to live in lowland areas and they should thus remain in their highland domain.[47] In fact this rhetoric in 1937 was principally intended to dissuade ex-soldiers from settling in the plains, particularly along the railway corridor where there were increasing disputes between Kachin and Shan communities.

Jinghpaw Gam objected strongly to this physiological construction of Kachin ethnicity and he refused to make allowances for it, not least because he was aware of its political implications and how it was being used to delineate the political future of the Kachin Hills. Upon his retirement, therefore, Jinghpaw Gam chose instead to settle on the plains and tried to encourage as many ex-soldiers and others to join him. His intention was that, if Kachin people could become established as a plains-dwelling minority, they would then be able to claim the right to have an elected member in the House of Representatives in Lower Burma. When officials tried to call him to meetings with other elders in the hills, he refused to go, turning the racial model upside down by claiming that going to the hills made him feel unwell.

Figure 2.3. Leaders of the *manau* dance (one of them a Baptist pastor) in Kachin State. (Photo: K. Dean)

Jinghpaw Gam's response reveals some of the tensions in interpretation of the term 'Kachin' that had been engendered by the colonial development of the term. Jinghpaw Gam was a Christian and desired the educational development of the Kachin peoples, as well as their economic, political and social uplift. However, he blended this desire for modernity with a critical approach to the model of Kachin ethnicity that he felt was still being defined predominantly by 'Other'. His response was to establish the first local development organization dedicated to the educational and social improvement of the Kachin peoples. In this he endeavoured to incorporate notions of modernity and Christian development as constructed by the missions and the military, but also to repossess the definition of the term 'Kachin' as a locally meaningful category. This meant indigenizing the term 'Kachin', not by reconstructing its folk etymology, but by repossessing the deep understandings of the social relationships which constituted its underpinnings through a local term that would act as its cognate. He named his organization Pawng Yawng Hpung. The ethnonym *Wunpawng* evokes a similar cognitive and semantic domain as this name, as will be shown.

INDIGENIZING 'KACHIN' – THE EMERGENCE OF *WUNPAWNG*

A very complex balancing act is still being played out by Kachin elites between the desire both to challenge the colonial construction of the Kachin ethnic category, and to make use of it as a means of authenticating Kachin alterity from the central discourses of the post-independence Burmese state. In this situation, the promotion of a local referent has been sought that could on the one hand take advantage of real political and geographical advantages of the term 'Kachin' as an official category but on the other would redefine it as a locally meaningful referent.

As previously stated, it is sometimes implied that *Wunpawng* has an archaic or primordial status. This is so in some senses of the word, but not in the strict usage of the term as an ethnonym. Again, studies of oral tradition can be used to demonstrate this. Using the same corpus of ritual language detailed earlier, it is possible to establish the cognitive boundaries of the term '*Wunpawng*' as an ethnonym.[48] *Wunpawng* in contemporary renderings of oral tradition typically has a quite restricted and specific usage, having two principal connotations: *Wunpawng Mungdan* [Wunpawng/Kachin Land or Country],[49] and *Wunpawng Htunghking* [Wunpawng /Kachin customs, ways, 'culture']. Both of these collocations are framed by contemporary nationalist meanings and can be shown to be modern inclusions in the recitations cited.[50]

Jinghpaw is a monosyllabic language that has a high facility towards word formation by its extensive use of affixes, suffixes and the juxtaposition of highly nuanced lexical items to create subtle inflexions of meaning.[51] *Wun* is a preformative that can convey many senses when attached to a variety of word types. However, significantly, in the historical dictionary written by the missionary Ola Hanson and first published in 1906, the term *'wunpawng'* is compared with that of *'wundung'*.[52] Both terms are referred to as meaning 'centre', the former as an adjective, the latter as a noun. The noun is further described in its ritual couplet form *wundung shingra* as 'the traditional "Eden" in Kachin lore', evoking its usage in 'creation myths' which identify the original homeland from which human beings migrated to the Earth.[53] Although this dictionary is extremely problematic as an historical document, it makes no mention of the term *'Wunpawng'* explicitly as an ethnonym of the kind that could be considered an indigenized equivalent of 'Kachin'. Even if it were Hanson's intention to downgrade this word as a local term of ethno-political identity, the local trajectories of the term in Kachin discourse also suggest that contemporary ethnonymic connotations have accrued to it rather than being innately embedded in the term historically and that this has developed out of a concept of an original 'homeland', albeit one which does not equate to 'Kachin' as an ethnonymic referent.

The development of the term *'Wunpawng'*, as stated, may be traced through a genealogy of local cultural, political and military organizations, and it seems reasonable to trace that descent from that starting with Jinghpaw Gam's *Pawng Yawng Hpung*. Because of the Jinghpaw pattern of word formation and euphony, *Pawng Yawng* may be associated with *Wunpawng* as they are based on the same root and are clearly derived from the same semantic and cognitive domain of oral tradition. *Pawng Yawng* may sometimes be used in a very similar way to that of *Pawng Yaw* and the relationship between these two terms therefore requires some explanation. *Pawng Yaw* is according to Jinghpaw oral tradition the common ancestor of all the Jinghpaw clans; *yaw* is typically used to identify a sixth-born son, and it is from the sixth-born son of the common ancestor that the Jinghpaw clans often claim to be descended. However, this has a lineage specificity that clearly excludes non-Jinghpaw lineages if it were to be considered a multi-group ethnonym. It becomes possible, however, to reconfigure this couplet while retaining its cognitive assimilation with the semantic domain of oral tradition. According to the tonality of the word, *pawng* can be translated as either something that is shared or held in common, or it can mean to be central or of chief importance.[54] *Yawng* can be translated as meaning all, or the whole of something. Thus, by reconfiguring the way these various components relate to each other, but maintaining the psychological saliency of the semantic domain of oral ritual, *Pawng Yawng* refers to an ancestor of central importance for all the lineages, Jinghpaw and non-Jinghpaw alike, who is held as a common ancestor.

It is unclear as to whether Jinghpaw Gam himself was a part of this reconfiguration of meanings, but the prevailing sense is that it probably did not emerge as a conscious rearticulation of 'invented' identity at all but had deeper roots that cannot be precisely determined. However, following use of the term '*Pawng Yawng*' in his modern, socio-political development organization, it came to be used in like fashion by other groups who sought to assert their ethnic identity within a broader political setting but in an inherently local discourse. For example, the name of one of the principal political parties following independence, headed by Duwa Zau Rip, was *Pawng Yawng Ram Rawt Hpung*.[55] However, after independence, and especially following the increasingly centralizing activities of the Burmese polity in the 1950s and early 1960s, the local discursive aspects reflecting local political affiliations seem to have been directed more and more towards central political events affecting the Kachin region as a whole. With this change in discourse one finds a change again to a different kind of identity label. In the early 1960s, a group of Kachin nationalist students, the Seven Stars, who later went on to found the Kachin Independence Army (KIA), established a Kachin Literature and Culture Committee at Rangoon University, which they called Jinghpaw Wunpawng Lailik Laika hte Htunghking Hpung. Here use of Jinghpaw was modified, although the term '*Wunpawng*' evoked the semantic domain of ancestry and archaism as well as the semantic specificity of coreness, centrality and unity. However, use of the term '*Wunpawng*' with that of Jinghpaw evokes also the contention, which many maintain today, that *Wunpawng* is essentially an adjective that needs to be used in conjunction with a noun: it cannot evoke by itself the notion of lineages and descent groups that are also vital to the functioning of an ethnonym. Certainly it would seem that at this time, on the eve of the outbreak of armed resistance to the central government, the term

'*Wunpawng*' does not seem to have been established as an ethnonym in its own right. It seems to have emerged in this style of usage with modern nationalist connotations, in parallel with the term 'Kachin', as a state-oriented discourse.[56] In this sense it seems quite coherent to represent *Wunpawng* as a local equivalent of Kachin. However, the fact that its usage is also locally contested demonstrates that this term in itself does not equate fully to indigenized models of identity formation.

This can also be seen in relation to the modern trajectories of this term. When the Kachin Independence Army was founded, it was initially called Jinghpaw Wunpawng Mungdan Shanglawt. However, the use of the term 'Jinghpaw' was dropped as local discourses and the need to uphold the unity of many peoples in the Kachin region determined that this could, after all, be interpreted with too narrow an ethnographic compass. Following the Cultural Revolution in China, there were increasing numbers of migrants into Kachin State from a diverse range of communities, but especially large numbers of Lisu peoples, who objected to affiliating themselves to the term 'Jinghpaw'. Not least this was because the term '*Jingpo*' had its own specific ethnographic connotations in the Chinese state, from which they distinguished themselves. There was also a concern that the Chinese government might be distrustful of the organization if they assumed its intention was to establish a broader geo-political Jinghpaw state as a nationalist project. Similar concerns relating to the perception of a pan-Jinghpaw/Singpho nationalist movement by the Indian government were also taken into account. Thus it was decided to use the term '*Wunpawng*' as an equivalent of Kachin as a multi-group category and to downplay any explicit reference to what might be deemed the specificity of the Jinghpaw lineage.

MULTI-GROUP ETHNIC CATEGORY IN THE POST-COLONIAL BURMESE STATE: THE CONSOLIDATION OF A SIX-GROUP IDENTITY, CIVIL SOCIETY AND THE POST-CEASEFIRE CONTEXT

However, in the post-colonial Burmese state, the problem of 'Kachin' has also become the problem of *Wunpawng*. Tegenfeldt (2002) has discussed how the transformation of ethnic conflict in the Burmese state depends to a great extent upon the degree to which minority groups feel less threatened by the central regime: that they should feel confident that their cultures, languages and historical perceptions of the state should be respected. One should also extend this analysis to the experience of conflict transformation at the sub-category level. Many non-Jinghpaw groups within the Kachin/ *Wunpawng* umbrella feel threatened by the dominance of Jinghpaw models of place/space, language, social and historical discourse and cultural forms. Kachin nationalists in a situation of extreme conflict developed prescriptive ethno-cultural symbolic discourses that made formerly permeable social and cultural boundaries appear concrete. Where these have resolved the dilemma of diversity through the promotion of Jinghpaw models of culture and society, they present as great a challenge to the principle of ethnic diversity in the present and a proper understanding of its dynamics in the past as any activities undertaken by the central regime in the eyes of some non-Jinghpaw communities.

While the new constitution of independent Burma written in 1947 consolidated the term 'Kachin' as a primary ethnic category and geo-political boundary, it was a constitutionally undifferentiated term juxtaposed straightforwardly with that of 'non-Kachin'. Paragraph 166 of the 1947 Constitution states that of the 12 seats in the Kachin State Council, six are for 'Kachins' and six are for 'non-Kachins'. The minister for the Kachin State was to be 'Kachin', but half of his cabinet had to comprise 'non-Kachins'. Non-Kachins were principally Shan and Burmese communities, while the Kachin community was an undefined catch-all for 'upland other'. As the colonial taxonomy of the Kachin ethnic category was neither wholly prescriptive nor wholly consistent, there was still much to be played for in how the ethnic composition of this category should be defined.

Initially the Jinghpaw predominance in the broader identity of Kachin prevailed and was largely unquestioned but, following the outbreak of conflict between the Kachin Independence Army and the Burmese government in 1961, the need to create multi-group coherence within the Kachin ethnic category became a priority. With the onset of armed opposition to the Burmese government, vigorous attempts were made to rearticulate the term 'Kachin' through the local ethnonym *Wunpawng,* which, as stated, involved dropping the term 'Jinghpaw' as a qualifier as being too group specific. 'Wunpawng' was thus promoted as an umbrella term for six sub-groups, known at the time as Jinghpaw, Maru, Lashi, Lisu, Atsi and Rawang.

Despite the nationalist claims of primordial authenticity, there was no reason why six groups *per se* should be deemed to comprise the Kachin composite and there were in fact other sub-group labels arising from the colonial period and elsewhere that could have been privileged. Although there is a neat concordance with the designation of six seats for Kachin representatives in the 1947 Constitution, these were not apportioned to specific sub-groups at the time and any impact this may have had on internal discussions within nationalist groups requires further investigation. However, by the time armed conflict broke out, the attempts that the new Burmese State had made to codify the extent of ethnic diversity in the Union had themselves been influential on the kinds of discourses in which ethnic groups engaged. This saw some groups being privileged over others and had led to the consolidation of set 'numbers' of ethnicities which the state could then seek to delineate and bring within its orbit. Undoubtedly the six-fold categorization was a response to this process.

The notion of six groups united as one, however, became increasingly fixed as an internal nationalist construct during the period of conflict. A generic example of oral tradition was transformed from the narrative of clans and family lines into a narrative of the common ancestry of the six sub-groups. There was also the development of multi-group ethno-cultural symbolism during the years of conflict, especially related to the *manau* and textiles. Increasingly from the 1970s onwards, when the indigenized Christian missions renewed their efforts across the Kachin region, Christian nationalism, both Baptist and Catholic, deemed there to be a common *Wunpawng* multi-group historical experience.

In constructing a prescriptive six-part ethnic category called *Wunpawng*, Kachin nationalist elites were responding to particular political circumstances engendered by long-term conflict. However, by linking this ethnonym dogmatically to a primordialist account of common ancestry and shared ethno-cultural symbols, certain difficulties relating to ethnic diversity at a sub-category level were created. During the time of conflict, the harsh and often brutal force of the Kachin nationalist military organization led to an authoritarian interpretation of *Wunpawng* ethnicity which obfuscated any discourse about the internal meanings of the term. Such discourse could only be considered a challenge to multi-group unity at a time of crisis. The effect after three decades was to narrow the expression of cultural and political diversity within the *Wunpawng* grouping considerably. In the post-ceasefire situation Kachin nationalist leaders state that they want to address this issue, but where expressions of cultural diversity intersect with traditional animist practices, and where political leadership is so intimately connected with church institutions such as the Kachin Baptist Convention, there has been a reluctance to engage fully with the implications of this intention.[57]

As of 2004, all armed Kachin military organizations were in ceasefire situations with the central government. Since the signing of the main ceasefire with the KIA in 1994, discussion of *Wunpawng* ethnicity and diversity in its sub-groups has started to be seen as an important issue in relation to future claims for political rights in the region. While the ceasefires do appear to have opened up a certain degree of cultural space in Kachin State, this has not been paralleled as yet by the creation of a comparable political space, and the dangers of opening up for public debate an agenda relating to internal political representation are perhaps too great in the circumstances (see South, this volume). The difficulties have thus largely been focused upon issues of cultural diversity. As a result cultural activities take on highly politicized sub-texts as this is the principal public sphere in which relations between the *Wunpawng* sub-groups, and their relationship with the state and with each other, may be represented and 'discussed'. For example, the status of the *manau* as an ethno-cultural symbol has been the subject of numerous committee debates across a number of communities; this debate has a substantive sub-text as a discourse on contesting Jinghpaw political dominance.[58] This reflects the continuing debate that is taking place within the *Wunpawng* public sphere about the relationship of the sub-groups to the umbrella identity.

Since the ceasefire, the creation of separate Culture and Literature Committees for each of the six groups has been permitted, and these tend to act as arbiters of cultural correctness for their respective communities. They have also promoted the use of different referents for themselves than the Jinghpaw-derived terms of old: thus La:cid is privileged instead of Lachik; Lhaovo instead of Lawngwaw/Maru; Zaiwa instead of Atsi; and so on. The creation of an official group committee offers distinct advantages to some groups in this situation: only by affiliation to officially recognized committees is it possible to organize cultural activities or make group presentations through publication; official status also conveys the right to censor what others may say about your group and the official committees have therefore acquired a considerable degree of power in relation to controlling the representation of their sub-groups. Their influence on the contemporary representation of ethnicity through dress is a good example of their influence.[59] Some groups have attempted to codify explicit numbers of designs of which they may then claim historical possession. This is usually accompanied by the assertion that a particular design originated from a particular sub-group, or else that it has been 'stolen' by others. There have even been discussions about copyrighting designs. This is not an uncommon response among 'indigenous' communities when they feel that outsiders are (mis)representing important cultural institutions, rituals or aspects of material culture.[60] However, given the impossibility of legally copyrighting these cultural markers, many of the committees have in effect cognitively patented the costumes of the sub-groups through their insistence on standardization.[61] Inevitably, in the hands of a powerful cultural committee, the right to claim cultural authorship of a design might be at the expense of smaller communities within the sub-group who feel that they have similar rights to such privileging and that they are not being given adequate recognition.

Debates over the possible extension of the six principal sub-groups to recognize the distinctiveness of a greater number of communities often focuses on dress and language as a form of documentation of identity. Dress and language are thus being used again as if they were discrete ethnic markers, replicating their status in the ethnographic analytical apparatus of the colonial state. Colonial period documentation is often cited as evidence in these claims. Recently there have been discussions over the status of *Ngawchang* peoples as a linguistic and ethnic identity in relation to the label '*La:cid*'. In response to this and to prevent further splintering based on linguistic classifications, Kachin linguists are attempting to produce a *Wunpawng* alphabet which can be used to transcribe the dialects of all the principal lineages, including Ngawchang.

There are plenty of colonial labels which could be used to contest the six-fold classification of Kachin. Many geographical representations of dress acquired distinctive labels in the colonial period (*Hkahku, Htingnai, Bhamo*); speech communities were also privileged with their own labels (*Gauri, Duleng*). In addition, local interpretations of group identity could be transformed endlessly to produce an ever greater sub-division of the *Wunpawng* category. This is exactly what the nationalist elites want to avoid. Unfortunately, however, as they have repeatedly emphasized the primordial common ancestry of six groups, they have taken on an air of immutability, and this has engendered its own difficulties for nationalist discourse in the post-ceasefire situation.

The difficulties encountered in trying to progress meaningful ethnographic discourse relating to ethnic diversity at a national and local level, and the significance of ethnonyms to such a process, is best demonstrated by a public debate that was held at the Myitkyina *manau* festival in December

2001. The intention of the debate was to decide finally upon an ethnonym which, it would be insisted, would replace use of the term 'Kachin' as a national ethnicity. Some nationalist Jinghpaw elites wanted to return to the appellation '*Jinghpaw Wunpawng*', as they objected to the term '*Wunpawng*' as being nonsensical as a stand-alone adjective. However, others objected to what they saw as the insensitive explicit restatement of Jinghpaw dominance in the *Wunpawng* identity. As the debate proceeded it became clear that the sensitivities arising from this issue were presently too great: a decision could not be reached in the present situation and the matter was left unresolved.

PRIMORIDAL AND MOBILIZATIONAL THEORIES OF ETHNICITY, AND THEIR EMPIRICAL APPLICATIONS

At a theoretical level, this problem to a large extent replicates the discontinuity between primordial and mobilizational factors in the construction of ethnicity – the degree to which it may be considered an innate and a-historical entity, or a politically malleable and manipulated identity. The tension between these two theories has been summarized by James McKay thus:

> [We] are told, on the one hand, that the continued salience of ethnic factors is because they are deep-seated, irrational, atavistic allegiances incapable of being altered and, on the other hand, because they are peripheral loyalties which can be readily manipulated in a rational way for pursuing political and economic goals.[62]

The intuitive response to this debate in relation to the Kachin ethnic category is that there is somehow an integration of the two, although the 'primordial' aspects are ineffectively articulated by local communities in the national political arena who strive to convey concepts of historic-ness as fully articulated histories.[63]

Part of the difficulty arises from the incompatibility between Western research models and local forms of self-expression in relation to ethnic category. Kachin elites, with one or two notable exceptions such as Maran La Raw, lack the secular academic training in historical and anthropological disciplines that would enable them to translate these local idioms into more globally understood conventions. The difficult political situation also constrains their ability to explore the subtleties of their own cultural experience as 'Kachin' or *Wunpawng* or whatever identity label they may choose and make that known on a wider stage. For example, presently the auto-ethnography of Kachin elites stresses not just commonality between groups but states that they are essentially indistinguishable. Inevitably this requires a significant suspension of disbelief if we are to accept this at face value, especially when it seems to be stated most frequently by members of the dominant Jinghpaw community. Yet this is in fact a traditional model of socio-cultural representation and should not be attributed to a form of Jinghpaw conspiracy theory. The failure of the explanation arises because the interpretive framework which permits these statements to be made with conviction is very different from that in which they are received and interpreted. In Jinghpaw discourse on cultural diversity, the distinction between saying that two things *are* the same or that they are considered to be the same because of a complex model of cross-cultural parallelism is never made explicit. Common ancestry is discussed as if it existed as a uniform account of oral tradition, as fact, rather than as a procedure by which lineages are equated with each other and subsequently rendered in a ritually dominant idiom. Traditionally this process of building cross-cultural parallels has enabled diverse language-culture communities to be brought under a common umbrella. On other occasions, an alteric model of social relations and behaviours establishes cognitive boundaries that can be used to construct difference.[64] While the assertion that all groups are the same seems politically bounded and historically inappropriate, it does in fact reflect a very important cosmological model of cultural and social relations between various groups in this region, and it is here that the psychological saliency of 'traditional' identity boundaries are best explored.

This cosmological model was expressed through the performance of ritual and related oral performance. The core of this system in this region was undoubtedly Jinghpaw, in that it cohered around a model of Jinghpaw lineage descent and was conducted in Jinghpaw ritual dialect. However, it also functioned historically as a ritual system that was integrative of other communities who came into ritual relations with it, the 'open system' that Leach strove to elucidate. Myth and ritual performance existed as a *process* of identity formation across the Kachin Hills. There were set cosmological boundaries within which this process could take place, but the process was essentially similar whether it functioned to forge a common 'identity' between two closely related clans or between two lineages. Inevitably, the socio-political relationship that existed between the communities concerned would influence the dominant idiom of ritual that was adopted and this led ultimately to a Jinghpaw system being generally dominant. However, this was an intricate ethnographic landscape and the local performance of ritual was inevitably complex as a result. Furthermore, each ritual performance would have to be negotiated each time it was performed, demonstrating the complexity of these forms across a broad social landscape. Thus it is inappropriate to consider mobilization and primordialism as inherent dichotomies: myth and ritual performance incorporated primordial aspects but they were also innately procedural, especially when they operated in complex situations of culture contact and had to be rearticulated in idioms that mimicked the experience of one group upon that of another.

An exploration of the integration or dissimilation of social systems at a cognitive level that has been demonstrated in the performance of ritual can be used to identify the boundaries of a coherent socio-political and socio-cultural system in this region. It is this which we might examine to appreciate what underpins local understanding of the terms 'Kachin'/ 'Wunpawng'. In different localities the level of integration to the dominant model would vary. In some situations there was a high degree of integration. Yet differing degrees of socio-ritual integration often served to maintain diversity rather than cause the subjugation of the 'alternative' model, thus adding to its complexity 'on the ground', about which Leach and most other observers have commented. The example could be given of festivals performed in Lachik or Lawngwaw communities in contact with Jinghpaw ritual idiom. In situations where the Jinghpaw idiom was dominant this could involve considerable submersion of the non-Jinghpaw form. It could, however, also result in the incorporation of a non-Jinghpaw ritual as a discrete element of the total performance, thus adding further complexity to the dominant idiom itself. In areas where the non-Jinghpaw ritual was the dominant idiom, Jinghpaw communities might alternatively assimilate themselves to it instead.

In some cases, integration of socio-ritual systems was more straightforward than others. For example, in reciting key traditions of the 'Creation Story (such as would have been recited at 'manau' festivals) there were important cognitive as well as practical differences in the integration of some lineages into the Jinghpaw model. For example, there is a very rich and distinct tradition of Lawngwaw and Lachik ritual orality, and genealogical recitations were structured very differently from those of Jinghpaw communities. As in other Lolo languages, the generations of lineages are linked through the naming system: syllables of the father's name are incorporated into the name of the son, and so on. Thus, a recitation of a Lachik clan genealogy might be: *Khao" Chang" – Chang" Yeing – Yeing Teing – Teing Khoo – Khoo Zung*, etc.[65] This does not happen in the Jinghpaw system and would necessitate considerable adaptation to the prosody of recitation. This was especially so as Lawngwaw prosody utilizes a system of triplet sentences, whereas Jinghpaw ritual is constructed through couplet sentences, and the use of odd numbers is seen negatively as a sign of loss in many Jinghpaw cultural contexts.[66] The styles would not preclude adaptation to the other form of ritual, but the level of integration towards one model or the other would be determined by local factors.

However, within this ritual system, kinship parallelism was fundamental to socio-ritual integration. For the socio-ritual system of this region, which was inherently bound up with knowledge of lineage descent, to operate effectively across groups, lineages would have to be made commensurate with each other. In recent years much importance has been attached to perpetuating knowledge of multi-group clan equivalencies as a means of supporting the notion of common Kachin ancestry.[67] However, the roots of this are not solely nationalist, but historical. Again the degree of integration to a Jinghpaw model could vary according to the locality. For example Colonel J. H. Green, writing in 1934, tells us that of two Lisu groups which were considered as 'Kachin' within the army, among the 'Black Lisu' who had migrated from the Salween Valley in China and were residing in British territory: 'The Triangular system of marriage does not exist and a Lisu is allowed to marry any woman of a different clan to his own'.[68] However, of the 'Flowery Lisu', who had migrated in greater numbers into the Kachin Hills region, he tells us:

Some of their clans claim parallel relationship with the Kachin[69] clans. Thus:

Tawn Kya	are called	Mitung	by the Kachins
Ngwa Hpa	«	Marip	«
Zaw Kya	«	Lahtaw	«

Gu Hpa & Waw Hpa are called Lahpai by the Kachins
In Myitkyina District the Lair Mair are known to the Kachins as Nhkum but in Bhamo as Lasang.[70]

Of the group defined by the colonial administration as 'Nung', which is another highly complex and oft contested label applied to a number of communities in upper Kachin State, Green stated:

> There are many clans which are generally named after the valleys in which they live. Local groups are generally clans, although some local groups containing two or three clans are found. ... Some of the clans compare themselves to the main Hkahku[71] clans as:

> | The | Nanhku | claim to be | Maran |
> |-----|--------|-------------|-------|
> | « | Sandong | « | Lahtaw |
> | « | Tingkan | « | Lahpai |
> | « | Yintangse | « | Marip |
> | « | Kumring | « | Nhkum |

> ... The triangular system of marriage, *mayu-shaw*i[72], is in force, but mayus are changed every five generations. The new mayus must not have acted as shawis during the past five generations.[73]

Thus there was clearly a regionally functioning socio-ritual system that was integrative and adaptive. It could be said to be primordial in some senses in that it was innate to a particular cosmology, world view and model of identity that seems to have existed over a historical period that is both extensive and indeterminate. However, when the notion of primordialism is stripped of its connotations of stasis, this system of identity formation, both within groups and across groups, is also innately mobilizational. This latter feature did not originate as a consequence of contact with the Burmese nation state or from the experience of colonialism (although these have produced adaptations in the way that this system was expressed). It is on these grounds that local elites claim that they should be considered sufficiently autonomous, coherent and historically authentic to warrant being privileged by the modern nation state. However, they have yet to determine how the local experience of diversity and difference can be rendered a cultural norm in the modern state without the fear of the disintegration of nationalist rhetoric of unity. For the limiting discourses of reified ethnicity to be transcended, it seems clear that the socio-ritual system, which is vilified by some Christian converts as a symbol of historical degeneracy, needs to be repositioned in historical discourses on the nature of ethnic category. Then, perhaps it might be possible to 'decolonize' the term 'Kachin' as a result and to determine what the psychologically and cosmologically salient boundaries of identity may have been according to another model of interpretation.

CONCLUSION – DECOLONIZING IDENTITIES AND TRANSFORMING THE PRESCRIPTIVE CONTEXT OF POST-CEASEFIRE ETHNICITIES

McKay has tried to integrate the primordial and mobilizational approaches to ethnicity at a theoretical level, but, as Hutchinson and Smith state, 'the question is really how far such studies can be empirically helpful'.[74] The integration of these two models might indeed provide the theoretical foundations from which Kachin elites could begin to discuss the complexities of 'Kachin/*Wunpawng*' formation without undermining its status as a legitimate ethnic category in the modern state, or make it vulnerable to accusations of historical artificiality. Such an approach is not simply an attempt to provide nationalist elites with the kind of theoretical justification for their cause for which they have long been searching. The approach would also require considerable modification by these elites of their stance relating to historical interpretation of ethnicity and the 'value' of traditional culture. Insofar as it would also necessitate a fuller engagement with animist culture, it is not necessarily an easy option for all interest groups to accept. In addition it would require some greater acknowledgement and acceptance of the value of cultural diversity at a sub-category level, and would necessitate an exploration and documentation of this diversity. However, this might indeed provide the degree of transformation in sub-category relations that Tegenfeldt (1974?) desires principally on the national stage.

If understandings of the Kachin/Wunpawng ethnic category are to become decolonized, this cannot be done by an ever more minute study of the documentation of the literate political authorities with which it came into contact, although these must play their part. It can ultimately only be achieved by the qualitative and quantitative study of oral ritual in context to elucidate the functioning of this system of ritual multi-group identity formation. This would involve the detailed analysis of a multiplicity of recitations from across language-culture groups and would thus engender significant challenges to the prevailing modes by which Kachin elites discuss the meaning of cultural diversity in relation to the broader ethnic category. The corpus that has been referred to thus far provides the means to begin considering how the core Jinghpaw idiom was constructed, and the means by which this dominant idiom negotiated its boundaries when in contact with other groups. This becomes a framework against which the important cognitive modelling of contact, how notions of mimesis and alterity, and the meanings and transformations of identities were made. However, beyond the Jinghpaw model, the same approach then needs to be taken with the ritual performances of non-Jinghpaw groups to see how these negotiate contact with each other and with Jinghpaw idiom in local areas.

The model would, however, enable local elites to discuss the broader meanings of their relationships, their status as a multi-group nationality minority, in ways that could be supported substantively with indigenized documentation. They would also be able to discuss historical and socio-cultural diversity in new and constructive ways that might lead to the transformation of conflict potential arising from the demands for an ever greater splintering into micro-ethnicities at a sub-category level. In this way it may be possible to decolonize understandings of ethnic relations, to reposition the importance of the trope of ethnicity as the definitive construct by which some communities may be politically privileged by the state, as well as to develop heightened awareness of the significance of diversity as an articulation of identity, rather than its nemesis.

NOTES

[1] Taylor 1982, p. 8.

[2] Ibid. p. 7–8.

[3] L. Smith 2001. The practical applications of this text have also informed the development of local projects in orality which form the background of research from which this chapter has developed.

[4] Ibid., pp. 2–3.

[5] This research has developed out of long-term engagement with archives of oral ritual sources collated by local researchers as part of a locally defined cultural documentation and research project. I am particularly grateful to Pungga Ja Li for his intellectual generosity in sharing this material with me, as well as many others in Kachin State who have facilitated and encouraged my research.

[6] Fuller discussion of this issue is the subject of my PhD thesis, Sadan (forthcoming a) SOAS, 'History and ethnicity: cultural contexts of the category Kachin in the colonial and postcolonial state, 1824–2004'.

7 The political centre states that Union Day was celebrated every year from Independence onwards, creating an unbroken continuity between those of their own celebrations and the endeavours of Aung San, as defined by the Panglong Spirit, to bring peace to the Union. It seems that all is not quite so simple. Current research suggests that Union Day was not celebrated on a grand scale (if at all) until 1953. The popular press at this time appears to make no mention of this event until that date – and it was habitual for the national press to mention every state-sanctioned festival that took place. For the first time in 1953, *The Nation* closed its doors for the day on 12 February as it was a national holiday. In its editorial, it discussed the need for a revision of the Panglong Agreement and it appears that this marked the shift from 'Agreement' to 'Spirit', which is really what is being celebrated through the ritual. In 1952 there had been a significant Union Conference which sought to redefine the economic relations of the whole of the Union. It no doubt seemed an opportune moment to create a public sphere ritual in which ethnic relations with the state could be idealized. In 1953 it was also hoped that discussions on the creation of a Karen State could be finalized.

8 Victor Lieberman (1978) helped to develop this hypothesis, although it does not deal with upland communities such as the Kachin or Chin peoples.

9 Although there were attempts to transcribe wordlists in Jinghpaw/Singpho from the mid-nineteenth century onwards, the first dictionary of 'Kachin' was completed by Ola Hanson in 1902 and the Bible was translated into Jinghpaw in 1927. Even by 1931, the official census of Burma stated that less than 1 per cent of urban Kachin people in the largest town of Myitkyina were literate in Jinghpaw.

10 Curach 2002.

11 This example was first given as part of Sadan (2002b).

12 This costume was given as an honour to the chief by the Burmese court.

13 For details on contemporary revisionism of the personality cult of General Aung San and Mahabandula, see Houtman, (1999a, p. 26). The Daipha Duwa (Duffa Gam in colonial archives) was a chief of the Jasen lineage.

14 This is an inversion of the common Burmese phrase often levelled at Christian ethnic minorities that they yearn for their aunt (the Western missionaries of the colonial period) and not their mother (the Burmese state).

15 See William Foley (2003).

16 Pungga Ja Li 'Bandu La (sh) Dumdu La', *Hparat Ninghkawng Meggazin*, 1994–95, Yangon, pp. 61–64.

17 This comment is derived from an extensive study of Jinghpaw ritual language that Pungga Ja Li and Hkanhpa Tu Sadan made from 1997–99, related to the corpus of oral traditions cited elsewhere in this essay.

18 'Auto-ethnography' is a term derived from the work of Mary Louise Pratt.

[19] This is still the most popular explanation within the Kachin Baptist Church, as was evidenced at the performance of a play on Kachin history put on by students at Nawngnang Theological College in Myitkyina in April 2002.

[20] La Raw (1967) and Wang (1997).

[21] Sadan (2002a).

[22] Some of the Kachin peoples also attach significance to a group of early humans emerging from a cave, which in Jinghpaw is *lungpu. Chin* in Burmese is written csif.

[23] The linguistic corpus referred to here was mostly compiled in the early 1990s by local researchers from the Kachin Baptist community headed by Pungga Ja Li and with the support of the rev. NNgai Gam and the rev. Gum Se. It does not claim to be a complete corpus and the findings are therefore preliminary and the corpus continues to be added to. The digitized corpus under consideration comprises more than a quarter of a million words (286,707 lexical tokens) reflecting a vocabulary of more than 7,000 items (7,100 lexical types) in Jinghpaw ritual idiom. Recordings before the ceasefire in 1994, were made at a time of highly emotive nationalist discourse. It is therefore reasonable to expect that the chances of finding references to the ethnic category 'Kachin' or any other indigenous group term of reference would, in the circumstances, be heightened as a result. This was especially so as most of the recitations took place in KIA-controlled territory or with the implicit or explicit approval of nationalist leaders.

[24] Preliminary research by Ro Soongchul (2002) suggests that the principal ethnic categories used by early British colonialists were adopted wholesale from the well-established geographical constructs that pertained at the Burmese court, which included the category romanized as *Kakiayn.*

[25] See Oriental and India Office Collection, British Library [OIOC] L/PS/7/18 – 'Entry of missionaries into the Kahkyen Hills', 1878, for contemporary accounts from Mr T. T. Cooper, the Political Agent at Bhamo, which give insights into how contact with the Kachin peoples in the Bhamo region was controlled and mediated prior to the Third Anglo-Burmese war in 1885.

[26] See Turton 2000. In a similar way, the Jinghpaw use the term *'Hkang'*, with similarly derogatory connotations in reference to both Naga and Chin peoples irrespectively and unspecifically.

[27] In China the term is transcribed in Pinyin as *'Jingpo'*, and has slightly different connotations within the Chinese state to either Jinghpaw or Singpho. As well as being an officially recognized ethnicity in China, Jingpo also refers to an autonomous administrative region that contains Jingpo and non-Jingpo communities. The Singpho peoples are today an official minority in Arunachal Pradesh.

[28] The use of the Jinghpaw language or the tendency to adopt Jinghpaw social and cultural behaviours is not a signifier of Jinghpaw identity however. This is deemed to reside in lineage affiliation. Each of the Kachin sub groups seems to

have a clear understanding of which lineage is part of which broader sub-group at an ideal level.

[29] Hannay (1847, p. 3).

[30] There does seem to be some metalinguistic structuring even of the term 'Jinghpaw' to give it such specific ethnographic connotations. Furthermore, as a *chyingtawt* drum is a drum of Shan origin, privileging of the term could still have emerged in a context of contact with 'Other'. The prefix *chying*, however, is a very common preformative denoting completeness and it could thus be associated with a range of verbs and nouns. For example, some elders from the Mali-Nmai 'Triangle' region north of the Irrawaddy confluence attest that it refers to the fact that humans originally emerged from the openings (*chyinghka*) of a traditional, recognizably 'Kachin' long house, rather than a drum. This term could also form a couplet with *chyinghpaw*. My thanks to Bawmwang Ja Yaw for his comments.

[31] This use is highly contextualized and dependent upon interpretation rather than a literal reading of the term. There are other terms in both ritual and colloquial Jinghpaw that can be translated as 'man' more directly.

[32] Hannay (1847, p. 3).

[33] Sadan (2002b).

[34] Today there is much significant new research being undertaken on Tibeto-Burman languages, and George Van Driem has recently postulated a new 'Kachinnic' category in his work *'Languages of the Himalayas'* (Van Driem, 2001).

[35] The Maru/Lawngwaw/Lhaovo: peoples have been referred to as the original Burmans because of contrived linguistic associations with the ancient Pyu; the Nung peoples have been called 'White Burmese' because of their linguistic 'descent'.

[36] Enriquez (undated, lecture I. p. 1).

[37] Ibid., p. 2.

[38] Enriquez (undated, lecture IV, p. 35).

[39] Sadan (2003).

[40] See Sadan (2002b) for discussion of the processes by which certain tropes entered and were interpreted by the imperial public sphere.

[41] For example, they are frequently reiterated in church youth fellowship meetings in the Baptist Church in order to give both nationalist and moral guidance to young Kachin people. Such Jinghpaw-language sermons were certainly an important extra-curricula activity for the young people at the college where Dean (this volume) conducted some of her research.

[42] A good example relates to the stereotype of laziness. One story relates that the dance of the *manau festival* was learned from the birds because a very lazy boy,

Ma Ding Yau, was sitting under a banyan tree one day, watching them, rather than doing his work.

43 Hannay (1847).

44 See Sadan, forthcoming PhD thesis for further elaboration of this point.

45 I am grateful to U Chit Hlaing (Professor Kris Lehman) for his comments relating to this term in a number of personal communications.

46 Turton (2000).

47 See Sadan (forthcoming b).

48 The term '*Wunpawng*' is to be found in this corpus on 153 occasions. Of these occurrences 34 arise in one recitation – that at an animist *manau* festival held in 1990 in KIA-controlled territory in the north of Kachin State. The festival had to have the sanction of local KIA commanders to take place; it was the first large animist ritual of its kind to be held in this area for more than 20 years. The *manau* has become a key nationalist symbol during the years of conflict and for this reason the KIA commanders were willing to permit the animist event to go ahead for the purposes of making a cultural record.

49 As opposed to *Wunpawng Mungdaw* – Kachin State/District.

50 This is discussed more fully in my forthcoming PhD thesis cited above.

51 I am grateful to U Chit Hlaing (Professor Kris Lehman) for his comments on this issue, albeit relating to other terms, made at the EUROSEAS conference in Paris, 2004.

52 Hanson (1954b, pp. 710–11).

53 Ibid., p. 710.

54 Hanson (1954a, p. 253).

55 Taylor (1982, p. 16) states that Duwa Zau Rip's party was an animist organization. This was not so. Duwa Zau Rip was a Baptist Christian, but he objected to some of the activities of the Christian missions.

56 Significantly, Hanson (1954a) does not cite this meaning in his dictionary entry for *wunpawng*.

57 Sadan (2000).

58 Sadan (2002b).

59 Sadan (2003).

60 Linda Tuhiwai Smith (2001, p. 101).

61 Sadan (2000).

62 McKay (1982).

63 I am grateful to Dr Maran La Raw for his comments on this subject in a number of personal communications.

[64] See Sadan, (forthcoming a), for discussion of this model of mimetic and alteric social behaviour and the way that this is expressed in oral tradition.

[65] My thanks to members of the Lawngwaw and Lachik Culture Committees for discussing these issues with me.

[66] For example, Jinghpaw *manau* posts must be constructed in multiples of two, whereas the modern Lhaovo: and La:cid posts both demonstrate that this is not an important cognitive model in their communities. My thanks to Pungga Ja Li and Bawmwang Ja Yaw for their comments.

[67] It has been mentioned that in the 1960s the KIA produced a book which sought to outline all the relationships between the various clans to enable people who had migrated to urban areas and who were encountering some clan and family names for the first time to be able to establish appropriate kinship relationships and thus adopt correct forms of address. This may be apocryphal, but the account reveals some of the difficulties engendered in maintaining this knowledge in an extended state of conflict. This kind of strategy is also very important in the kind of conflict resolution processes that Gowler (2002) has described.

[68] Green (1934, p. 254).

[69] In this case he uses 'Kachin' to refer to Jinghpaw clans on the east of the Kachin region.

[70] Ibid.

[71] 'Hkahku' is principally a geographic term used to distinguish Jinghpaw peoples living in the Mali Nmai region and Hukawng Valley.

[72] '*Shawi*' is the Hkahku term for *dauma/dama* (wife-takers). The preponderance of the term 'dauma' today for this status term reflects the dominance of the easterly dialect in discourse on this issue.

[73] Green (1934, pp. 193–195).

[74] Hutchinson and Smith (1996, p. 9).

Chapter 3

RESHAPING KARENNI-NESS IN EXILE: EDUCATION, NATIONALISM AND BEING IN THE WIDER WORLD

Sandra Dudley

I really want to improve my English because I want to tell the world about our independent Karenni Historical. I want to fight the SLORC or SPDC by non-violence. Today I'm a student. I can't hold a gun. I can't fight with violence. We can't defeat the SPDC because we are [an] ethnic group. So we need a lot of educated people in our country. I want my nation [to] return to our motherland ... my nation's gotten big problem[s] and faces hell ... My village was burned and my nation was kill[ed] ... Burma military keep ethnic cleansing in Burma. They keep nepotisms in their organization so that become soon mutiny in troops. I so much glad with East Timor. Because East Timor get independence from Indonesia. Teacher, I want to become a good or a great leader ... I will study more and more during the school. I'm the hope of the future for Karenni people. (Extract from a letter, in English, from Eh Ka Lu Taw[1], a Karenni refugee camp high school student to the author, 18 October 1999)

In his letter, Saw Eh Ka Lu Taw neatly expresses some of the issues central to the ongoing re-formulation, in refugee camps in Thailand, of what it is to be 'Karenni'. He is convinced of the importance of learning English, rationalized as it is in terms of being able to spread information about the Karenni to a wider world. He has accepted the inevitability of the *Tatmadaw*'s military superiority, and believes that all he and his people can use effectively is education. He is clear about the belief in the political independence of

Karenni (Kayah) State as taught in camp schools, and about his desire to return to an independent homeland. His use of the phrase 'ethnic cleansing' demonstrates familiarity with some of the potentially impactful language of international politics and human rights. His familiarity and association with recent events in East Timor indicate the extent of his international awareness. And in his aspiration to be a 'good or a great' leader of his people and his acknowledgement of the importance of the next generation, he demonstrates a combination of ambition and sense of duty common amongst refugee Karenni school students, especially young men.

INTRODUCTION

This chapter focuses on the over 22,000-strong[2] Karenni refugee community in Thailand, examining some of the ways in which Karenni refugees conceive of and interact with the world beyond the camps, and how they perceive their place in the wider world and construct and re-construct Karenni identity in exile. The chapter does not explore Kayah or Karenni ethnogenesis (cf.cf. Chit Laing, this volume), pre-exile historical constructions of identity, the role of religion in pre- or post-exile imaginations of Karenni-ness or wider issues in the theoretical modelling of ethnicity. With specific reference to the Karenni, these matters are discussed elsewhere by myself (Dudley 1999, 2000, 2002, forthcoming a and b) and by F K L Chit Laing (Lehman 1967a and b, 1979).

Karenni refugees are highly diverse in various ways. Ethno-linguistically, most Karenni belong to the wider Karen family. Nonetheless, they are politically and historically distinct from, albeit often intimately involved with, the much more numerous Karen groups further south. Under the wide 'Karenni' umbrella are grouped perhaps a dozen self-distinguishing but related groups, principal among whom are the Kayah, Kayaw, Paku Karen and various Kayan sub-groups. The boundaries of these groups are ambiguous and fluid. Furthermore, the population of Karenni State, Burma's smallest ethnic state, is disparate not only in ethnicity and language but also in socio-economic and educational background, religion, awareness of the world beyond, political aspirations, and, in the refugee camps, in the experience of displacement itself and in future expectations. Experiences at the hands of the Burmese army or others inside Karenni State and subsequent displacement have brought together people who all originate in

Karenni State but who are in many other ways disparate. That is, diversity is a characteristic of the population inside Karenni State and has been concentrated still further by the distillation process of displacement and subsequent coming together in the relatively confined spaces of the refugee camps. Yet despite this, all the refugees refer to themselves as 'Karenni', although, as I have elaborated elsewhere, 'Karenni' is itself an ambiguous and fluid label, its meaning dependent upon whom one talks to, variously defined in terms of ethnicity, territoriality, and history (Dudley 2000, Dudley forthcoming b).

Amidst their displacement and the concomitant diversity of their own community and in their engagements with both, then, Karenni refugees in Thailand are active in continually defining and redefining what it means to be Karenni, a process that involves highly self-conscious appropriations and rejections of elements of tradition, ideas of history and future aspirations. In particular, they are mostly engaged in an ongoing nationalist agenda dominated by a largely Christian,[3] political elite known as the Karenni National Progressive Party (KNPP), a self-styled 'government-in-exile' that continues to fight a guerrilla war against the Burmese military regime. The KNPP has the official objective of independence for Karenni State or, more accurately, international recognition of what they see as Karenni State's *existing* independence compromised by illegal invasion by an alien aggressor (Burma). This official position on independence has in the past led the KNPP to refuse to participate in talks with other Burma opposition groups on federalism and a pluralistic, democratic constitution for a future federal Burma that would include Karenni State: why, the KNPP have argued, should they participate in such dialogue if they are not, as they insist they are not, really a part of the country of Burma at all? More recently, however, under the current KNPP Prime Minister Hte Buphe,[4] the approach has been considerably more pragmatic, so that although the KNPP's official position on independence remains the same, in practice the leadership is prepared, for example, to endorse the draft federal constitution drawn up by opposition groups for a future, democratic Burma that would incorporate the Karenni. Most importantly for present purposes, however, this nationalist KNPP group dominates the processes whereby what it means to be 'Karenni' and 'modern' is deliberately reformulated in exile.

Exile itself is also a key component in reformulations of identity. The spatial and other constraints of living in the camps of necessity mean that life in displacement is in many ways very different from life before it; subsistence farming, for example, the main occupation of the majority of Karenni refugees prior to exile, is impossible. Political awareness and activity too are different in displacement, as is the extent to which refugees feel themselves part of wider, (post)modern global networks. Nonetheless, far from being passive victims of circumstance, Karenni refugees are active in making the best of their situation both conceptually and practically. What is more, they work hard to preserve some sense of continuity with 'home'; in turn, this idea of 'home' and of continuity with it is important in what it means to be Karenni in the first place. Rather than *losing* collective identity because of violent upheaval and migration, it is for many in the refugee camps that a collective sense of Karenni-ness is *born* (cf. Malkki 1995). Refugee camps provide theatres within which the complexity and lack of clarity in what 'Karenni' means are made explicit but are also, to an extent, resolved.

The pan-Karenni identity formulated by dominant groups is continually challenged, however, by real diversity in tradition, history, religion, levels of education, etc. There are also occasional resentments and rivalries between groups. Indeed, there are many tensions and conflicts in the processes of defining a pan-Karenni identity, stemming from the challenges of diversity and from imbalances of power and political consciousness across the population. This is particularly so as some of the different Karenni groups in the not-so-distant past were little more than neighbours or distant relatives; i.e. there is some degree of shared history, and often shared language and/ or other cultural traits, but the idea of all the groups being members of one community is relatively recent (cf. Anderson 1991). Some groups are more effective than others in advancing their highly politicized models of a shared future and of what it means to be Karenni. These dominant groups come from the longer-staying refugee community, and mainly comprise relatively well-educated, Christian, politically conscious individuals who are in the highest levels of the social and political hierarchy. Yet other groups, rather than being simply subsumed into an emerging pan-Karenni national identity, sometimes find that it is their socio-cultural 'traditions' – e.g. the annual *ka-thow-bòw* ritual so important to recently arrived non-Christian refugees – that are appropriated by otherwise more dominant groups, perhaps transformed, and incorporated as central, defining elements of what it means to be Karenni (Dudley 2000 and forthcoming a).

The Karenni identity being discussed here is, like all identities, a relational artefact: I am only who I am because of how I and others define me *in relation to* others (cf. De Vos 1995). And in the Karenni case particularly, it is essentially an 'ethnic identity' or 'ethnicity' (here treated as synonymous).[5] Diasporas such as Karenni refugees, and those to whom they relate 'back home', by definition consist of groups sharing a sense of identity primarily thought of in ethnic terms. Sharing an ethnic identity means belonging to a group with a common name, myth of common ancestry, memories of a common past, several elements of a common culture (religion, customs, language), a link with a homeland and a sense of solidarity (A. Smith 1986), all of which may be real or, often more likely, imagined (cf. Chit Laing, this volume). In fact, for Karenni refugees much of the pan-Karenni identity may indeed be imagined. Important for groups such as the Karenni is the degree to which political aspiration such as nationalism combines with migration, forced displacement or other means of increasing and altering one's engagement with the wider world (such as use of media) to strengthen and/or modify senses of ethnic or other identity and political and economic agenda. Furthermore, as the influence of global cultural forces increases, there is an associated, increasing awareness of the international political importance of *having* an 'identity' in the first place (cf. Handler and Linnekin 1984). The articulation and re-formation of 'identity', be it defined in ethnic, religious or other terms, thus becomes a very self-conscious and deliberate endeavour indeed.[6]

More generally, it is now well accepted that the genealogy of ethnicity, like that of the nation, is traceable to the imaginings of colonial state and associated anthropological, historical and other constructions.[7] Nationalism and ethnicity are seen as products of the modern world (Anderson 1991, Gellner 1994), although ethnicity tends not to be prioritized as an important part of the development of nationalism (A. Smith [1986, 1994] being a notable exception), at least not until the influence of colonial constructions of ethnicity took hold in most parts of the world. Indeed, it is now a commonplace to refer to the totalizing, controlling and categorizing needs of the imperial system as leading to the self-consciousness and politicization of ethnicity and, inevitably, ethnonationalist conflicts and collective violence (e.g. Tambiah 1989 and 1996; see also Horowitz 1985). Nonetheless, however recent may be self-conscious constructions of ethnicity (and 'nation'), and whatever the part played by colonial and post-colonial history and politics, it is a fact that *now* ethnicity *matters* to many groups. That the Karenni, for example, now call themselves 'Karenni' and define it in certain ways, matters in itself (Dudley 2000). The 'truth', if it exists, in what 'Karenni' actually means, matters far

Figure 3.1. Mae La refugee camp, Thailand (Photo: M. Gravers)

less to this analysis and is far less of an interesting question to me, than the way in which the KNPP and their supporters seek to manipulate such claims not only in their relationships with potential members who share their ethnicity or religious identity, but also in their response to wider global cultural influences.

Karenni refugees are part of a large population of around half a million refugees and asylum seekers from Burma residing in neighbouring countries, including over 335,000 Karen, Karenni and Shan in Thailand.[8] Ethnic minority parties and organizations consider that it is the non-Burmans who 'have always paid the highest price for the political volatility in [Burma] at large' (M. Smith 2001: 23), as evidenced by internal displacement[9] and outpouring of refugees on a massive scale particularly (but not solely) after 1988. Nonetheless, internationally, ethnic minority situations have received less coverage and sympathy than has the general pro-democracy cause. Many ethnic group members attribute this relative international neglect to their geographical marginality, their longer history of struggle, and, above all, their relative lack of education that has made it harder for them to convey their predicament to an international audience. But whatever its origins, it is a neglect that is felt sorely and contributes significantly to Karenni and other ongoing constructions of identity.

One way in which some outsiders have attempted to make up for this general neglect of the ethnic groups has been by working extensively with and focusing on the displaced groups based on and around the borders. This is especially so in Thailand where groups in exile, and their ethnic relatives inside Burma but near the Thai border, have received an especially high level of contact, support and attention from Western governments, agencies, and individual activists, journalists and scholars. As M. Smith (2001) has pointed out, this is problematic from the perspective of some ethnic leaders inside Burma: for them, focusing on border politics means not seeing the ways in which internal ethnic minority struggles have changed and moved on. On the other hand, one way in which analysis of the experiences of those living in exile can enhance wider understanding is by exploring the effects of increased contact with the outside world. Such increased contact comes via interaction with NGO staff and other visiting foreigners, through access, albeit still limited, to computer-mediated communication and opportunities outside the camps, and through the greater availability in Thailand of globally distributed material objects, images and ideas. Foreigners, and foreign objects and images, can play a significant part in people's constructions of their own identities and their ideas of the world and of their place in it. Moreover, there is often created a sphere of transnational discourse that rests on the international acceptance of the apparent authority of refugees and exiles.[10]

To return to Eh Ka Lu Taw's letter at the beginning of this chapter, the issues with which he deals, together with the extent to which his beliefs and aspirations have been engendered and nurtured in displacement, particularly in camp schools, run through the remainder of this chapter. The first section deals with the education system in the camps and its relationship to nationalist ideas of the future. The second addresses ways in which Karenni refugees contextualize themselves and their experience both in a wider world and against the backdrop of KNPP political aspirations. Together, both sections explore how Karenni refugees perceive their situation within wider temporal and spatial contexts *beyond* the confines of present life in the camps. 'Beyond' is itself a relative concept operable on a number of different levels; 'traditional' Kayah refugees from very remote areas of Karenni State who have been arriving in Karenni refugee Camp 2 since forced village relocations in the Shadaw area in 1997, for example, have a very different experience and idea of the world beyond Karenni State and Camp 2 than do members of the KNPP elite. Furthermore, any one person or group does not always adhere to the same view of a particular 'beyond'. Members of the KNPP elite, for example, sometimes see the outside world primarily as a potential source of assistance and, ultimately, legitimation; at other times, they see it as something that has failed to fulfil its obligations; and at yet others, as something which may in various ways threaten Karenni security and communal values. What matters to the discussion in hand is the extent to which certain 'beyonds' and/or Karenni perceptions of them, impact upon and have agency in the ways in which the Karenni construct and reconstruct their sense of who they are.

LOOKING TO THE FUTURE: BEING EDUCATED, BEING 'A MODERN KARENNI'

Education has taken on enormous importance in Karenni refugee life. Refugees see education as the one thing they can usefully pursue – albeit within the constraints imposed by displacement – both to make the present more bearable and to prepare for possible futures, individual and communal. It is at once something to occupy otherwise idle hands, something that will be of practical use in the future, and a powerful tool to mould minds and work towards political ends. It serves existing aspirations, reinforces them, and sets up others. Indeed, the importance placed by refugees on education as part of a process of change far exceeds that placed on the military struggle, in both aspirational and everyday terms.

Positive Karenni attitudes towards education are common not only to those involved in running the formal education system and to those senior in KNPP and camp hierarchies, but also to other members of the refugee population. Whatever their own educational background, during my field research almost everyone I spoke to emphasized the importance of children and young people availing themselves of the educational opportunities in the camps. Karenni leaders and teachers in particular, however, articulate specific reasons for the importance of formal education. As parents rather than as leaders and teachers, they recognize that to attain as good an education as possible improves future prospects for individuals.

Accomplishments considered especially useful include good spoken and written English and, to a lesser extent, information technology (IT) skills. Whether or not refugees are able to return to Karenni State in positive circumstances in the imaginable future, an increasing array of internship opportunities with foreign NGOs (see below) means that there are some possibilities for gainful employment outside the camps as well as in them, and in order to be successful in obtaining one of these placements students need to demonstrate English and other skills. Hence, parents and teachers encourage students to work towards this sort of goal in part at least for themselves. Much more important, however, is the emphasis on education being of value because of the need to work in the future for one's people, whether in exile or back inside Karenni State. Speaking English and being able effectively to use information and communication technologies, is perceived as crucial to propagating the KNPP nationalist message to a wider world beyond the camps. Language, IT and the overall education agenda all ameliorate the present (not least by providing a focus for one's time) and simultaneously are geared towards the future – both coping with it and having the potential to change it – and towards improving communication with the non-Karenni world.

The value of formal education is enthusiastically promulgated by parts of the Karenni leadership and by senior schoolteachers (the boundary between the two groups in fact being blurred). Nonetheless, because of the wide variety in the adult refugee population's experience of formal education prior to coming to the camps, ranging from a postgraduate university education to no schooling whatsoever, people's reasons for valuing education, the sorts of ambitions they have for their children, and the degree of actual commitment, vary widely. New refugees with no or very little school education of their own, for example, while all delighted to have an opportunity to send their children to school could neither explain *why* they considered education important nor articulate any post-school ambitions for their children. Furthermore, their attitudes to schooling were not strict and they were unlikely to force a child to go to school if he or she did not want to (Dudley 1997: 15). Members of the political elite with relatively extensive educational backgrounds of their own, on the other hand, can posit numerous advantages of education both for individuals and for the community as a whole.

The message that education is for the good of all is continually repeated to students by their teachers, in normal classes and in addresses to the whole school given at morning assembly or on some special occasion by the headmaster or, occasionally, the KNPP education minister or his deputy. The message inculcates a strong sense of duty in school students. Obligation to 'try hard' is felt keenly, as is a duty to use what one learns 'for the Karenni people'. The sense of duty is not, however, abstract and reified: it is personalized and strengthened with the emphasis on the need for today's good students to be tomorrow's leaders. Karenni leaders also convince their students that it is only in education that the Karenni have a chance of 'defeating' the Burmese military. This student's comments in 1997 are typical:

> We couldn't compare to [the Burmese] with arms. So we must try hard and make up our Education.
>
> At first, I wanted to fight but our leaders didn't want [it] because we couldn't believe we could win against them in the field. All of the students ... are going to be many leaders for the future...
>
> ... So I want to learn ... English is the most important and is used all over the world. (Extract from an essay by James, 10th standard, January 1997)

Things had come a long way since a few years previously when the children of the deputy education minister, already quite proficient in English on first arriving in Camp 5, were teased for 'eating English shit'.

By targeting all young people within the refugee community (the KNPP require that all children attend school up to the age of 18), the education system is set up for success in its aims not only of providing a forum for teaching and learning, but also of being a focus for the reproduction of a particular set of social values (cf. Bourdieu and Passeron 1977) and, especially, for the promulgation of nationalist ideology. Education provides refugee young people (and teachers) with something to do, but it also secures them as a target constituency for the KNPP-dominated ideology of Karenni identity and nationalism justified along certain historical lines:

> The few authoritative persons who have read the several documents relating to the Karenni people, their past history and their political status, agreed that the Karenni people have been politically wronged by the British Government when it allowed Karenni to be ceded to the independent Burma. It is the British Government which refused to admit the injustice fraudulently committed by the Labour Government which passed the

86

Burma Independent Bill knowing the 1947 constitution was criminally fabricated ... (Karenni government, n.d.)

The tone is similar in a number of KNPP documents, for example:

Karenni is a tiny small independent state. It is situated between Burma and Thailand on the longitude 97.10 to 97.50 east and from north Latitude 18.50 to 19.55. It has an area of 4582 square miles with a population of 300,000 approx. Throughout the history of Karenni we have never been subordinated to Burma kings or other neighbouring sovereign states. In August 1948 Burma invaded Karenni then we, the Karenni people fought back to defend our sovereign and independence. The national liberation war against the successive regimes of Burma and now Myanmar counts 48 years and it continues to this day. Over the many years many of us were tortured and killed. Many of our villages were burnt down from year to year and villagers fled to live in thick jungles.

Through blood, tears and sweat, we, the Karenni people had survived after having suffered an unaccountable hundreds of violations of human rights at the hands of the racist Burmese regimes. However, we continued our steady and sturdy support to our resistance. Since the racist regimes could not subdue us they tried to relocate us to confined locations, where they could be able to set up a rigid control on us. In 1976, 61 villages in No. 2 District area were force relocated to Mawchi town. We refused and our villages were destroyed and burnt down. We had to build hide-outs and lived in jungle to continue our support to the resistance. (Karenni government 1996)

Both the texts from which the above citations come were written largely for an external readership, and intended for distribution to outsiders: either those who turn up and express interest, or international bodies and others whom the KNPP wish to lobby. There is also, however, a repetition of this historico-political message and tone in a history textbook produced in both Burmese and Karenni by the KNPP for use in Karenni refugee-camp schools (KRNRC 1974/1997).[11] All of these sorts of publication, despite their different intended readerships, have as their focus a description of the KNPP view of Karenni history and its relationship to the KNPP characterization of a politico-military struggle for independence, and the more or less explicit need for KNPP interpretations of history to be accepted by a wider, international public. The KNPP-run education system in the camps is actively and continually involved in the politicized propagation and reinforcement of this set of ideas, with the specific aims of inculcating tomorrow's adults and leaders with certain beliefs about who the Karenni are, why they are in the situation they are in and what they should be doing about it. A Ma, 10th standard student, explained:

> I was born in Loikaw [capital of Kayah State] [but before I came here] I didn't know I'm Karenni ... I never heard about the Karenni. I know it as the Kayah. I never learned the history of the Kayah [but] I have some knowledge of Burmese history ... Only when we arrived here we have learned about the history of the Karenni and are proud of being a Karenni. (Essay, January 1997)

The formal education system is central to the reinforcement, propagation and continuation of the KNPP's interpretation of history and a KNPP-determined sense of pan-Karenni nationalism and purpose (cf. Anderson 1991, Gellner 1983). Methods include singing of the national song in school assembly every morning, the central part played by school students in national days and festivals, the teaching of a particular interpretation of history using KNPP-produced text books (e.g. KRNRC 1974/1997), the teaching of Karenni (Kayah) language and frequent reference to the Karenni struggle/history/future aspirations by the headmaster and others in addresses to the school and in classes. On national days, for example, all but one of which mark the anniversaries of particular events in the post-1948 period,[12] schools close, and there is a formal parade and opening ceremony in which the school students are the most active, central group. It is they who make up those on parade, and for whom and by whom most of the day's activities are centred. On Army Day, for example, after an opening ceremony involving senior members of the KNPP and speeches – made to an audience consisting mainly of school children – about the history and importance of the Karenni Army, there is an atmosphere of fun and mischief-making focused on competitive games such as tug-of-war, *chinlon*,[13] badminton and, especially, volleyball. Certainly, Army Day and other annual commemorative occasions are not solely targeted at school students, but this group does comprise the main constituency from which the main participants in the day's activities are drawn and the bulk of the audience for speeches from KNPP leaders. It is KNPP and camp leaders, and schoolteachers, who largely organize the events. In so doing, they ensure that young people, especially school students, hear the message to be given out on that day. And, by definition, on commemorative days this message always directly concerns some aspect of Karenni history, interpreted from a KNPP perspective and intimately tied to KNPP aspirations concerning an independent Karenni State.

Commemorative days, like other central aspects of the formal education system, thus serve as effective forums in which KNPP interpretations of history and nationalism can be promulgated and, thereby, further disseminated and reinforced. That is not to say, however, that every detail of the KNPP message will be immediately taken in and remembered by everyone. On Army Day in 1996, for example, many of those to whom I spoke after the opening ceremony, did not know the precise reason for celebrating on 17 August, despite it having been explained to them earlier in the day. But they did still understand that the day was about celebrating the Karenni Army, and showing support for its part in the ongoing Karenni struggle for independence. And from a KNPP perspective, this is enough: it does not matter that many people do not know or understand the details of the historical rationale that lies behind the KNPP's nationalist aspirations. It is sufficient that the refugee constituency – especially its younger members – is regularly reminded of what and how central its political objectives are. Of course, the official organization of these events, especially such as Army Day that are a great deal of fun, also reinforces the KNPP's standing and authority within the refugee community at the same time strengthening bonds of commonality and solidarity between students, soldiers and other young people.

Ambition and opportunity

Both ambition and opportunity refer to potentialities that have not yet necessarily acquired concrete reality, but are distinct: ambition is a vision, an internal thing with reality only inside the minds of those holding it; opportunity, on the other hand, here the existence or potential existence of possible work, is an external thing that has reality or potential reality outside of mental life. It is in the interface between these two things that the relationships between Karenni attitudes to education and Karenni perspectives of the outside world and their place within it become apparent.

Before reaching the upper end of the school, students tend to have developed but unfocused ambitions. A combination of their own personal experience, and the ongoing reinforcement by school authorities and others of the message of duty and obligation, ensures they have a strong sense that they must not only try their hardest in the present, but that they must also aspire to 'help' or 'work for' the Karenni people in the future. Precisely what this might entail is vague, however, encapsulated in such typically general statements as 'so the Karenni Government has opened schools … where people can learn. And then their people will be useful for the future … we must try to succeed for the future' (extract from a joint essay by five 9th standard students, February 1997). This conviction in the need 'to succeed for the future', if it is further focused at all, usually centres only on a minimal set of possible future occupations including soldier, teacher and medic. In other words, personal ambitions are largely restricted to the sorts of jobs for which students have existing role models all around them; i.e. there is a clear relationship between subjective expectation and objective probability (cf. Bourdieu 1977). These ambitions are not only imaginable but are also directly related to Karenni perceptions of the current political, military and humanitarian situation and what might be done to ameliorate it .

As students grow older and more educated, their ambitions are consolidated and refined. The subject of ambition does not necessarily change, but the way in which individuals see their role becomes more aspiring. Most students still hope for posts within education, healthcare and/or 'the struggle'. Now, however, rather than simply wanting to be a teacher, they may want to be a 'very good teacher' or a 'headmistress' (essay by Ni Ma [10th standard], January 1997), or a 'very good doctor ... to take care of the wounded soldiers during the war ... like Florence Nightingale' (A Ma [10th standard], January 1997). And rather than simply wanting to be a soldier, ambition to be seriously involved 'in the struggle' is defined in terms of wanting to be a politician, a great leader, or a senior military officer – 'a manager of soldiers' (Klaw Reh [9th standard], February 1997), or even 'a good dictator' (James [10th standard], January 1997). This consolidation and refinement of ambition is due to increased encouragement and reiteration of the need for today's students to be tomorrow's leaders by teachers and other members of the Karenni elite. But there are discrepancies between individual students, perhaps unsurprisingly related to gender.[14] While they aspire to help their people, female students are far less likely to articulate ambitions unprompted. They are also most likely to restrict ambitions to education or healthcare, whereas male students often visualize themselves playing an important part in future politics. Nonetheless, female students may still see themselves being able to help publicize the Karenni situation to the wider world – it is just that they do not think of or describe this sort of activity in terms of politics, whereas male students, who also may perceive their future role as being in communicating with members of the international community in some way, immediately describe it in terms of political life.

By the time students reach the top of the school, they are aware of the existence of various opportunities. Realistically, for most students these opportunities are restricted to employment within the Karenni refugee community, as teachers, medics/medic assistants or clerical and political assistants within one of the Karenni government ministries. Involvement in the military, for students who have reached 10th standard or above, is likely to comprise clerical, political and intelligence assistance to senior officers, although students who drop out of school at a much lower level are more likely to become soldiers; in either case, involvement in this sphere is largely restricted to males. But beyond these Karenni jobs, there is also the possibility of getting an internship, furthering one's education or at least attending some training with an outside organization. Such opportunities include fixed-term internships with NGOs in Thailand (in a few cases with the possibility of an ongoing job afterwards) and training periods outside the camps with NGOs in Thailand. Very few individuals are able to take up study and training opportunities abroad. Since 1997, when the first Karenni interns began work at the local International Rescue Committee office in Mae Hong Son, the availability of such opportunities has mushroomed. Nonetheless, they are highly competitive, and often open to all groups along the border (i.e. the Mon and Karen as well as the Karenni). They are eagerly sought after – from a communal perspective they present an opportunity to widen not only skills but also knowledge and experience of the wider world beyond the camps; and from a personal perspective for young individuals they constitute a chance to get out of the camps and away from the relatively restrictive and boring life there. The possibility of acquiring office skills, management skills, familiarity with information technology, increased proficiency in English, greater political sophistication and knowledge of the machinations of the international community, and using this experience to the benefit of the Karenni, is highly valued by all.

Outsiders' involvement in Karenni education

For most refugees, the outside world is most immediately experienced in interactions with visitors to the camps. A disproportionate number of these outsiders come in connection with education, and they have a significant influence on Karenni attitudes to formal education. Visitors include miscellaneous foreigners who stay for periods ranging from a few weeks to a year or more to teach English or, occasionally, some other subject such as music, art or politics. Also included are NGOs such as Jesuit Refugee Service

(JRS), who conduct occasional training inside the camps. Those who stay more than a few weeks usually make the most impact. In general, the increased level of interaction with outsiders implied not only by increasing numbers of internship and other training opportunities, but also by the involvement of outsiders in the camps' education system, has numerous impacts upon the Karenni community. One is the potential of some internships and similar opportunities to exacerbate existing inter-camp or other rivalries. The selection of individuals to take part in the International Rescue Committee's (IRC) original internship programme in the late 1990s, for example, became enmeshed in and in turn exaggerated existing bones of contention between the Camp3/Nai Soi nexus and Camp 5. The candidates preferred by IRC did not exactly correlate with those preferred by the two Karenni leaders also involved in the selection process. Both leaders resided in Nai Soi, and their preference for candidates from this nexus rather than from Camp 5, together with an initial insistence that all successful individuals should be able to speak Kayah, was evident in their final choice.[15] Eventually, the creation of an additional internship place by the IRC allowed a satisfactory outcome whereby both the IRC and the Karenni leaders were happy that their chosen candidates had been successful. Nonetheless, before this point was reached, it looked as if the Karenni leaders would get their way; among Camp 5 students, this led to considerable resentment.

Another significant impact of the involvement of outsiders has been the beginning of a change in Karenni attitudes towards opportunities for women. A number of NGOs now make it either an explicit condition of offering an internship that they are able to select a woman candidate, or at least indicate a preference for doing so. From the NGOs' perspectives, emphasizing opportunities for women goes some way towards raising the profile and role of women in refugee communities. In turn, this trend has not gone unnoticed by the Karenni leadership. Their reaction has been characteristically pragmatic: they have recognized that currently there are more opportunities available to young women than to young men, and that taking up such opportunities still means that some young Karenni people have the possibility of furthering their education. Beyond this, however, to recognize the internships being taken up by young women as potentially useful for the Karenni has also entailed having to acknowledge that these young women should subsequently play a significant role in Karenni communal and/or political life on their return to the camps. In turn, because it is still assumed that marriage will mean the woman's departure from her job, male Karenni leaders and teachers have also begun to recognize the need actively to encourage young women not to get married too early.[16] Such shifts in attitude on the part of a few leaders are thus far small, and women are still regarded as secondary to men in the political sphere. Nonetheless, the shift is there, albeit more because of pragmatism in maximizing the use of available opportunities rather than because of a clear ideology of equality.

How far foreign teachers reinforce certain received ideas of Karenni-ness is inevitably less than the effect of Karenni teachers. Nonetheless, it is significant. Within a short time of being in the camps foreigners learn Karenni versions of the current humanitarian and political situation, making no out-loud critique of what they are told and then in turn reinforcing it. In my own teaching, for example, I often asked students to write essays about their individual backgrounds, their views of the Karenni situation and about hopes and fears. While I did not stand in front of the class and presume to tell them about Karenni history, in getting them to write down a combination of personal experience and the historical rationale and political aspirations they had already been taught I was reinforcing a particular perspective on the past and future. I was encouraging its confirmation in writing, and in my subsequent expressions of shock and sympathy to individuals when I read of their own experiences, I further contributed to strengthening a certain way of *interpreting* that experience. I am not suggesting that what my Karenni students wrote and said was untrue, rather that in my encouragement and reaction, like other foreign visitors, I indirectly strengthened the received relationship between individual suffering and a particular historical and political explanation. I did not ask my students to write in their essays about Karenni history and politics, but invariably they did so, at once demonstrating the effectiveness with which it had been taught to them and, in the very act of writing it down for me, reinforcing its strength and validity not only in their minds but as something in need of further dissemination, for which purpose they should develop their abilities in English. Hence, in the process of inadvertently reinforcing a certain set of ideas about Karenni-ness, I and other foreign teachers also reinforced a certain approach to the reason for education and – especially – learning English in the first place. As representatives of the outside world encouraging interaction with us about ideas of what it means to be a Karenni refugee, we crystallized our students' ideas of the nature and desirability of similar interactions with the rest of the non-Karenni world.

On a more short term-basis than teaching for a year or more in the camp schools, foreign teachers are also often involved in training programmes such as teacher training by outside organizations. Karenni attendees take training sessions seriously. They are seen as opportunities to make Karenni education more effective. Karenni participants also see them as emancipatory by comparison to the situation inside Karenni State/Burma. First, it is allegedly very difficult for members of the Karenni and other non-Burman ethnic groups inside Burma to gain access to adequate teacher training (and other further education). Second, whether one has access to it or not there is a general refugee perception that the level of training received in the camps is far superior to anything inside Burma. Whether or not this is true is irrelevant. Teachers and students alike feel that education is better in the camps. Furthermore, positive attitudes towards training reflect general Karenni conceptions in which they see themselves as 'simple' and uneducated in comparison to the outside world, representatives of the latter therefore being perceived as able to teach the Karenni many useful things.

Overall, education is something Karenni refugees consider positively. It is not just something that whiles away the time and prepares the young better to face the future; it is also something that in itself is worth being glad about. In part, this entails attitudes towards the outside world, and it is to these that the chapter now turns.

LOOKING AND BEING 'BEYOND' THE CAMPS

NGOs and other foreigners are for most refugees the only points of contact with a wider, outside world. Furthermore, they are generally seen and interacted with inside the camps – that is, they stand for an outside world that for most refugees is otherwise unknown. Visiting NGO staff and occasionally NGO donors, foreign teachers and other outsiders such as journalists and religious groups, are for most refugees transient beings who come and go between the refugee camp and another, unfamiliar realm. Meanwhile, most refugees themselves stay put, unable to move freely. For them, particularly recent arrivals such as those in Camp 2, the outside world *is* foreigners who come to the camp and are perceived simultaneously as actual or potential sources of help and as fleeting symbols of another, richer, stranger world. It does not take long for the comings and goings of such foreigners to be taken for granted, and while many refugees expressed anxieties about not wanting to have to accept help at all, dependency is a concern on all sides (Dudley 1997). Furthermore, in the course of their assistance NGOs unwittingly and perhaps unavoidably reinforce the sense of displacement and all it entails. Many organizations, for example, are unwilling to provide funding to assist internally displaced persons (IDPs) in Karenni State, on the grounds that such assistance could not be accurately evaluated.[17] This reinforces the distinction between 'home' or 'inside', on the one hand, and refugee camps on the other. It also reinforces Karenni refugee perceptions of themselves as beholden and subordinate to donors. To be told that one may not have funds for projects inside Karenni State because the money's destination and use cannot be confirmed by the NGO, while understandable in terms of NGO accounting, from a refugee perspective makes one feel mistrusted.[18]

For a minority within the refugee population, relationships with NGOs and other foreigners extend beyond seeing outsiders in the camps and perhaps being involved in their assistance programmes. Primarily, this minority comprises camp and KNPP leaders with whom the IRC and others regularly meet, and young people who may be selected as NGO interns or employees or for study in Thailand or beyond. In the case of leaders, their interactions with foreigners still mostly take place within the bounded spaces of the camps, although some need sometimes to travel out of the camp to Mae Hong Son or occasionally elsewhere for meetings. It is, however, among young people selected to move outside the camps to fill positions as NGO interns, trainees, employees or university students, that relationships with outside organizations and individuals, indeed, with the outside world as a whole, reach their fullest development and impact. The possibility of acquiring expertise and of subsequently using it 'to help the Karenni people', is highly valued. Particularly appreciated acquisitions are office skills, management skills, familiarity with information technology, increased proficiency in English, greater political sophistication and knowledge of the machinations of the international community, and general experience of the outside world so that the Karenni may benefit from and become increasingly involved in it.

Older members of the Karenni elite are now enthusiastic about such opportunities for young people. This kind of enthusiasm for younger people gaining experience and knowledge away from their communities, especially abroad, has not always been shared by all members of the Karenni leadership, however. It was claimed to me that even by the end of 1996 some Karenni leaders thought it unnecessary, extravagant or generally undesirable to send anyone abroad at all – and this despite the fact that some of them had enough personal wealth to make it possible for one or two young people.[19] For other Karenni elite, however, this reluctance was incomprehensible, because in their view without getting young people out to learn as much as possible, 'who is there here [sic] now who is able to run a country?'[20] Nonetheless, some Karenni leaders feared that if young people went abroad to learn, they would not come back again, though others pointed out that if the camp education system was successful enough in instilling in young people a political consciousness and sense of duty, then most if not all would return to their people. More recently, however, like wider attitudes to education (Dudley 2000), attitudes to the value of gaining experience away from the displaced Karenni community, have become more positive. And as the number of such opportunities increases, and as young people gradually return to the refugee population from partaking of them, so do general awareness and imagination of the international community and of ways to communicate with it also increase.

GLOBAL VIEWS AND GLOBAL EXPOSURE

Interaction with tourists, whether in the 'Long-neck' villages or in passing in Mae Hong Son market, is but one way in which Karenni refugees come into contact with representatives of a wider, international community outside the camps. Indeed, tourists are of relatively minor importance in comparison to such other global vehicles as video, radio, printed media and NGOs. Interactions with, and Karenni imagination of, the international community bring a varied sense of the global into Karenni ideology.

On a political level, it seems clear that the Karenni, or at least the KNPP leadership, have little sense of much of the outside world's opinion of their hard line on Karenni State independence. The KNPP emphasizes the distinctness of its own political standpoint on this, and at the same time feels aggrieved at the apparently poor understanding and support of it by the outside world. The KNPP leaders on the whole do not perceive that differing foreign views of them on the one hand and, say, pro-democracy Burmese student groups on the other, may have something to do with the difference in political standpoints. So, while the Karenni are right to feel aggrieved that human rights abuses in their and other ethnic areas tend to be reported less than those affecting the mainly Burman population of central Burma, they may not be wholly correct to assume it is simply lack of awareness that is responsible for the relatively low level of international sympathy they receive. Indeed, this sympathy seems low in comparison to other ethnic groups such as the Karen, as well as in comparison to pro-democracy groups such as the National League for Democracy (NLD). This is partly a function of relative size (the KNPP is small in relation to the Karen National Union [KNU]), but it may also be a result of the KNPP's stance on independence, a political objective that to many outsiders seems worthy of little support.

From an outside, practical perspective, then, the KNPP seems unable to recognize what it is that ensures their continued international marginality. But from the inside, ideological perspective of the KNPP, the greater the marginality the greater must be the insistence on the objective of independence: it is a point of principle that is hard to compromise. For the KNPP it has also become a definitive characteristic of who the Karenni are, and a principal element in the explanation of their suffering. It is through such mutual misunderstanding that the Karenni have frequently been left out of NGO and other border initiatives. Negative Karenni responses to certain projects, made on the grounds of independence, often result in the Karenni not being included in subsequent projects. An example is the responses of some KNPP leaders to the efforts made in 1997 by the Burma Lawyers' Council (BLC) to provide training sessions to all groups along the border, facilitating understanding of a draft-written constitution for a future democratic Burma. The BLC simultaneously tried to involve their target groups in discussions about the composition of this draft constitution. For some KNPP leaders, however, this process was irrelevant to the Karenni: if Karenni State should not and will not be a part of Burma, then how can it be included in the latter's constitution? They did not, however, prevent the training from taking place, and those Karenni who actually took part – mostly young, reasonably well-educated people drawn from all the camps – were positive in their response. Indeed, the grassroots reaction from involved youth was that the process was a useful one in which the Karenni should most certainly be involved. Unfortunately from a Karenni perspective, however, the apparent negativity of some KNPP leaders towards such projects does not always encourage outsiders who might be planning further efforts (nor, as I discuss elsewhere [Dudley

2000] does it always make for agreement between generations of Karenni refugees). It seems, for example, for precisely this reason that the Karenni were not as significantly involved as other groups in the 1999 onwards National Reconciliation Program.[21] Furthermore, apparently negative responses from KNPP leaders sometimes give the impression to outsiders that the Karenni are not very concerned with the wider world. But this could not be further from the truth. International legitimation of and support for Karenni political objectives are important to the KNPP, as is the dissemination of information about the humanitarian situation inside Karenni State.

More abstractly but perhaps most significantly, for younger people especially the wider world is both a source of knowledge, and itself something about which they wish to know more. The acquisition of knowledge from and about the wider world not only allows it to be better understood, but also alters Karenni perceptions of their own place within it. Tantalizing glimpses of parts of this wider world are had in the camps, not only through the visits of foreigners but also through radio, video, and printed media. Short-wave transistor radios are highly valued items, and those who do not possess them (the majority) often visit the houses of those who do to listen to news broadcasts. Inevitably, news about Burma and the border is of particular concern, but there is also a general awareness of and interest in international current affairs. There were numerous occasions on which I was asked, unprompted, my opinions on current situations in Northern Ireland, Bosnia and the Middle East. Discussions often extended beyond immediate 'news' – educated, young people, for example, wished to explain their admiration for such figures as Yasser Arafat, Che Guevara and Fidel Castro.[22] Furthermore, interest in persons and events elsewhere in the world goes beyond politics: sport, in particular the English football league, is of major interest to well-informed young men, who are often able to discuss not only teams but also individual players. Any fashion magazines or other Western images, together with British or American popular music, are eagerly consumed by the young whenever possible. For a few individuals who have previously lived in urban areas in Burma with access to cinemas, Hollywood films and the Oscars are also of major interest. For most, however, films are familiar only through the showing of videos in the camps. These showings, usually out of doors in the evening, in Camp 5 at least are usually organized by KNPP leaders using their own equipment. The TV screen is invariably of normal size, yet despite this, and despite the fact that most watching the video cannot understand the dialogue, scores of people crowd together to watch. Sometimes the films are Thai or Chinese, but more often they are American, ranging from violent war movies such as *Full Metal Jacket*, through blockbusters like *Jurassic Park*, to quirkier films such as *Babe* or *The Gods Must Be Crazy*. Occasionally too, smaller student groups are shown educational videos, or taped British TV programmes (including, on one memorable and surreal evening for me, an *Inspector Morse* episode based in my old workplace, the Pitt Rivers Museum, University of Oxford).

It is all these sources of information pertaining to a modern world beyond that contribute to a continually growing curiosity in and knowledge of both the international community and its machinations, and of cultural diversity around the globe. This is 'consumption' in its wider sense of being conscious of 'living through objects and images not of one's own creation' (Miller 1995: 1; see also Appadurai 1986, Bourdieu 1984). As more knowledge, images and sounds are consumed, so are more desired, and so grows the realization of being a *part* of a wider community. Becoming refugees and coming to the camps has hastened and intensified this process for all, but perhaps particularly for young people: their interactions with foreigners, video and printed media are often greater than among other members of the refugee population. Furthermore, the increasing availability of internships or other opportunities outside the camps means greater numbers of educated young Karenni people are gaining experience of the wider world through physical interaction with a part of it, and, once out there, through email contact with other parts of it. Such experience is by its nature partial, so that ideas of the outside world are part knowledge and part imagination; by extension, so too are conceptions of Karenni-ness in relation to the wider world and of the place of the Karenni within it. As experience of the wider world increases, so do its impacts on constructions of Karenni-ness.

Ideas about the wider world are important too for ways in which Karenni refugees conceive of their current situation *as refugees in camps*. That is, the camps themselves are seen not alone but in relation to the world beyond. Particular glimpses of the wider world heighten awareness of disjunctures between local poverty and social realities on the one hand and global materialism and possibilities on the other. In direct comparison with life inside and beyond the camps, however, the commonest idiom is that of 'the jungle'. On one level, this entails emphasizing the paucity of opportunities for educational advancement, political expression and material acquisition, and other palpable disadvantages of jungle living. Relative isolation, ignorance, hardship and boredom are all variously pointed to as problematic results of camp-based exile, and 'the jungle' becomes shorthand for all of them. The feelings of young people in particular about being confined to such a life at times reach desperation, although such strong emotions are often couched in irony and humour. Paul, for example, while talking to me of his depression at being stuck in the 'jungle' and his desperate hope not to have to spend the rest of his life in such a socially, politically, intellectually and materially restrictive environment, added that he supposed it was not all that bad as at least there was lots of fresh air. Most importantly, expressions of unhappiness at the current situation are invariably counteracted by statements about having to put up with it out of duty to one's country and people; that is, living in the jungle is a price that must be paid for being a positive part of the Karenni struggle. And here, of course, there is a circularity: refugee-ness is a price that must be paid for being a Karenni nationalist, yet simultaneously Karenni nationalism as it is manifested in the camps can be perceived by an outsider as an elaborate way of ameliorating the experience of displacement.

Negativity about 'jungle' living is mostly expressed by young and/or relatively well-educated people, and by the minority who lived formerly in urban areas. 'The jungle' is used by such people as shorthand for a situation in which intellectual, political and sophisticated cultural activities are almost impossible. For many other members of the refugee population, however, the jungle is in some ways not that different from the area they came from. It may be topographically a little different, but it is similar insofar as it is a rural surrounding from which may be gathered a variety of food and other useful items such as leaves for thatching, natural dyestuffs, etc. However, for these refugees one important difference remains: here, nearby areas of jungle may not be cleared for cultivation and thus in this context 'jungle' is indeed symbolic of restriction.

For all refugees, then, living in the 'jungle' symbolizes a degree of restriction, be it constructed primarily in intellectual, political, agricultural or other terms. The response to such restriction is often rather passive. In part, this is unsurprising – there is little that refugees can constructively do about not being able to farm properly, for example. But for some passivity also becomes a more generalized way of talking about things, even an affectation. When, for example, I asked Saw Eh Gay if the Karenni tried to make contact with outside groups (e.g. religious organizations), he replied, 'Oh no. They contact us, because we don't know how to. We are quite content and when things are needed God sends them – like he sent you.' Yet in reality various Karenni individuals and organizations *do* make and maintain contacts with a number of outside groups. Indeed, by 1999 the Karenni were successfully and actively using email to seek replacement English teachers. Admittedly such organized efforts, and knowing where to start in making them, are relatively new. Admittedly too, Saw Eh Gay's apparent Christian fatalism is more marked than most. Nonetheless, it is also slightly disingenuous. Many Karenni portray themselves as poor, ignorant jungle-dwellers, yet do not always behave or really see themselves as such in practice. Indeed, the simplicity and ignorance so often claimed by the Karenni, and so often rationalized as being due to having to live in the jungle, is sometimes a useful tool in the effort to win outside sympathy and assistance. Living in camps in the jungle is problematic, but is also part of a wider way in which a separateness from the outside, the non-Karenni, is asserted (cf. Malkki 1995) and used, both in reinforcing what it means to be Karenni and in relating to what is non-Karenni.

CONCLUDING REMARKS

Engaging positively with the future through education and outside contacts is envisaging that future as the hoped-for end-point of 'the struggle' with which many Karenni refugees have been actively engaged for a long time. Eventual return home, at its most positive, is dreamt of as return to a place free of Burmese oppression, a future manifestation of an idealized past not personally experienced by any of the refugees in the camps; in other words, the object of the myth of return is itself a myth. As time passes, it appears to more and more refugees to be less and less of a real possibility. Nonetheless, it is a part of the KNPP's political agenda and aspirations, presenting refugees with a possible future, a politically constructed, hypothetical alternative to staying in the camps indefinitely or returning to a Karenni State still under a Burmese fist. Furthermore, the dissemination of KNPP ideals to 'outsiders', and the training and encouragement of young people to participate in this dissemination, helps to keep alive in Karenni minds the possibility of fulfilling the nationalist dream.

The fact that there *is* a dream, and that part of trying to make it come true is to disseminate it among both the Karenni and the international communities, not only reinforces political ideology in a positive feedback cycle but also helps make displacement itself more bearable. It does this indirectly by providing something for people to work towards and focus on, and directly by conflating the dissemination of ideology with the need for material assistance. Many of those outsiders with whom the Karenni interact comprise relief agencies and individuals wishing to help on humanitarian grounds. In the process of assisting, they are made aware of KNPP-driven Karenni views on why Karenni refugees are in the position they are in, and where ideally they would like to be. Conversely, other outsiders initially become interested in the Karenni because of their history and political agenda, and subsequently become drawn into a process of assistance. Outsiders themselves, by their very involvement, perpetuate further the dream of return to a free Karenni State. NGOs, for example, frame capacity development programmes in terms of developing skills for refugees to use when they eventually return home, in the NGO's view perhaps including preparation for a worst-case scenario such as forced repatriation but from refugees' perspectives often simply reinforcing the hope, nay belief, in the successful outcome of current nationalist agenda.

As time spent in the camps increases, inevitably so too does the level of refugee exposure to and conviction in political aspirations of an independent Karenni State. Putting it another way, as others have joined the original, politicized, pro-KNPP core of the refugee population, they have provided a means to widen the KNPP constituency. In general, the spreading of nationalist ideology and ideas of common pan-Karenni bonds is part of a wider dynamic system in which the refugee community is fertile ground for the propagation of ideas. But the same community is also a pool from which are drawn both people to serve the system and the reason for the system to exist. The dissemination of nationalist ideology is a self-sustaining, self-serving, dynamic process. The inculcation of a sense of belonging and duty, or identity and purpose, among the refugee population, and especially among young people, particularly through education, is an important part of this process. Education and nationalism are both intimate parts not only of shaping and reinforcing what it means to be Karenni but also of coping with being a refugee.

World-wide education, outside contacts and transnational solidarities,[23] media and new media, and forced migration itself are all pathways of multidirectional cultural influence between the local, regional and global. Members of refugee populations such as the Karenni may perceive themselves as liminal, marginal to a globally hegemonic system of nation states (Dudley 2000), and this self-image may help to initiate and maintain nationalist movements such as the KNPP: that is, nationalist movements often comprise people who rather than challenging the order of nation-states to which they perceive themselves as not properly belonging, seek to join or reproduce it. At the same time, forced migrations like that of the Karenni bring together in the relatively narrow confines of refugee camps, etc., ethnically and otherwise heterogeneous populations, the diversity of which for most first-generation migrants has little or no precedent in pre-migration life. Exile often provides a context for the strengthening and transformation of collective identity, as is clearly happening for the Karenni refugee population. Simultaneously, identity is also continually modified by the increasing engagements with a wider world that exile often brings. Fascination with Western media and personal images among young Karenni, for example, draws them into a wider world from which their present liminality as refugees seems to separate them, making more porous the boundary around them, at the same time accentuating the demarcation between refugee and non-refugee, poor and rich.

In sum, displacement and dynamics of ethnicity and nationalism are interwoven with each other and with knowledge of and attitudes towards the wider world in order continually to reshape what Karenni-ness is. As 'symbolic universes merge ... people become more similar in terms of practices and representations ... [and they become] more liable than before to reflect upon and objectify their way of life as *a culture* or *a tradition* ... [thus becoming] *a people* with an abstract sense of community and a presumed shared history' (Eriksen 1993: 85, emphases original; cf. Chit Laing this volume). Presumed or not, imagined or not, the Karenni of the refugee camps in Thailand are indeed focused upon becoming 'a people'.

AUTHOR'S NOTE

Thanks to the Carnegie Foundation and Queen Elizabeth House, University of Oxford, for support in the writing and presentation of a much earlier version of this chapter at the 1st Collaborative International Conference of the Burma Studies Group (BSG), 'Burma-Myanma(r) Research and its Future Implications for Scholars and Policymakers', University of Gothenburg,

Sweden, September 2002. Parts of this chapter have appeared in different forms in Dudley 2000, Dudley forthcoming (a) and Dudley forthcoming (b).

The chapter is based on ongoing communication with Karenni refugees in Thailand, and, primarily, on my field research in Karenni refugee camps from 1996 to 1997, and again 1998. I am grateful to the grant-making bodies who made this field research possible: Jesus College, Oxford; the Emslie Horniman and RAI/Sutasoma funds of the Royal Anthropological Institute; the Peter Lienhardt Memorial Fund, University of Oxford; the Cha Fund, University of Oxford; the Board of Graduate Studies, University of Oxford; and the Evans Fund, University of Cambridge. My greatest debt of gratitude, however, is owed to the many Karenni friends who shared their lives with me.

NOTES

[1] Since I last saw him, Saw Eh Ka Lu Taw has changed his name. He was previously known by a Karen religious name, but his new epithet expresses his nationalist aspirations. In his letter, he explained it thus: '*Eh* is love, *Ka Lu* is nation, and *Taw* is truth or faith.'

[2] Christian Solidarity Worldwide (2004). http://www.csw.org

[3] I do not have space to discuss religion and identity in the camps here. Suffice to say that Christianity has become a central component in this view of positive ways to be Karenni in the world. Spreading the Christian faith among the Karenni refugee population is seen not only as a Christian duty, but also as a way of spreading a wider message about the hegemony and benefits of things generally thought of as 'modern' and 'moral' and associated by the Karenni with Christianity. In particular, these include ideas about education and female propriety. See, for example, Dudley (1997, 2000 and forthcoming).

[4] Hte Buphe's most recent occupation of the KNPP premier office began when he succeeded Aung Than Lay in the party elections of December 1996.

[5] On ethnicity and the relative importance of an ethnic group's boundaries rather than content, see Barth (1969), Barth (2000) and Cohen (2000), but cf. Glazer and Moynihan (1975). For overviews of anthropological perspectives on ethnicity, see Banks (1996), Jenkins (1996).

[6] Cf. Barnes (1995: 1) on the self-conscious assumption of the identity 'indigenous people' because of its 'currency in contemporary international legal and institutional activities'. See also Dudley (2006) on increasingly self-conscious uses of internationally familiar human rights language, such as 'genocide'.

[7] In Africa, for example, Malkki notes that 'there is a chilling traffic back and forth between the essentialist constructions of historians, anthropologists,

and colonial administrators, and those of Hutu and Tutsi ethnic nationalists'
(Malkki 1995: 14).

[8] *US Committee for Refugees Country Report: Burma*, 2002, http://www.refs.org/
world/countryrpt/east-pacific/burma.htm

[9] In Kayah (Karenni) State alone, in October 2004 there were estimated to be up
to 88,000 internally displaced persons (IDPs).

[10] Cf. Tibet: see, e.g. Korom (1997).

[11] This textbook is also given to outsiders and includes the KNPP address and
telephone number for those requiring more information.

[12] These days include Resistance Day (9 August; commemorates the day in 1948
on which, according to the KNPP Karenni State was invaded by the Burmese),
Martyrs' Day (18 September) and Army Day (17 August; commemorates the day
in 1948 that the Karenni National Resistance Army [KNRA] was formed). One
other annual commemoration, National Day, is held on 21 June, to mark the
anniversary of the Anglo-Burmese signing of the 1875 agreement recognizing
the independence of (Eastern) Karenni.

[13] *Chinlon* is a South East Asian game of skill played with an open-structured
rattan ball, the aim being to keep the ball in the air by kicking it. The Karenni
generally refer to it by its Burmese name, although one or two use the Thai
name, *takraw*.

[14] Education itself is also affected by gender. While all adults, for example, said
education was equally important for girls and boys, in practice it is more likely
that in any one family girls will receive less schooling than boys. It is also more
likely that older siblings, especially if they are girls, will receive less education
than their younger brothers and sisters as they are required to help in the house.
(Dudley 1997; CCSDPT 1995).

[15] Kerry Demusz, personal communication (1996).

[16] Saw Doh Say, personal communication (1999).

[17] Christina Fink, personal communication (2000).

[18] Cf. Daniel and Knudsen (1995).

[19] Teddy Buri, personal communication (1999).

[20] Ibid.

[21] Christina Fink, personal communication (February 2000).

[22] Cf. Eriksen on the effects of 'globalisation of culture and relativisation of
boundaries', on which he cites as an example Mauritians talking about Chernobyl
(1993: 148–9). Karenni conversations in 1998 about the death of Princess Diana
provide similar examples.

[23] Transnational solidarities in the form of NGOs and more informal networks
provide valuable support and advocacy for many groups. In particular, 'a much
sought after strategy for transnational political networks' is the co-opting of

NGOs 'since such organizations facilitate contact with levels of policy making which are otherwise difficult to gain access to for a diaspora organization' (Østergaard-Nielsen 2001: 16). Østergaard-Nielsen gives the examples of Andean indigenous and Kurdish political organizations, and although not discussed in this chapter it is a strategy common to many other groups as well, including the Karenni (Dudley 2000), who appeal to and depend upon the lobbying of the United Nations and other international bodies by organizations such as the Unrepresented People's Organization (UNPO). But transnational social movements and international organizations do not just function as conduits, supports and targets for lobbying. They also 'provide a normative frame of reference for those [groups] advocating democratization and human rights agendas' (Østergaard-Nielsen 2001: 16) and, one might add, a normative frame of opposition for those groups advocating rather different agendas. In the case of pro-human rights/pro-democracy groups such as the Burmese pro-democracy movement, for example, they increasingly take on the language and values of international human rights rhetoric in order both to explain their cause to a wider international audience and thereby to attempt to garner additional international support of various kinds (Dudley forthcoming a).

Chapter 4

SOME REMARKS UPON ETHNICITY THEORY AND SOUTHEAST ASIA, WITH SPECIAL REFERENCE TO THE KAYAH AND THE KACHIN

F. K. L. Chit Hlaing

I was not a participant in the panel at the 2002 Burma Studies Conference at Gothenburg at which these chapters were first presented, though I was present and made some comments from the floor; but I was an outside reader of the resulting manuscript collection for the publisher, and it is on the basis of my remarks in that capacity that I was asked by the editor, Mikael Gravers, to contribute this brief additional chapter. He also thought that it would be useful if I could respond to some of his questions concerning the Kayah and the ethnic categories, since I did ethnographic field work among them in 1961 and wrote a monograph on Kayah ethnography (Lehman 1967b) and have in addition (Lehman 1963, 1967a, 1975, 2004a, b) written at some length upon the general theory of ethnic identity on which the present volume focuses.

My work on ethnicity is grounded in cognitive theory and more particularly in a cognitively based theory of social systems. Now, as all the chapters here and the recent literature they cite make clear, ethnic identity is one way or other a political relation and not any kind of primordial category; not only is it not 'who any group of people or communities "really is" ', but also people are commonly able to claim alternative ethnic identities in such a way that two communities who claim one identity may alternatively claim contrasting identities. Some Thai are Khon Müang (Northern Thai), while others are Thai, *tout court*; some Kachin are Jinghpaw, while others are, respectively, Maru, Atsi (Zaiwa), etc. These are all well-known facts, especially in the literature on Southeastern Asia. This phenomenon is not at all limited to that part of the world, of course. All the indigenous population of the Netherlands is Dutch, except that some are Frisian and so on; but it is pointless to continue such examples, as the world is replete with them.

What is especially interesting, however, and far less widely appreciated, is the relation between ethnic identity and 'culture'. Leach first argued this clearly (1954) with regard to Kachin. It turns out that, as I have pointed out many times (see earlier citations), there is hardly any cultural trait or custom that meets the following conditions: that is universally shared by all the communities claiming a given identity, and that it is unique to just the communities claiming a given identity! The sole exceptions seem to be customs and practices associated directly with making the claim to the identity in question: flags, formal litanies of identity, and the like, which, if not always universally shared, are certainly unique to the identity claimed. I dare say these are largely what Barth (1969) called 'boundary markers' of ethnic identity, although, as I pointed out long ago, sometimes these are mere markers and sometimes they are customs around which communities coalesce as 'ethnic' to protect such customs. For instance, though hardly all Jews follow or even believe in the rules and regulations of that religion, all acknowledge those religious doctrines and customs as something that somehow makes them all Jews. Not all Burmans are Buddhists and yet all recognize and acknowledge the centrality of Theravada Buddhism for their Burman identity – which is what is really meant by the common view that 'to be Burman is to be Buddhist' (see Spiro 1970; it is true, as he says, that a villager will sometimes say of someone that he/she does not like that that person is 'not really Burman' if happening not to be Buddhist, but, when then asked if the person is of this or that 'other' ethnic category, the respondent tends to rapidly say 'no').

Yet it seems a well nigh universal fact of human social life that people claim for any given ethnic identity 'a culture', i.e., a 'way of life' belonging to them as 'the so-and-so people'. Indeed it is a well-documented proposition that modern nation states do everything they can to create and/or promote a 'national culture'. Nowhere has this been more repeatedly shown than in thee literature on Southeast Asia, with particular reference to Indonesia and Thailand. In fact Anderson's (1991) well-known and much cited notion of the nation state as an 'imagined community' is based on just this sort of situation. Any attempt, however, to extend this analysis to 'the state' in general must fail because history shows us innumerable states (monarchies) with widely commanded loyalty that were not nation states, that did not claim or try to promote a uniform cultural identity amongst their subjects. All the pre-colonial states of Southeast Asia were like that and, in fact all mercantilist states, meaning that almost all states prior to, say, 'modern times' were states with a formally and jurally acknowledged plurality of cultural and ethnic communities. One of old Siam's most distinguished subjects was Greek, Constantine Phaulkon (Gerakis being the Greek name, which, translated, means falcon), who was prime minister in the seventeenth century (Wyatt 1984: 112), whilst Burman kings had their Portuguese Catholic subject communities from the sixteenth century, and its politically important Armenian Ministers as well, even though the king derived his legitimacy as patron-protector of the Buddhist religion (see Lieberman 1984).

In any event, it is common – if not indeed universal – for any ethnic identity to define itself historically, and not relationally. For most such identities at least, and certainly for the many 'tribal' peoples of Southeastern Asia, there is a mythology purporting to derive 'their customs' from some sort of primordial assignment or dispensation by some sort of deity or original human ancestor. So, for me the central question is why people in general do and always have attributed to themselves 'our true, primordial cultural identity'. The question obtrudes for at least two closely related reasons. First, because clearly 'we' do not all subscribe to the same customs, and second because it is also clear that ethnic identity is in fact what I have called 'relational' i.e. one is not, for instance simply, say, a Chin, a Lai or Hakha Chin; rather to be a Chin is explicitly *not* to be a Burman. They are all ultimately in the Lai language Zo, and this word explicitly means something like 'remote and relatively uncultivated', in contrast to the word *Vaai*, which means, for Lai Chin, 'Burmese'. I recall asking what the difference is, and being told again and again that '*Vaai* have towns and writing and kings while *Zo* do not' (they added 'horses' too, but Chin had at least some horses). Let me now deal in turn with each of these two considerations before coming to the most central question about ethnicity: why have people (and anthropologists, too) persisted in imagining ethnicity as a system of essentialist – which is ultimately to say taxonomic[1]– categories and in supposing that each such identity 'has' a real thing called 'its culture'? Let me elaborate here, if only as a gloss upon chapter 8 in this volume by Lianhmung Sakhong.

First, it is necessary to explain that *Vaai* does not *mean* Burmese; it *refers to* Burmese among Chin within Burma, but among Mizo (Lushai – 'Mi<u>zo</u>' = Zomi, where 'mi' means just 'people') it refers to the civilized lowlanders that *they* related to most closely, those of Assam-Bengal, and India more generally. *Vaai* clearly means civilized, elaborately cultivated and the like. So much so that the special blanket used by men giving a high-ranking Feast of Merit was called *vaipuan* (*puan* = cloth, blanket) because the weaving of its embroidery is technically very sophisticated.

Second, there is a related pair of correlative words involving zo,[2] namely, the pair *Zo/Laai*. The Hakha Chin proper, those of the dominant centre of Hakha, call themselves *Laai*. Those of Falam call themselves *Laaizo*. Now, in these languages, *laai* means simply 'central', cognate with the Burmese word *(a-)le* (spelt alay), 'middle'. In the Hakha area, the Hakha themselves refer to their subordinate villages to the south and east (some speaking practically the same dialect as that of Hakha, others not) as *zo*, but as one proceeds away from Hakha town in those directions, especially eastward, people refer to themselves as *Laai* but to their neighbours, even farther off in the same direction, as *Zo*.[3]

Third, it is interesting to look at the word 'Chin' in this connection. Now this word we get from the Burmese, which spells it 'khrang'. This word first appears in Burmese in some stone inscriptions erected in the early tweflth century by the Pagan king Kyanzittha. Those inscriptions in the Middle and Upper Chindwin valley state that the Burmans claim jurisdiction up to the left bank of the river but will leave the Khrang in the hills beyond to their own devices (in fact as a sort of buffer between Pagan and the kingdom of the Sak (modern Burmese *Thet*) in and around what is now Manipur, across the border in India. Now (see Lehman 1979) it was once suggested that Khrang might have been an archaic Burmese word for 'other folk', but it turns out that it is in fact an old Chin word meaning just 'people' (of any ethnicity!), as found in southern Chin languages, such as N'Men, where it surfaces as *k'khFang*. So, almost as a mirror image of the Chin view of their relation to the civilized Burmese, we find the old Burmese treating their Chin neighbours terminologically as 'those other people'.

With regard to 'a culture', it is usual for people or communities who claim a given identity to dismiss the aforementioned (often considerable) variations in custom and as mere 'variations on a common theme'. This is done often in spite of the fact that, for any two or more communities claiming that identity, the cultural similarities may be no greater than those between or among neighbouring communities claiming different identities. The example of language-and-dialect is instructive: for example, consider Burmese. One commonly speaks of Arakanese as a language, if only because Arakan (Rahkain) was once a separate kingdom, and yet in terms of mutual intelligibility, Arakanese is demonstrably more mutually intelligible with the 'standard' Burmese of Yangon or Mandalay than are the 'mere dialects' such as Yaw Burmese just below the Chin State, or Dawe (Tavoyan) in the far south. Such examples can be multiplied endlessly. In northern mainland Southeast Asia, there is a chain of mutually very similar incantational-mediumistic cults, all centring upon a practitioner called '*bimo*' and similar sounding names in such languages as Akha, Nuosu (a kind of 'Yi'/ Lolo) and so on. But in each case the usual claim is that of 'mere similarity' among religions of different cultures.[4]

The lesson to be learnt from all this is that 'a culture' as 'a distinctive way of life' is, as is 'a language', in fact something that any set of communities systematically *attributes to* itself. Any attempt to establish objective criteria for determining the 'real' boundaries of a culture, e.g., the 'common language' criterion, is bound to fail because cultures are not things out there but rather attributional categories. Two things follow from this. First, that a 'true' taxonomic catalogue of cultures, or a non-arbitrary answer to the common question of 'how many cultures are there?' is not possible. Second, that any common language criterion is necessarily circular![5]

It is rather well understood these days that ethnicity is what one may call 'a political fact'; the various chapters in the present volume make this clear, with all the necessary references to the literature on this matter. However, it is common along these lines to hypothesize that ethnicity is a phenomenon strictly associated with the presence of hegemonic states. Indeed, in the case of the Chin of the Burma–India borderland, I have given myself (Lehman 1963) a good instance of this sort of situation (see above with regard to the correlative terms in Lai Chin, *Zo* and *Vaai*). Better-known is the way in which China, both imperial and republican China and the People's Republic have literally created ethnic groups and labels and categories, a fact so widely documented (and referred to in my earlier papers, cited above) that I need not go into it here. The Kayah case is especially instructive.

As I showed in my monograph upon these people, a Central Karen-speaking people of the southern end of the Shan plateau (Lehman 1967b; on Karen linguistic classification, see Solnit 1997), they literally came into existence as such in the latter half of the eighteenth century as a confederation of dialectally related communities formed by charismatic leaders in order to wrest control of the increasingly lucrative teak trade from the Shan for whom they had been working. Furthermore, they modelled their new polities upon the example of Shan princely titles and rulership, and they secured their political existence as a 'people' by making compacts with the Burmese throne in Ava and then Mandalay, and subsequently with the British colonial administration that ended up granting the Kayah (Karenni) States the status of protectorates. Furthermore still, their existence as a people was given symbolic focus by the creation of a ritual cult associated specifically with these charismatic leaders, now rulers (*sophrya*, the title itself a refiguration of the Shan and/or Thai princely title of *Caopha* [Shan]/*Caophrya* [Thai or northern Thai]). This was the cult of the *iyluw*, the elaborate pole with its rotating top and its decorated streamers that is in all details the same as the Shan and Burmese Buddhist 'flagpole of the victory' of the Lord Buddha over the host of Mara (though Kayah generally refuse to acknowledge any similarity). This cult and its apparatus in fact is common to all Kayah and *only* the Kayah among the central Karen (including the farthest eastern Kayah on the Thailand side of the border who did not themselves belong to any Kayah State although they were cross-border extensions of Kantarawady Kayah historically).[6] Indeed and significantly the Manumanaw (a Burmese name based on the Kayah word *Manœ*, meaning 'western') who speak a dialect indistinguishable from that of the western Kayah of Kyebogyi but who live in the adjacent western hills and were never incorporated into the Kayah identity, do not have this cult. Above all, the basis for the symbolic authority of these charismatic leaders is their claim to be, or to have been, *phrey phrow*, i.e., persons who have appeared suddenly and from the outside world with the powerful knowledge of that outside world of the Shan, Burmese and Mon kingdoms (the term means literally one who has sprung miraculously from out of nowhere).[7] Two points emerge here: (a) that the ethnogenesis of Kayah gives evidence of considerable agency on the part of the Kayah themselves and cannot be attributed to state hegemony at all, and (b) that the Kayah considered themselves to possess specifically Shan-style principalities for the purpose of dealing with the outside world, but for internal purposes considered their leaders to be only religious-charismatic 'chiefs' and not actual rulers. Indeed, as the former wife of the Kantarawady State ruler, the Kantarawady Mahadewi (the term is Shan-Pali for a Shan prince's chief queen and means, in Pali, 'great goddess')[8] once mentioned with great emphasis that her father, the then Kyebogyi ruler (probably around the transition from the nineteenth to the twentieth century), was hardly much of a real prince because each morning he went out into the fields with his oxen like any other village man.

I have been asked by our editor, Gravers, to elaborate upon the Kayah case in certain matters. First, as to the *phreyphrow*, were they prophets or – considering that the system of principalities founded by *phreyphrow* was in the sense explained above modelled upon the system of Buddhist statecraft among the Shan, Burmans and Mon – were they like what in Burmese is called *mìn laùng'*, literally 'immanent kings', which is what in Burmese characterized a proper occupant of the throne? No, *phreyphrow* cannot be compared usefully to *mìn laùng* because the latter word derives its significance from specifically Theravada Buddhist *samsaric* cosmology: a king is above all patron–protector of the Buddhist religion and its Order of Monks and, as such, in a position to earn immense Merit. Therefore, by the economy of Merit, he must have earned so much Merit in previous existences that he was 'bound to become a king', and indeed eventually, should he, as king, earn great Merit, gain supreme enlightenment, so that if he is *Mìnlaùng*, he is also *Hpaya:laung:*, an immanent Buddha' (see Spiro 1982). The *phreyphrow* were indeed prophets in many ways, though: they 'prophesied' a millennial change for the better in the circumstances of the people's lives. Moreover, for not all *phreyphrow* were political leaders, now and again there arose such figures among the Kayah, as among so many Karen (see Hinton 1979, Marlowe 1979; Marshall 1922; Stern 1968, 1979). And when, as usual, their predictions failed to materialize, they were not infrequently killed. One such case occurred some years before my arrival in Kyebogyi, and I was shown the burial site. In this regard let me relate a story told by the far-eastern Kayah in Thailand (who were not part of any of the Kayah principalities although speakers of the dialect of Kantarawady State) about the origin of their version of the *iyluw* cult.[9] Long ago there came miraculously to the Kayah village such a man. He stayed on because he fell in love with a girl there, and he lived with her and her mother. From him the people learnt all sorts of useful things and could look forward to more of the same. However, this man became bored and departed, rising up on some sort of log or platform towards the sky. The mother and daughter ran out and begged him to return, but he refused, and when they said to him that they would not know how to do all sorts of things, he told them to just pray to God. But they asked, 'How does one do that?' He then said, 'That is the problem with you people, you don't even know how to pray to God!' And he continued, 'Look, just plant a long pole in the earth and decorate it atop, and pray to that!' whereupon he left for good. And the people did that, and the pole is the *iyluw*, which means, literally, something 'implanted vertically'.

Regarding this cult, it is interesting that it exists, at least in Kyebogyi and Kantarawady, side by side with another cult, that of *kéy*, which means 'the land'. The cult of the *iyluw* (also known as *kathowbow*) is intimately connected with the lineage of the ruler. In fact this line is understood as intertwined with the priesthood of the *iyluw*, while that of *kéy* is associated with the kindred of the common folk. I mention this because Gravers (personal communication on 13 January 2004; cf. also his Chapter in the present volume on Pwo Buddhist ethnicity and ritual) has reminded me that there are several striking similarities between this ritual complex and the religious complex among Buddhist Pwo Karen, where, as he remarks, 'they identify with the larger world while maintaining a separate identity'. That neatly characterizes the Kayah situation also, obviously. Furthermore, it is well known that the Pwo were closely associated with the Mon, and that Pwo Buddhism owed much to the Mon model. It seems clear, historically, that the Burmese *tagundaing* (and the Shan *tam-khon* – loanword from the Burmese *tagun* – see above), on which the *iyluw* is modelled, owes much to an apparent Mon Buddhist origin. Is this significant? I think so. For Kantarawady legend, for instance, gives the distinct impression that their first prince, Papaw, came up from the south, from among the Yangtalai, the Karen people of the southernmost Kayah State of Bawlakhe. The Yangtalai (see Lehman 1979 for speculations on the etymology of this ethnic label, where 'Yang' = Karen, and 'talai' means 'south/downstream') are known to have had close geographic and economic relations with Pwo and Mon down in Burma proper. So, in considerable degree, it seems likely that there may have been a distinct Mon source, by way perhaps of Pwo, for the *iyluw* cult ritually defining Kayah and its attendant form of Karen millenarianism.

I must point out that states are certainly not at all the only source of ethnic categorization. When Europeans first encountered the aborigines of the New World, it is clear that the latter were uniformly divided into many self-designated different 'peoples', with no states in sight or even known for the most part except on the northern borders of Mexico. In Southeastern Asia, for all sorts of historical, political and 'ecological' reasons such as, say, who controlled which trade routes (see Fiskesjö 2000 on Wa) and access to which salt wells (see Hutton 1921) and because of different local 'arrangements' and relations with lowland states as well, various communities of non-state, 'tribal' areas defined themselves ethnically in relational competition and contrast with one another. And, of course, local tribal politics banded some communities together ethnically as against others. There is ample documentation of this practice and it is a common ethnographic fact that each ethnic 'group' sees itself always in contrast with neighbouring groups. This is also an aspect of the relational character of ethnic categorization. But of course what is special and important about the state-hegemony context of ethnic categorization is that the state can often manage to create, by power, authority and formal law, not only formal categorizations of 'minority, 'tribal' populations but in fact a sense of ethnic identity on the part of the communities so formally categorized. For, to put it bluntly, if a powerful state treats a set of communities as an ethnic group, and if, in particular, it results in those communities being able to manage their relations with the state only under such rubrics, these communities not uncommonly end up actually thinking of themselves as 'the same people'. This has been documented again and again in the case of the People's Republic of China and its official list of 55 ethnic 'nationalities' Maybe the best known instance is that of the 'Yi' (see, e.g., Harrell 2001).

Prior to the 1950s, when China first initiated this system of official minority nationalities, there was no such category recognized by China or by the people in question. 'Yi' collects together various groups of Loloish/Yi-speaking groups for which, moreover, the various languages – though closely related – are often quite mutually unintelligible (see Matisoff 2003). There were of course, certain obvious family resemblances among their various systems of social order, ritual practice and so on, but these too varied widely, from the egalitarian social order of some to the rigidly stratified political social order of the Nuosu (see, e.g., Hill, (2004), while some of the groups did not have the 'characteristic' cult system in question (incidentally, a situation quite similar to that of the Akha mentioned above, who are not officially Yi but Hani, and speak a southern Loloish language within Tibeto-Burman). It is now, however, increasingly the case that when one asks someone from these communities what kind of people they are, one will get the answer 'Yi', given in such a way and in such a context that it is clear that they take it seriously and as a matter of personal identity. And yet, if one probes more carefully, these same respondents will switch around to asserting, just as strongly, that they are 'really' Nuosu', or Sani, or Lolopho' or whatever. This last is of especial interest. For, the creation of the Yi category was in part predicated upon the proposition that Luolo (Lolo), the traditional, strictly *supra* ethnic Chinese word for most of the peoples in question was a hegemonic and therefore pejorative designation. 'Yi', by the way, is simply a variant of the universal Loloish word meaning 'people' (actually a *collective* plural of the word for person, usually *su, hu* and the like – the *-su* of Nuosu, one of the Yi groupings, cognate with, e.g., the *thu* third person pronoun of Burmese), Comparative Tibeto-Burman linguistics reconstructs a proto-form **nyi* or **ñi*, and in the various languages under consideration it surfaces as *yi, nyi, yi* etc., where, moreover, this word is found also in the name of the officially different Hani ethnic nationality (Hani is the same word, given the common s~h alternation, as Sani, who are officially Yi) , as well as in other far flung-branches of the Tibeto-Burman language family (e.g., in southern Chin languages). This is a nice case inasmuch as just about the only cultural or language fact they have in common is simply the increasing habit of calling themselves Yi (see, e.g., Liu 1998).

Now I shall turn to the facts showing that ethnicity is far from being an essentialist, primordial identity inasmuch as: (a) there can be ethnic identities within other ethnic categories; and (b) sometimes one of the 'included' identities will be that of another, entirely separate ethnic category. The central observation here is that for each such situation, the grouping claims for itself 'our way of life/culture'!

My first case will be that of the Kachin.[10] Leach made the Kachin famous among anthropologists in general in his *Political Systems of Highland Burma* (1954). Now, it is well understood that Kachin is what I called above 'a sort of super-ethnic category'. In Burma, certainly, 'Kachin' is the common response to the question of one's ethnicity; in Burmese one's *lu-myou:* literally, 'kind-of-people'). In China the equivalent, official category is *Jingpo* (the Pinyin romanization of what is otherwise written Jinghpaw). But in fact, Jinghpaw is the name only of the majority members and communities speaking the language so named, in which this word means simply 'person', just as 'Kayah' does.[11] Kachin, however, is from the Burmese, based (*pace* Leach) on the name of the area where the most classical 'thigh-eating' chiefs had their domains: the *ga khyen*, literally, 'red earth', while the Jinghpaw name for this group is in fact *Jinghpaw Wunpaung Amyu ni*, literally 'the Jinghpaw and associated peoples'. These comprise the Jinghpaw on the one hand, and, on the other the Maru (Lawngwaw in their language), Atsi (Zaiwa in their own language) and so on, where Jinghpaw is distributed among at least three quite different branches of the Tibeto-Burman family – Maru, for instance, being closely related to Burmese and the Loloish branch. What is held to bind them together culturally is their model of political order and asymmetric marriage among recognized Kachin clans that is specifically a Jinghpaw model with Jinghpaw as its formal, ritual language. While this is, in its way, 'the culture' or way of life they attribute to themselves *qua* Kachin, in local contexts they acknowledge different myths and rules, e.g., when Zaiwa are 'being' Zaiwa and asserting that ethnicity for themselves. In this connection there is a wide-ranging system of clan equivalences: each Maru, Atsi or any other clan is held to correspond to a specific Kachin clan, although there is some disagreement about which local clan equals which Kachin clan (Ho 1996a, b, 2004; Zhang 2004). So we see that while *Wunpaung Jinghpaw* is indeed felt to be an ethnic category, it contains various different groups, each of which *also* an ethnic category. More important still, Kachin includes some Lisu communities.

Now Lisu is an official nationality in China and Lisu is a set of mutually intelligible southern Loloish Tibeto-Burman languages, most closely related to Lahu (yet another ethnic people in China and mainland Southeast Asia) and fairly closely also to Akha-Hani (see above). But not all Lisu are, or even can be Kachin, and those Lisu who are Kachin are just Lisu when among those other Lisu, who know nothing about being Kachin or the relevant clan-equivalence system. In fact Lisu as such own a model of political order strikingly at odds with the Kachin one: radically egalitarian as against the traditional Kachin system of social stratification. Apparently it was necessary at some not very distant time in history for Lisu settling in Kachin territory to adapt to the Kachin system and, for that purpose, to adopt a quite new cultural identity in this regard. Ethnic categories can therefore also even intersect. There are other instances around the world, but this may be the most explicitly dealt with in the ethnographic literature. Another kind of Kachin are Nung Rawang, who are otherwise linguistically and culturally closely connected with the Dulong (the Chinese name, otherwise known as Taraon) of the high mountains where Burma's Kachin State borders on the southwesternmost corner of China's Yunnan Province, who have no connection whatever with Kachin; but this case is less well understood or documented. In some sense at least, Nung are just those Rawang (*Rvang*) who are also Kachin. The complexities of these ethno-linguistic categories of people can most directly be surveyed from references in Matisoff (2004) and Thurgood and LaPolla (2003). I come now once again to the central and northern Karen, but let me briefly first return to the Kayah. From their beginnings towards the end of the eighteenth century they have called themselves Kayah-Li (Red Karen). When Burma became independent again in 1948, it was decided to call the territory of the old, colonial Karenni States 'the Kayah State', because 'Karenni' is a Burmese word (Anglicized). It is notable that in the recent and current insurgency, the Kayah insist upon the political designation 'Karenni'. The reason seems to be that this is what their territory was called during the British colonial period, when the Karenni States were quasi-sovereign protectorates rather than part of Burma proper (administrative British Burma). This usage seems to ignore the fact that it is not in their own language, but also indicates a rejection of the official, Burmese name for them.

In this connection it is useful to observe that change of ethnic *label* may be less a change of identity than a political emphasis upon different relations that define the identity. Thus, consider the northern Karen people, whose women wear the long stack of brass neck rings. In Burmese they have always been known as *Padaung*, meaning roughly 'mountain folk'. In their own language, they have always been *Keykong*, meaning 'people of the land/country' (more exactly, *Keykong duw*, 'greater Keykong' as distinguished from their closest linguistic relatives, the *Keykong phuw*, or 'Lesser Keykong'). These people were actually the ruling population in one of the early Kayah States, or rather in a statelet in the north, between Shan and Kayah (Moeng Pai), and they have always had close political relations with the Kayah, in whose language 'Keykong' becomes *Lachie/Lakhie*. Currently, however, at least within the secessionist or insurgent movement, they insist on being called *Kayan*. This is, in their northern Karen language, the same as 'Kayah'(see above) , and the name does no more than signify, as a 'political statement', their association with (a) the Kayah, and (b), more broadly, Karen in general. Moreover, it is worth noting that this is part and parcel of a new Kayah 'Karen cosmopolitanism'. Before he last few decades following Burmese independence, Kayah largely downplayed, sometimes even rejected, identification as a kind of Karen. However, the insurgencies since the military coup of 1962 have brought them politically closer to the older Karen National group – although in the earliest 1950s this was problematical and the KNDO (Karen National Defence Organization, as it was, the precursor of today's KNU (Karen National Union), was rumoured among Kyebogyi Kayah to have killed their former prince (Sophrya) in the jungles, where his small force had in some way joined with the KNDO.[12]

Another northern Karen example goes even farther towards making clear how much variation in ethnic names can exist within and for the same ethnic identity. I refer here to the Pa-O. This is their name in their northern Karen language. In Burmese they have always been called *Taungthu*, 'hillbillies', as it were. After Burmese independence, in the era of increasing sentiments of ethnic self-determination, they insisted upon being known as Pa-O, if only because the Burmese name is clearly demeaning for a people who had their own Shan State (around the chief Shan town of Taunggyi) and who were staunch Theravada Buddhists. Nevertheless, traditionally, e.g., during the late nineteenth and early twentieth centuries, the matter was more complicated. These people were important itinerant traders all around the Shan–Thai borderlands in very close association with the Shan traders and Shan principalities of the neighbourhood. Amongst the Shan they were in fact widely respected, not least as fellow Buddhists. When, in the late nineteenth century, the deposed prince of the southern Shan State of Moeng Naai made his incursion into what is now Thailand's northwesternmost Mae Hongsorn Province, and founded the short-lived state of Mae Hongsorn, one of his closest supporters was a Pa-O trader. The prince built one of the *chedi* (pagodas), atop Loi Kongmu ('Pagoda Hill', above Mae Hongsorn town), whose impressive ruins remain to this day. So important was he that the founder (known in the chronicles only as *Ko Lan* 'Six Leagues', because of his mythical prowess in being able to jump great distances while fully armed) married his niece or daughter (the record is confusing here) to this Pa-O, who is known in the records (the manuscript Mae Hongsorn Chronicle) as (in Shan) Kyong Tonghsu, i.e., 'the Taungthu who donated a Monastery'.[13] (For this history, see the obscure reference in Keyes 1979: p. 42; p. 60 footnote 62). In effect, then, we can say that, at least in those days, these people were Pa-O at home but Tonghsu when 'abroad' as Shan traders.

Finally, I come to the most central question of all: why is it that people seem universally to categorize themselves and one another into ethnic groups, to which they systematically attribute a whole culture, a whole way of life? This is not the place to go into the matter in detail; I have done that elsewhere (Lehman 1975, Chit Hlaing 2004). Briefly, the answer is that ethnic identity is always relational and hence an ethnic identity is invariably a sort of maximal social role (properly, social identity). Now, any social identity ((hereafter SI) is necessarily endowed with roles, content having to do with behavioural norms, expectations and the like. One cannot 'be a ...' (fill in the ... with the label for any SI whatever) without it being expected that one knows *how to* 'be a ...'. This is necessary for the proper ordering and orderliness of SI–SI interaction. Therefore two or more persons may have some way of fairly smooth interaction with one another, knowing what should be expected and how to understand each other's actions and react appropriately. But why maximal (ethnic) SIs? The answer seems to be that it is a matter of essential cognitive processing efficiency. It is, after all, demonstrably impossible to keep track of all the innumerable different local variations, let alone individual variations, in customs, and the like. Basically, the only way to have some sense of how to deal with anybody is to have some expectations concerning him or her – expectations as to behavior, as to characterization, and so on; expectations as to what to make of his or her behaviour and so forth. It is a matter of meaning-assignment! And as such, it is particularly so for persons claiming to be 'of the same group'. Obviously this is a complicated matter in cognitively based social theory, but nonetheless it is basically as simple as I have just outlined. One needs some illusion, at least (and it is often just that, convention rather than actual beliefs, knowing what clichés to utter and so on) of common beliefs, knowledge and expectations about social relations, if one is to know how to be 'of the same group' with others. It is the same ultimately as what is required for *any* social interaction: one assumes certain things about any person that one relates to in order to make sense of, assign meaning to, the other person and his/her behaviour.

NOTES

1   Consider what a taxonomy is. For every living creature or plant, it *is* (a dog, cat, potato, pine tree, and so on) in the sense that membership does not cross lines. It is *either* a dog *or* it is not, and, if not, then a cat or a duck or a ... . The categories are mutually exclusive and exhaustive (see Chit Hlaing 2004a). They are, in short, 'natural kinds' (see Atran 1990).

2   Note that *zo* is not only an ethnic label. Of the two sorts of swidden field among the Chin of Hakha and Falam, the more crudely cultivated, the higher-elevation fields, are called *zo lo*, where *lo* means swidden field (see Lehman 1967).

3   This was confirmed for me by two Chin scholars during a discussion in 2004 at a meeting of Laai Chins at Martinsvillle, Indiana, USA.

4   The Akha case is striking inasmuch as this cult is for them a central aspect of *Akhazang*, the creator-established customs that are held to define being Akha (see Kammerer 1986).

5   In technical linguistic terms, a language is defined by a grammar, the cognitive knowledge that makes anyone a native speaker of something. But it is known that even in a relatively homogeneous community, different persons, e.g., across adjacent generations, will have some differences as to which constructions are or are not 'acceptable', while some will be 'mixed' with respect to such matters, so that in fact the number of languages at any moment is possibly a small multiple of the number of currently living persons who speak anything at all!

6   Curiously, for the easternmost Kayah isolate communities in Thailand's northwesternmost province of Maehongsorn, have a non-state-centred *iyluw* origin legend that, nevertheless, still invokes an 'ancient' *phreyphrow* (for this, see Lehman 1967b).

7   It is a curious fact that the founder of the western Kayah State of Kyebogyi was held to be a *prey phrow*, even though he was known to have been born in the nearby village of Maphrowshie (or Makhrowshie) with the ordinary Kayah male name of Sha-re. The point is that he supposedly went out into the wider world, acquired all that powerful civilized knowledge and then returned.

8   Kantarawady, the eastern Kayah State, with its ultimate capital at Loikaw, present seat of the Burmese Kayah State, is itself a throne-title in Shan Pali, in the Buddhist tradition of statecraft (literally Gandharavati, 'possessing the [heavenly] perfume') reminiscent of the classical Greco-Sanskritc kingdom of Gandhara during the Buddha's own time, in which are now the Afghanistan–Pakistan borderlands. Kyebogyi is named after its charismatic founder, the aforementioned Sha-re, whose title was *Keyphowduw*, signifying 'great (*duw*), one who sprang fully formed (*phrow*) from the face of the land (*key*).

9   Gravers (2001c) makes it abundantly clear that much of the Kayah 'royal' and *iyluw* cult has a lower Burma source; for the Buddhist Pwo Karen, whose Buddhism has a historical Mon basis, have *tagundaing*-like poles just like the Kayah *iyluw*, while their 'prophets' bear a remarkable resemblance to the Kayah *phreyphrow*, not least in their pretensions to royalty.

10   Much of what I say here is closely connected with the material in the chapter, in this volume, by Mandy Sadan; I owe her and the other panelists at a conference in Paris in 2004 much on our discussions concerning Leach and his Kachin work. I thank her for including me in that panel. Thanks also are due to my external pupil Zhang Wenyi for his discussions of his work with Jingpo in China (see Zhang 2004). Gowler (2002) does a fine job of putting the subject of conflict resolution into a jinghpaw context, with her idea of *Wunpawng* as a sort of 'global' ethnic category rather than being simply an 'artificial' ethnic category, a reflection of Jinghpaw hegemony (see Sadan's chapter). Likewise, Karin Dean's chapter in this volume does much to place the Kachin in the context of the political science literature on ethnicity, politics and mapping; as such it relates closely to my own remarks here.

[11] 'Kayah' can refer to a person of any ethnicity, including European, and is cognate with *Ka(r)iang, from which comes the Burmese designation 'Kayin', spelt 'Karang', and hence the English 'Karen'. The full name for the Kayah is *kayah-li*, meaning Red (*li*) Karen, in Burmese *Kayin-ni* (Karenni, *ni* meaning red), referring to the traditional red short trousers that men wore in battle to distinguish their side in the fight.

[12] When, in 1961 I was asked by the then Kayah parliamentary secretary, Kayah Oo Sein, to make an ethnographic study of Kayah, he said he hoped I would be able to demonstrate that the Kayah are *not* Karen (i.e., not 'Karenni' but 'Kayah').

[13] *Kyong* (from Burmese Kyaung) is a Buddhist monastery. One of the most respectful ways to address any older Shan man is as *lung kyong* (*lung* is the honorific word 'uncle') implying, at least pro forma, that he has earned the title *kyong taga*, Shan-Pali-Burmese for Donor of a Monastery.

Chapter 5

MAPPING THE KACHIN POLITICAL LANDSCAPE: CONSTRUCTING, CONTESTING AND CROSSING BORDERS

Karin Dean

INTRODUCTION

The most essential components on political maps are boundaries. These lines arrange the world space on the map into orderly and fixed patches of adjacent territorial units whose different colours are supposed to manifest the distinctiveness, autonomy and sovereignty of each such entity. It does not require one to be a geographer of the modern school to recognize that the world's lived-in space is not spatially disconnected. Nevertheless, such territorial lines have today become determinants, in extremes of prosperity or poverty, of enhancement or suppression of cultures and ethnicity, of nurturing freedoms or persecution – and sometimes, of life or death. In Southeast Asia these territorial lines were drawn mostly by the British, French and Dutch authorities to delineate their colonial empires without much knowledge or regard to the dynamics, flows and territorialities on the ground. Such imposition could not wipe out automatically the *de facto* geographies that continue to persist, in a modified way, under the present system of states. Nevertheless, the assumption that state territories are set or fixed units of sovereign space to be taken for granted has somehow become the most powerful assertion of certainty in the modern world.

International relations theory and practices recognize only the language of states and sovereign territories, those that are bounded by the so-called 'international' boundaries. In our socialized perceptions and normative maps, the primary and 'natural' characteristic of a state is its territory, an artificially bounded place whose definition in political geography includes the persistence of control over behaviour and access.

Burma fails this primary characteristic of a state because several mostly ethnic-based groups, such as the Kachin, the Karen, the Shan, the Wa, by maintaining arms and armies, control parts of its territory and access to the so-called 'international' boundaries.[1] Thus Burma presents a case that is an epitome of the rigidity and taken-for-grantedness of the modern international system of states. Burma is sovereign but only externally – i.e. as recognized by other states – while internally, it contains several (contested) sovereignties.[2] Bound by the prevailing language, some geographers have started to label the phenomena that counter the *de jure* meaning of boundaries and sovereignty as 'challenges', 'unbundling', 'hidden geographies' or counter-territorialities.[3]

A look at the Southeast Asian political map displays Kachin State in northern Burma and Dai-Jingpo Autonomous Prefecture of southwestern China in different colours and divided by an inter-*national* boundary. The Kachin are territorially 'trapped' since their historic domain on the hills of the South Himalayas is now mapped into India, Burma and China.[4]

This chapter will explore how the Kachin today define their space. It will suggest that the Kachin social space that crosses the international boundaries has become more meaningful than the 'truly' Kachin territorial places, which have been reduced to only a few. In the strict politico-geographical definition of territory, a 'true' Kachin territorial place is a territory controlled and administered by the Kachin. In the deconstruction of the territorial domain, the term 'Kachinland' seems to be beginning to shift towards being less of a reference to the Kachin-inhabited areas but rather to a disconnected space similar to the Karen Kawthoolei in that it does not refer to any distinct connected geographical area but rather to a symbolic space (with the traditional heartland).[5]

The chapter will introduce a perspective that scrutinizes territorial and social boundaries in juxtaposition. The comparison of the Kachin territorial places and social space is used as a key for understanding the Kachin ethnicity and nationalism in our modern spatialized world and seeing beyond the coloured patchwork of the world political map. In short, consideration of the territorial place/social space relationship can be a theoretical tool for understanding the intra- and inter-state dynamics, interactions and interrelationships that the imposition of the 'modern' language of states, nations, sovereignties and international boundaries has created.

Figure 5.1 Manifestation of the SPDC territoriality: Kachin manau festival in Myitkyina under the Myanmar flag. (Photo: Karin Dean)

Territory is generally defined through boundaries. Robert Sack, who has greatly influenced the understanding of human territoriality in his *Human Territoriality: Its Theory and History*, is quite strict in his definition of territory – it is not a cause but an effect: 'Unlike many ordinary places, territories require constant effort to establish and maintain. They are the results of strategies to affect, influence, and control people, phenomena, and relationships.'[6] Territory is a bounded, organized space or area whose boundaries are controlled by a certain kind of power; thus it is a juridico-political notion.[7] It should be easy to see state boundaries as artificial human constructs because no matter how natural some boundaries (e.g. following rivers, mountain ranges) might seem, their demarcation is always determined by people.[8] Thus the notion of territory, defined through human-constructed boundaries for the purposes of exercising control, is itself an artificial human construct.

Juxtaposing places and spaces to territories heightens the recognition that territories are always artificial human constructs. Places and spaces are less rigid notions, and for that reason these are also more contested than territories. Places, spaces and boundaries 'spring up' if we follow Grundy-Warr's suggestion and turn political maps inside out to see the '... hidden *de facto* geographies that are not reflected in the brightly colored blocks of sovereign territorial states'.[9] On an inside-out map, peripheries and border(land)s turn out in the centres; places previously seen as bare dots, if at all, loom large in the foreground, and with a little of imagining it is easy to see that the spaces-of-flows and spaces-of-places have no correspondence to the different colours of the various territories fading away in the embrace of *de facto* dynamics. In fact, space has been the favourite central notion in geographical thinking just because of its greater level of abstraction, Taylor speculates.[10] Places and spaces have both actually been recognized as involving human and social dimensions in addition to spatial ones – although the social component has been veiled in the definitions by heavier emphasis on the spatial.[11] Territoriality is seen as involving three basic human behaviours – a form of classification by area, a form of communication by boundary and an attempt at enforcing.[12] The bloodiest conflicts and disputes over territories and places have occurred between rival ethnic groups or nations. For contingent historical conditions some nations have evolved with states, while others in today's world system of states form a category that can be labeled as 'nations without states.'[13] In both cases, people are grouped and bounded similarly to spaces – through boundaries. Equating the states with nations is one of the most serious flaws in the modern language of international relations theory and practice. The reality today is that the world has fewer than 200 states but more than 800 nationalist movements, many of which are 'small, weak, dispersed, nonviable, but not necessarily resigned to their fate' – although it is out of the question that all these nationalisms can be accommodated by grants of statehood.[14] The following questions arise: 'Weak and non-viable' by whose standards? Is the quota of statehood for ethnic (national) groups full at the present time? Was it on the first-come-first-served basis? Where is the dividing line between those ethnic groups (nations) deserving a state and those which do not deserve one? Who decides? Should a state be the all-underlying aspiration? Why is it seen as the only option by many? These questions are also very relevant to the Kachin ethno-political situation. Nevertheless, while various social groupings in the world have started to define and redefine the relations between social and physical space by demanding recognition, autonomy or independence, studies on the links between territorial lines and symbolic boundaries are missing in the academic field.[15]

This chapter is concerned with the theoretical relations between spatial and social and, specifically, with the links and relationship between a territorial place and its symbolic counterpart social space. A place is regarded as territorial when it is bounded by territorial lines – while acknowledging that territorial lines are not necessarily visible in lived-in space but can be conceivable or perceivable. Examples of territorial places are a state, an administrative unit or any functional bounded compound or area. Like territorial places, symbolic spaces are bounded and defined by symbolic boundaries. Social space is symbolic in the sense that it is not literal, factual or 'seen', as it constitutes shared feelings, beliefs and attitudes, and is defined through intangible but perceived symbolic boundaries – while it is rooted in relational and social networks. Where ethnicity and identities are involved, these usually constitute a social space whose boundaries are defined by tangible ethnic markers and intangible characteristics. Symbolic boundaries might appear to be more evasive and contested, and more subject to manipulations than territorial boundaries, since they do enjoy neither conceptual nor material support from authorities and institutions. Jenkins has noted that '...the boundaries of collective identity are ... taken for granted until they are threatened'.[16] The role of ethnic boundaries in identity construction and maintenance has occupied an important share in anthropology since Fredrik Barth's influential work.[17] Ethnic boundaries are created through ethnic identities or, conversely, boundaries can create identities. 'Identity and boundaries thus seem to be different sides of the same coin.'[18]

While all territorial – particularly the so-called international – boundaries in the global space carry certain analogous sanctioned meanings, the status and functions among different symbolic/ethnic boundaries within one state often vary. Symbolic boundaries can diverge and fluctuate in their meanings and in the intensities of enforcement between different groups. It is useful to try to identify *what kind of boundaries* the ethnic groups construct to distinguish 'Us' from the 'Others', and then compare the maintenance and enforcement of such boundaries between 'Us' and the several 'Others.' By examining ethnic/social group boundaries, much can be learned about socio-political and power relations among and affecting the different groups. This helps to reveal hidden tensions in the society. The aspects to consider when comparing territorial and ethnic boundaries are their *construction*, *contested-ness* and/or *crossing possibilities*. For example, crossing symbolic boundaries based on group affiliations (ethnic identities) or religions can be much more difficult than crossing 'international' boundaries between states. 'The necessary visas' for crossing such boundaries often require ritual behaviour, processes of conversion or exchange of one identity or affiliation with another.[19] Thus the crossing of symbolic boundaries can be a significant socio-political manifestation.

Starting the discussion with the historical relevance and contingency *vis-à-vis* the construction of states and nations will make the point that '... the plot of history is written, retrospectively, by the "winners" '.[20] This chapter avoids taking the state for granted and does not analyse the Kachin social space within the framework of the state of Burma (or China) but rather in relation to other spaces – the Kachin own past territorial domain as well as the present spaces of the 'Others' – that have persisted in the geographical area that the Kachin inhabit. It is rather this geographical area, the loosely defined historical territorial Kachin domain, that is taken for granted – as the starting point – because this space contains Kachin-ness and the Kachin networks, if one wishes to see the 'inside-out' political map. Social boundaries have evolved – that is, have been constructed – as effects of certain socio-political contexts, often due to unequal power balances that have caused deprivation or threats to the group in the disadvantaged position – in the loser's position from historical perspective. The chapter will now proceed to examine how the Kachin territorial places have transformed and the social space become to signify the Kachin domain and Kachin-ness. This signification process is implicit in the Kachin opting for constructing, contesting or crossing *certain* boundaries while dismissing others.

RELEVANCE AND CONTINGENCY OF HISTORY

The point about the contingency and relevance of historical factors in the processes of nation formation and territory construction will also serve as an introduction to the Kachin, who have evolved as a self-conscious and recognized group in the context of the larger historic processes. The latter include the dynamics of the Chinese empire at its southwestern peripheries, the British colonial practices, the Second World War, Burma's independence movement and the deliberations of China's Communist Party. Nevertheless, the Kachin history today is largely regarded as a part of Burma's (or China's) history.

The development of the 'Kachin' as a nation out of the diversity of the tribes inhabiting the south-western foothills of the Himalayas has been very successful, especially if compared to that among many other ethnic nationalities such as the Shan in today's Burma, China and Thailand, or the Mon, the Karen, the Karenni or the Chin. The initial categorization of the hills and the tribes as the 'Kachin' by the 'outsiders', the creation of the written script for the Jinghpaw language and the success of the Kachin Independence Organization (KIO) in forging feelings of unity and common (Christian) identity among the six tribes considered to be Kachin – can be identified as the main factors contributing to the formation of the Kachin nation.

Carving out 'Kachin territories' from the Kachin Hills of the southern Himalayas into Kachin State before and after the newly established Burma, and 'internationally' between Burma and China in the late 1950s has, on the contrary, been rather unsuccessful. It has left the Kachin with a (Kachin) State in Burma where they are hardly in majority. Similarly, in China, the areas of the Kachin concentration have arbitrarily been bounded into Dai-Jingpo Autonomous Prefecture (AP) where the Kachin (categorized as the Jingpo in China) make up 13 per cent, the Shan (Dai) 14 per cent and the Han Chinese 48 per cent of the population. The British colonial 'order without meaning' is directly to be blamed for the carving out of Kachin State in Burma with large non-Kachin populations with no right to secede in order to protect the latter's interest.[21] In the Dai-Jingpo AP, the Kachin share 'power' in the prefecture government with the Dai, the deliberations behind such spatialization being the Chinese government's objective to dilute the dominance of the Dai (Shan) in south-western China by separating them into different autonomous prefectures. The deconstruction of the historic Kachin territorial domain exemplifies the significant role of contingent historic developments.

The settlement of the 'international' Sino–Burmese border that cuts through Kachin-concentrated areas epitomizes the arbitrariness of drawing boundaries. All parties involved in determining the location of the territorial line – Britain, Burma and China – laid 'historical claims' to certain areas by presenting 'historical evidence' of their respective authorities in the past. However, the very different historical concept of establishing authority and territoriality in the domain that had no experience with territorial borders puts all claimants in a rather equal position. It was the British power position that determined the location of what later became the Sino–Burmese boundary that in the late 1950s surfaced as a problematic issue between the newly established Burma and China. Both states showed patience and a conciliatory approach in order to solve the dispute. The final deal in which three Kachin villages were 'given' to China in exchange for the Namwan Tract in the southern part of Kachin State was not unfair by international standards. However, the failure of Rangoon to clarify the nature of the border agreement helped to prompt the Kachin nationalistic 'rebellion'.[22] The border settlement together with U Nu government's insensitive attempts to establish Buddhism as the state religion were the main reasons that precipitated the KIO insurgency in 1961.[23]

Consideration of the palimpsest qualities of present political maps is vital for understanding the dynamics of today's Kachin domain. Even without detailed knowledge of historical facts other than the establishment of the Union of Burma in 1948 and the People's Republic of China in 1949 that spatialized the Kachin into the two states, it is clear that the Kachin feelings of belonging and loyalties to the newly created spatial units could not be taken for granted. The Sino–Burmese border was in fact settled by Burma and China in 28 January 1960. Although the function of a border is to separate, it did not separate anything from the Kachin point of view as their domain extended on both sides of the boundary. Nevertheless, the power of the conceptual boundary, even immediately following its settlement, cannot be overlooked. For example, state jurisdiction delimited by the boundary determined that the Kachin in China and in Burma were to attend schools run by their respective authorities, among other new policies that were going to affect the lives of the people. China has generally opted for appeasing the ethnic 'minorities' in Yunnan, including the Jingpo, and has provided economic, financial and technical support and expertise, especially to the remote and marginalized ethnic 'minorities.' This is highly visible today in the higher living standards of the Kachin in China when compared to their kin just across the boundary. In China, additionally, the state permits and supports the ethnic material culture, the teaching of the ethnic languages at schools (at primary level) and publishing magazines and broadcasting radio programmes in the ethnic languages. In Burma this has been rather the opposite. The states' monopoly over impacting people in most aspects is what Paasi calls 'socialization'.[24] Socialization by the state can shape people's thinking and identification and create loyalties if carried out with careful deliberation and wise decisions – or it can create counter-loyalties and ideologies. Ashley South in this volume shows that the impact of the state extends even to the methods and practices that the opposition groups and ethnic nationalist movements choose in pursuing their objectives. State socialization that certainly impacts on ethnicity can be carried out with different levels of success as comparison of the Kachin socialization by Burma and China respectively reveals. However, state socialization through education and other non-coercive operational vehicles that the state possesses cannot be carried out (successfully) without full internal sovereignty. Burma, although recognized as a sovereign state, does not have full internal sovereignty since a number of contested territorialities challenging the *de jure* meaning of sovereignty and the international boundaries characterize Burma today.

KACHIN TERRITORIAL DOMAIN

The patchwork of territorialities that characterizes Kachin State today, resulting from the KIO ceasefire in 1994, includes the territories controlled by the SPDC and those controlled by the KIO/KIA, while in some areas 'authorities' overlap. Challenging the *de jure* meaning of a sovereign state, the KIO/KIA maintain control over about one-fifth of Kachin State, and most of these territories are located along the Sino–Burmese boundary. The KIO/KIA Central Committee acts as a government and is divided into several departments, while the KIA maintains arms and army bases. Along the Sino–Burmese border between Kachin State and Dai-Jingpo AP in China the KIO/KIA maintains *truly international* relations with the Chinese authorities as well as with the SPDC. KIO/KIA international relations point directly to the fallacy in common practice in international relations, whereby the word 'international' does not refer to what it describes, that is, the relations between nations, instead referring to relations between states.[25] Following the strict political geographical definition of 'territory', only the areas under the administration of the KIO/KIA can be regarded as the Kachin territorial places as these are the territories under *de facto* Kachin administration and control.

Figures 5.2 and 5.3. Kachin cultural symbols (the *manau* posts – *manau shadung*) in Myanmar (above) and in China. (Photos: K. Dean)

Special attention in these territories is devoted to the manifestation of territorialities that involve marking the borders. Kachin State is infested with markers of territoriality – the SPDC/*Tatmadaw* have set up countless checkpoints run by state departments or the army, while the KIO/KIA marks its territory rather similarly, by 'gates' and checkpoints. Thus another unofficial international border has emerged – between the SPDC and the KIO, marked by respective checkpoints, guards and hoisted flags. This border is often marked more explicitly than the so-called international Sino–Burmese boundary, and while the border-crossing procedures are similar, the Kachin cross the SPDC/KIO territorial line more reluctantly than the Sino–Burmese boundary and given choice, opt for the latter. Nevertheless, the Kachin territorial places are enclaves, and thus dependent on restrictions that Burma and China both impose on the KIO/KIA from their respective power positions. Thus the KIO/KIA power is strictly limited and even the real autonomy in these Kachin territorial places is rather questionable. The recognition of external sovereignty in the international system of states is the overruling factor, and provides the Burmese state with power and legitimacy to determine the developments of these true Kachin territorial places.

If viewed less strictly, Kachin territorial places can be found scattered all over Kachin State and Dai-Jingpo AP. These are the Kachin inhabited villages or neighborhoods in towns, while several Kachin-run institutions in the SPDC-controlled territory also enjoy a certain amount of autonomy in administration and management. The latter include the Kachin Baptist Convention (KBC), the Kachin Theological College (KTC), the Young Men Christian Association (YMCA) and the numerous church congregations. These places are managed by the Kachin, where they can mingle and the Jinghpaw language is predominantly spoken – thus serving as important nodes of communication in the maintenance of the Kachin social space.

THE KACHIN SOCIAL DOMAIN

Kinship and lineage system with centuries' old roots, having survived the recent turbulent changes in the Kachin historical socio-political environment, is the underlying foundation for the present Kachin social space that continues to persist and certainly defines a large share of Kachin social relations today. Significantly, too, without any regard to the socio-political context or the effectiveness of state socialization, it determines the inclusion/exclusion to the Kachin social space. It is typical of most Kachin today (as in the past), for both young and old, to introduce one's family name first when meeting a stranger in order to establish knowledge of one's *mayu/dama* relationship.[26] Without knowing each other's lineage a Kachin does not know how to relate to another – as a brother/sister or mother/father, depending on one's age, or as somebody one can potentially marry or be regarded as an in-law. 'It needs to be emphasized...that the *mayu/dama* relationship is a very real one...[T]he division of all Kachin society into three groups – one's own clan, the clan or clans from which one takes wives, and the clan to which one gives wives – determines much of one's social relationships.'[27] Hugely significant from the aspect of the Kachin border construction and maintenance is that the lineage, kinship and family relations extend on both sides of the Sino–Burmese boundary. Similarly, Carol Gowler (2002) emphasizes that the *mayu, dama*, and one's own clan are the three cornerstones of the Kachin society, and that the clans cutting across all the different tribes [in addition to the international boundary] constitute the foundation of Kachin society today.[28]

Thus the Kachin social space extending across the Sino–Burmese boundary is mostly the effect of the past Kachin territorialities. Slash-and-burn farming, frequent feuds between clans, military service for the Chinese court and the system of ultimogeniture, according to which the elder sons after marrying moved out of their parents' home and the most ambitious individuals established new villages with the collected followers, are the causes for the spread of the Kachin territorial domain.[29] The links between marriage and trade also ramified the Kachin kinship network as women were occasionally handed out as pledges of economic co-operation by the chiefs.[30] At the present, the Kachin extended kinship relations firmly establish a part of the Kachin identity, and the stability of such relations weaves the territorially disconnected members of the tribes into a web of social links and relationships.

The extent of cross-border bonds today is well illustrated by a Chinese Jingpo author who has titled one chapter of her Yunnan-published book on Jingpo women 'Cross-Boundary Marriage'.[31] According to the author, almost all Jingpo villages and 'quite a number of Jingpo families' have blood ties and relationship by marriage with Myanmar's Keqin (Kachin) nationality.[32] In the typical patriotic, embellished style, it reads: 'women living separately on both sides of the national boundary have woven a solid bond through their

Figures 5.4 and 5.5. Typical Kachin feast in a village in China (left) and near Myitkyina in Myanmar (below). Photos: K. Dean)

own marriages which closely links compatriots living separately in the two countries and have erected a bridge of friendship with love for the peace and tranquility of the two peoples'.[33] Such expression of cross-boundary social ties by a Chinese Jingpo in a state-sponsored publication is highly significant because the Chinese government has generally rather eagerly discouraged any cross-boundary comparisons of its transnational ethnic groups, this implying that the Chinese Jingpo today cannot be characterized without their cross-border contacts, activities, networks and visits, and that this forms a part of being a Jingpo in the present day China. Plenty of empirical examples further confirm that Kachin ethnicity crosses the international Sino–Burmese boundary. 'The Jingpo are all same family but live in different countries.'[34] The Kachin unilaterally claim that the Kachin, or Wunpawng in the Jinghpaw language, are a federation of six tribes in Burma, China and India – or 'all kinds of Kachin combined'.[35] Highly important in a discussion of ethnicity and ethnic/symbolic boundaries is how the members of the group under scrutiny define/characterize themselves. The purpose of the survey of how Kachin-ness is defined by the Kachin themselves was to study the Kachin internal definition/self-perception – before following the conventional approach of defining an ethnic group through common ethnic markers such as religion, language, traditional dress, ceremonies and customs. While obviously important, the conventional ethnic markers do not necessarily have to constitute the essential factor but rather help the outside observer to identify the nation/ethnic group.[36]

Internal definition, self-perception, self-images – whatever label one uses – although constituting in some instances personal experience, amalgamate with collective representations and become depersonalized 'assumptions regarding national character'.[37] Although stereotypes are 'simplified beliefs', these should not be dismissed as overly simplistic, general or arbitrary for two reasons. First, stereotypes can be created and manipulated; thus these can be rather powerful.[38] Second, as 'the ideological dimensions are inevitably important in their constitution and manifestation',[39] the differing stereotypical perceptions of 'Us' versus the 'Other' signify social/ethnic boundaries. In order to define 'Us', the 'Other' is the necessary upon which the difference that rhetoric effects boundaries can rest. Each nation is defined 'not only in terms of its own, but in purely relational terms as well'.[40] Difference presupposes comparison between at least two groups. In the Kachin social space, the Kachin include themselves as constituting 'Us' and exclude all the 'Others'. In the particular socio-political context of Burma and southwestern China, the 'Other' is not a monolithic group. There are several 'Others', while the Kachin perception of the Chinese, the Shan and the Burman is the most relevant when constructing the Kachin social space. A group of 44 Kachin students (average age 22 years) were asked to describe the 'Kachin', the 'Burman', the 'Chinese' and the 'Shan'.[41] All respondents, mostly Jinghpaw but including a few from other tribes or from mixed families consisting of a Jinghpaw and a member from another Kachin tribe, are all Christian and speak Jinghpaw. It is recognized here that a relatively small group of Kachin youth cannot be wholly representative of the Kachin nor their generation. However, many of these respondents are expected to be future leaders or teachers in the Kachin society; thus they will be in a position to influence to an extent the Kachin consciousness.

CONSTRUCTING BOUNDARIES

Jenkins, who views ethnic identities through two interdependent social processes – internal definition and external categorization – has called on including the considerations of power and authority in order *not* to result in 'a model of ethnicity which is as trivial as it is one-sided'.[42] External categorization has previously been mentioned as a contributor to the successive formation of the Kachin as a nation. The best example of this is the label 'Kachin': before the six tribes had developed a consciousness of constituting a people called 'the Kachin', they were referred to as such by the British officials and missionaries. Only later did 'Kachin' develop into a political term (as a name of the state), to be further fixed by their nationalist movement when included in the name of the independence organization and army.

The challenges to the *de jure* state in Burma, and its contested sovereignties and territorialities can be expected to present power imbalances. The group that perceives its culture, religion, language, social position, economic resources or territory threatened by another group is inclined to construct and maintain boundaries for protection. Knowledge of power relations also helps to recognize internalized external factors as part of self-perception. The following will show that power relations and the positions of authority enter boundary construction and maintenance in a very explicit way.

The notion 'Kachin' was described as having the following contradictory connotations: 'poorly educated', 'poor farmers', 'always helping', 'quite lazy', 'loving traditions'/'very friendly', 'honest', 'kind', 'loving forests and (living in) mountains', 'wanting freedom, independence and democracy from the Burmese', 'envious of the wealthier', 'poor and unstable workforce', 'liking alcohol and drugs', 'simple', 'collectivist', 'not smart', 'sharing', 'poor due to the Burmese control/influence [of the Kachin natural resources]'. The first two features, 'poorly educated' and 'poor farmers' dominate overwhelmingly over others, and these are obviously not ethnic identities but presumably internalized socio-economical categorizations. Their 'successful' internalization – i.e. featuring as the top two defining characteristics of the Kachin by the Kachin in Burma – implies a greater power, authority and legitimacy on the part of the categorizers and, indeed, reveals more about the categorizers and their policies/objectives than about the categorized. During informal conversations in Kachin State, the most dominating rhetoric among the ethnic elites and the 'common' Kachin is that of 'underdevelopment'.[43] The powerful rhetoric of underdevelopment generates a psychological need to balance or counter it – or to justify and legitimize – and 'poor and honest' fits very well. A highly positive Kachin 'national character' compensates for the large share of negative self-perception, or rather, the internalized external categorization ('poor farmers', 'low level of education', and 'poor, unstable workforce'). The national character is good in most senses – helping, kind, honest, hospitable and friendly. The high ranking of 'lazy' in Kachin self-perception – the fourth in the successive list – is probably 'helped' to such a dominant position by the 'agreement' between internal and external definitions. The Kachin like to emphasize that they are lazy, and although 'officially' denounced as negative by the ethnic elites, this quality in informal communication definitely enjoys some positively naughty connotations. The Kachin self-definition 'loving traditions' – in the top five – is a general designation that includes the adherence to kinship and marriage rules and the references to Kachin food and dress.

As seen from the above, most relevant are the seemingly personal characteristics that try to capture something intangible, the presumed essence of Kachin ethnicity. Myths of origin, claimed as one of the defining characteristics of a nation, are irrelevant to the respondents.[44] In everyday practice where ethnicity is threatened, the exact location of an ancestral homeland or myths of origin do not help as a source of identity that defines, preserves and fosters ethnic space. Conventional ethnic markers may but do not always mark ethnic boundaries, especially in the context of multi-ethnic states and globalization. Among the conventional ethnic markers, the

Figures 5.6 and 5.7. Symbols of Kachin culture: an animistic burial site in China (right) and a Catholic home in a village near Myitkyina. Photos: K. Dean

Jinghpaw language and Christianity, and certain components of 'culture' are highly relevant in defining the Kachin social space by the Kachin elites.[45] Nevertheless, it is interesting that the respondents did not mention a common language as the defining characteristic – suggesting that this is taken for granted. Christianity as a marker of Kachin-ness was mentioned by only two respondents in Kachin State – thus not making it to the list – suggesting that this, too, is taken for granted.

Comparing Kachin self-perceptions in Burma and China should help to depoliticize Kachin ethnicity as the socio-political context in the two states differs. Burma is characterized by a context of bewildering and perplex relationships, links and boundaries between ethnic, state-led and majority (popular) nationalism. In China, popular nationalism supports the state-led nationalism (Zhao, 2000) and effective dissemination of state ideology due to successful socialization has entered the 'unsuspecting minds' of ethnic nationality elites.[46] The state in China has enshrined ethnic boundaries in the state policies – most obviously through positive discrimination – and it supports material culture as defining ethnicity at the expense of the intangible spiritual emotional expressions. This is also reflected in the Chinese Jingpo self-perception, where 'liking to sing and dance', 'having distinct dress, food and lifestyle', occupy the most important positions. The Kachin in Burma define themselves through less tangible characteristics and seem to take tangible features such as language and religion for granted.

The following lists the Kachin perception of the Burman in order of the frequency of the mentioned characteristics: 'hypocritical and pretending' (mentioned by exactly half of the respondents), 'dishonest, lying, cheating and tricking others' (mentioned by one-third), 'suppressive government', 'committing atrocities', 'some are good but most are bad', 'cheating and stealing money from other peoples like the Kachin and the Shan', 'selfish', 'bright, intelligent, very clever'. Given the civilizational distinctiveness of the Burman from the Kachin in culture, religion, origins, it is surprising that only a tiny share of the Kachin respondents use cultural characteristics – which do not even make it to the top list – to describe the Burman. The Kachin perceive deep differences between themselves and the Burman *not* in general cultural components, social status or religious beliefs – which one would expect in an apolitical context – but in (politicized) personal and straightforwardly political characteristics.

The Kachin perception of the Chinese relates to money and business. The dominating characteristic is 'hard-working', elaborated further that the Chinese work harder than other nations. The second distinguishing feature is the love and importance of money for the Chinese, they 'do anything (risk, smuggle or work hard) to make money'. Politically, China has a 'good government that wants to improve the living standards of its people by providing education, machinery, financial support and advice;' equally frequently mentioned is that 'they [the Chinese] help the Kachin'. The relatively positive attitude towards China reflects the relational dominating relationship with the Chinese – which is historically symbiotic but so generously positive in comparison to that with the Burman. In the encounters with the Chinese or Chinese Jingpo, and when crossing the

Sino–Burmese boundary that manifests most starkly as an economic line, the 'underdevelopment' rhetoric of Kachin State is magnified through its contrast to China. The root of its cause is blamed on the economic neglect of Kachin State by the Burmese government. The demographic, economic, cultural and political threats by the Chinese to the fragile social structure of Kachin State are overlooked, in spite of the fact that the Chinese have bypassed the Kachin in seizing business opportunities, especially in jade and gold trade and logging. Although this other 'Other', the Chinese, can be perceived as overly positive in order to balance the Burman, there are some distinct and contrasting differences between the Chinese and the Kachin, such as, respectively, 'hard-working/lazy' and 'love for money'/ negative connotations of wealth.

In the Kachin perception of the Shan the most dominating theme is that 'they [the Shan] are the same as the Kachin (in their opinions, character and nature)'. This designation is enhanced further through the label 'ordinary farm workers'. Characteristic of the Shan is that they are always 'involved in Buddhist celebrations and rituals', 'live historically together and/or mixed with the Kachin'; many are *also* uneducated and *also* want freedom from the Burmese government. The Shan are 'friendly', 'good and kind' and 'united' (that is, not mixing with other groups). The Shan are perceived as similar to the Kachin and are 'almost like Us'. This perception is not even altered by the fact that they follow another world religion, Buddhism, as opposed to the Kachin Christianity.

The socio-political context and power relations in a society are relevant and significant for analysing the dynamics in the self-definition and its negative or positive, or irrational/contradictory, contents. Only in this context can we understand why the Shan are perceived to be 'just like "Us" '– as this has not been the case historically when contrasts between hill–valley agriculture and ways of life have defined the character of the Kachin–Shan relationship.[47] There has always been a lot of interaction through food and commodity trade, while the protection fees were asserted by the hill-Kachin onto the lowland Shan villages. The Kachin as freemen of the highlands probably did not perceive the Shan, bound subjects within their aristocratic princely/serf system, 'just as Us', although their relationship was close. The relationship has also been close and symbiotic also with the Chinese but nevertheless does not make the latter 'just like Us'. The political developments in Burma have resulted in the same setting for both the Kachin and the Shan as 'ethnic minority nationalities' in the same state with the Burman majority; in this sense the Shan are 'just like "Us" '. The Kachin relationship with the Burman has historically been strained: the latter were distrusted as a result of experiences when the Burmese had taken advantage of the Kachin in politics or trade.[48] The Kachin today can claim that the 'undelivered promises' of the Panglong Agreement, attempts to establish Buddhism as the state religion, the Sino–Burmese border agreements, the dilapidated state of infrastructure in Kachin State with no promised development since the 1994 ceasefire – while resources, mainly gold, jade and trees are being extracted at an accelerating pace – continue to be affirmations of the untrustworthiness and lies of the Burman. As in the case with the Shan, the supposedly personal characteristics of the Burman derive from the socio-political context. The Burman is a referent for the government and the army.

For the Kachin ethnic space and boundaries to exist, the contents of difference seem to matter less than the *need* to create such difference, and thus the boundaries, in order to 'protect Us' from the dominating 'Other'. The Kachin ethnic boundaries are the strongest with the Burman, while with the Shan the boundaries in some 'areas' are not 'demarcated' at all. The boundaries are 'delineated' between the Kachin and the Chinese because the latter differ in their national character and values, especially as the Kachin do not have a tradition of working hard to accumulate wealth and save money – however, there is a working and understanding, truly international relationship. The situation differs greatly with regard to the Burman who are extremely distrusted, and therefore the boundaries must be constructed, marked, maintained, conserved – and protected. Such strong ethnic boundaries stem from the highly negative stereotyping and perception of the Burman 'national character'. Even 'bright, intelligent and very clever' takes on a negative connotation – and with the preceding characteristics becomes a deadly combination. The Kachin self-perception as honest, kind and simple is contrasted straightforwardly with this dreadful combination and reinforces strong boundaries that need to be protected. Thus the contents also matter less than the boundaries that range from the vigilantly protected ones (with the Burman) to the 'undemarcated' ones (with the Shan) – manifesting varying power relations. Such boundaries exist in the conceived and perceived spaces, created by stereotyping and assumptions about 'national character', and these are further subject to manipulation.

CONTESTING BOUNDARIES

Contesting an imposed colonial boundary that arbitrarily divides land comprising the same social structures and people needs no further elaboration. From the Kachin point-of-view, it is easy to contest a boundary that makes them a trans-border nation belonging to different states with relatives and members of the same clan (with the same family name) living on both sides of the boundary. As such family and social contacts continue to persist, nurtured by economic and political circumstances, the phenomena on the Sino–Burmese boundary can be described as unbundling, countering and challenging the *de jure* meanings of an international boundary.

The least that can be said about the contested-ness of social boundaries is that these are based on tangible and perceived differences that have been enhanced by external and internalized external categorizations. As the Kachin are the ones who construct and maintain such boundaries, an outside observer is not in a position to contest these. State support and enforcement of the tangible and perceived differences in its policies also help to keep social boundaries from being contested. This is the case in China, where social boundaries are less contested due to the preferential treatment afforded to minority nationalities. In the context of Burma, the links and borders between antithetical nationalisms, the state-led and the (popular) majority nationalism provide more opportunities for contesting. As far as the Burmese government's policies are effective, social boundaries are being rubbed out with the state's efforts at homogenization. As emphasized earlier, however, the state of Burma has not achieved an internal sovereignty, and this is a major hindrance to successfully carrying out government policies.

It is also important not to see – to impose – ethnic boundaries everywhere. In the life-world, lived-in space, daily life, such boundaries often decrease or cease to exist and trans-ethnic solidarities occur. Towns in Kachin State such as Myitkyina, Bhamo and Loije and many others are rather multi-ethnic, multi-cultural or plural places, and have historically been as such. As says a Muslim man (of Indian origin) in Myitkyina, owner of a bookbinding and tailor shop just next to a mosque, pointing to a *Karen longyi* that he is wearing: 'This is a Christmas present from my [Kachin] friend. I usually celebrate Christmas with my Kachin friends.' Most of his customers are the Kachin who bind bibles in his shop. He was born in Myitkyina, and can understand and speak '25 per cent' of Jinghpaw. 'The Kachin are nice and friendly people. *Like anybody.*'[49] The latter seems to support Bloul's claim that the concept of 'identity' is (sometimes) 'overthick', referring to the preoccupation with ethnic identities and difference, and the exaggeration of their role. She says that the continuing obsession with ethnic identities and identity politics negates the possibility of 'intercultural reflexivity' and makes the already existing occurrences invisible.[50] There is always a danger of (mistakenly) imposing social boundaries based on the (outside) observer's conceptions and perceptions, thus the example above is meant to serve as a reminder.

CROSSING BOUNDARIES

The above-described trade, marriage and kinship routes having followed long distances and connecting far-away places have resulted in large numbers of Kachin relatives across the territorial boundary – thus in visits and contacts. Another reason for such cross-boundary links is the change of jurisdiction of several areas near the present boundary. The three Kachin villages 'given' to China in 1960 have already been mentioned. In addition, other areas near the present border have changed jurisdictions or several clans have migrated for various reasons. In short, a lot of Kachin have relatives on both sides of the present Sino–Burmese border, and cross-boundary marriages continue to take place.

In addition, the immediate zone on both sides of the border has been woven into a tight network of criss-crossing practices. One such practice is the five-day market system where a market moves around from village to village for the convenience of buyers and sellers. The imposition of the border that now divides the participatory villages into Burma and China has not interfered with the tradition – consequently, the villagers cross the 'international boundary' every day. The practices of crossing the territorial Sino–Burmese boundary are further enhanced by the maintenance of the KIO/KIA enclaves. The KIO/KIA uses the boundary in ways that challenge most *de jure* meanings of an international boundary and tate sovereignty.

It should be implicit by now that the Kachin cross the Sino–Burmese boundary more readily than the social boundaries. Marriages across the boundary help to epitomize the case in point.[51]

The traditional kinship and marriage relations that connect places on both sides of the border, and the older trade routes, can be seen as criss-crossing lines, some more faded than others, establishing the political map as a palimpsest. On this palimpsest the Sino–Burmese border also fades away as more and more cross-border networks and links surface. Territorial international boundaries, states and sovereignties are often taken for granted, although historical contingencies have been involved in their imposition. For the Kachin, the past territorial domain has been deconstructed into a few enclaves, while the past Kachin territoriality has not disappeared but is disguised in the modern language of nations and states as the Kachin social space. The notion of social space best represents the politics and dynamics of the domain where the Kachin operate in the present day Burma and across the inter-state Sino–Burmese boundary.

The variety of spaces – ethnic, religious, political, social – might cause confusion and frustration. For that reason the chapter suggests 'social space', which also refers to social construction that ethnicity, to a considerable extent, is argued to be. Social space as it is being conceptualized in the chapter and in the on-going research involves both, territorial and social components, where the 'territorial' is part of the 'past territorialities'. In the modern globalized world, where the territory is losing relevance and social identification gaining importance, discussions on social space become relevant to wider social science debates.

NOTES

[1] The name of Burma was changed to Myanmar (and Rangoon to Yangon) in 1989 by the State Law and Order Restoration Council (SLORC), the 'government' of the Union of Burma, which in 1997 was reconstituted into the State Peace and Development Council (SPDC). In the chapter, the name 'Burma' will be used in order to follow the choice of most respondents.

[2] On distinguishing two kinds of sovereignties, external and internal, see Taylor (1995), pp. 1–15. Taylor's designation of 'internal sovereignty' refers to the state's 'effective control of a territory'. He says that 'external sovereignty' – recognition by international community – is the basis on which a state is considered sovereign. Recognizing the sovereignty of a state while it lacks internal sovereignty exemplifies the flaws in the 'modern' language of states.

[3] 'Unbundling' is used by Agnew and Corbridge (1995) and by James Anderson (1996). For discussion on 'hidden geographies', see Grundy-Warr (1998).

[4] Agnew and Corbridge (1995) have coined the term 'territorial trap'. They claim the International Relations theory to be in a 'territorial trap', led there by three geographical assumptions, the most powerful of which is that state territories have been reified as set or fixed units of sovereign space. Territorial space and

sovereignty have been regarded as 'natural' characteristics of states, linked together by the concept of security – not the security for humans, culture or ecology but the defence of the state's territorial space that preconditions sovereignty.

5   See Mikael Gravers (Chapter 9 in this volume) for a brief discussion on the symbolic and real meanings of Kawthoolei.

6   Sack (1986, p. 19).

7   Paasi (1996, p. 17).

8   Newman (2003).

9   See Grundy-Warr (1998, pp. 73–74, note 2).

10 P. Taylor (1999, p. 13).

11 Agnew, who has studied the definitions of place, concludes that most geographers have defined place through one or two of these three elements: locale, location, and sense of place. The latter is 'the geosociological definition of self or identity produced by a place' See Agnew and Corbridge (1987, pp. 5–6, 27–28).

12 See Sack (1986), and Thongchai (1995, p. 16).

13 For a thorough treatment of the nations without states, see Guibernau (1999). Guibernau predicts the rise of the role of nations without states in the future as alternative global political actors.

14 Richard Muir quotes Falk (1997, p. 49).

15 See Paasi (1996) about redefining relations between social and physical space, and Newman (1994) for his call to study the links between territorial lines and symbolic boundaries.

16 Jenkins (1994, p. 200).

17 Barth (1969 pp. 10–19).

18 Newman and Paasi (1998, p. 194).

19 Ibid., pp. 9–11.

20 Christie (1996, p. 1).

21 See M. Smith (1999, p. 43) for the quote by Aung Thwin, who characterized the British rule as an 'order without meaning'.

22 Lintner (1997, pp. 123–124).

23 M. Smith (1999 p. 154, note 21); Lintner (1999 pp. 123–124, note 22) and Tegenfeldt (1974, p. 70). All agree on these two reasons as triggering the Kachin revolution.

24 Paasi (1996).

25 Taylor (1995, p. 1 note 1).

[26] M*ayu-dama* [wife giver/wife taker] is the Kachin marriage alliance system based on kinship. *Mayu ni* refers to the lineage from which males of one's lineage take brides, *dama ni* is a lineage into which females of one's lineage are married. A man may not marry into his *dama*, and a woman may not marry into her *mayu*. A man ought to marry his mother's brother's daughter, and a woman her father's sister's son. See Leach (1954, pp. 73–85) and Wang (1997, pp. 99–100).

[27] Tegenfeldt (1974, p. 31, note 22).

[28] See Gowler's chapter in this volume for a more thorough description of how the marriage patterns work.

[29] Wang (1954, p. 59–60, note 26).

[30] Leach (1966, p. 66).

[31] Jin Liyan (1995, pp. 38–41).

[32] Ibid.

[33] Ibid., pp. 40–41.

[34] Conversation with Marip Gam Awng, Yingjiang, Dai-Jingpo AP, PR of China, 16 October, 2000.

[35] Conversation with Nang Tawng, Kachin State, 18 November, 2000. The term 'Wunpawng' is used when referring to the six tribes in Jinghpaw language conversations and expressions. 'Kachin', originally an external categorization, has nevertheless been widely accepted, but more so when talking to 'outsiders', including the Burman.

[36] Connor (1978, pp. 389–390).

[37] Paasi (1996, pp. 59–60, note 6).

[38] Ibid., pp. 59–61.

[39] Ibid.

[40] Ibid., p. 59.

[41] Interviews, Kachin State, November 2000.

[42] Jenkins (1994, p. 219, note 15)

[43] November–December, 2000; April, December, 2001; January 2002.

[44] Anthony Smith argues that 'the special qualities and durability of ethnie are to be found neither in their ecological locations, nor their class configurations, nor yet their military and political relationships ... [but] one has to look at the nature (forms and content) of their myths and symbols, their historical memories and central values, which we can summarize as the "myth-symbol" complex'. See A. Smith (1986, p. 15).

[45] Mandy Sadan presents a very detailed discussion of the current promotion and censoring of the Kachin culture by their ethnic elites. She also discusses how

the Burman categorization has shaped the Kachin nationalist censorship. See Sadan, (2000, pp. 58–77).

[46] On nationalisms in China, see Zhao (2000). For a discussion on insemination of ethnic elites in China with state ideology, see Litzinger (2000, pp. 238–259).

[47] Leach, (1954).

[48] Tegenfeldt (1974, p. 62, note 23)

[49] Conversation with Myo Razim, Myitkyina, 17 December, 2000, *emphasis added*.

[50] Bloul (1999, p. 24).

[51] This is not to claim that there are no or few marriages across the ethnic lines. Multi-cultural environment in towns such as Myitkyina and Bhamo and the state encouragement and propaganda in China provide hundreds of examples of mixed marriages and the number is increasing.

Chapter 6

CEASEFIRES AND CIVIL SOCIETY: THE CASE OF THE MON

Ashley South

INTRODUCTION

'Civil society' may be defined as 'the set of intermediate associations which are neither the state nor the family'.[1] These include more-or-less formally organized religious and cultural networks (traditional and modern), and community and social welfare groups, as well as more overtly political organizations. However, political parties and other organizations seeking to assume state power are not part of civil society.[2] The term may, though, include some types of business support organization, although it is normally restricted to the non-profit sector.[3]

According to de Tocqueville and others (especially American theorists), the existence of civil society is central to democracy. These forms of association act as a check on both state power and undue private influence, encouraging the participation of social groups in political processes (understood in the widest sense). According to David Steinberg,

> the significance of the term... lies in the hypothesis that if civil society is strong ... then this ... somehow translate[s] into overall trust in the political process of democracy or democratization and leads to the diffusion of the centralized power of the state. Civil society is thus seen as an essential element of political pluralism.[4]

In her influential essay, *Bringing The State Back In*, Theda Skocpol outlines a Tocquevillian concept of state–society relations: '[T]he organisational configuration (of states) ... affect[s] political culture, encourage[s] some kinds of group formation (but not others), and make[s] possible the raising of certain political issues (but not others).'[5] According to Skocpol, the forms of association adopted by social groups ('civil society') are conditioned by the structures and strength of the state. We should therefore expect that changes in state structure, whether gradual or revolutionary, will result in the emergence of new forms of social identity and organisation (whether more or less 'progressive').

This chapter will examine the manner in which Burmese political culture and concepts, particularly in the field of ethnicity, have been influenced by the development of the state. It will also examine the emergence of new forms of (post-ceasefire) state–society relationship, and what affect these might have on political culture in ethnic minority areas.

However, social groups' relationship with the state is not passive. Although the manner in which agents of political change *conceive* of their task may be determined by – or in reaction to – existing configurations of the state, social and economic groupings may nevertheless influence, and precipitate the transformation of, state structures. This chapter will examine the extent to which the re-emergence of civil society networks in ethnic minority areas might contribute towards processes of political transition in Burma.

Discussions of social identity and organization in Burma have tended to focus on the topic of ethnicity. Is this complex phenomenon a product of historical state formation, or does it have an independent existence? Conversely, how have concepts of ethnicity affected forms of social and political organization, and with what consequences?

The historical development of ethnic identities in Burma

The Pre-colonial era

In *The Ethnic Origin of Nations*, Anthony Smith (1986) asks whether state structures determine ethnicity. He reviews Anderson and Gellner's accounts of the development of nationalism, and the related concept of ethnic identity, within the context of an emerging modern bureaucratic capitalism. Both share 'a belief in the contingency of nationalism and the modernity of the nation.... Yet there are also difficulties with this view. For we find in pre-modern eras, even in the ancient world, striking parallels to the 'modern' idea of national identity and character.'[6] Smith demonstrates that many contemporary nations and nationalist movements are closely related to – if not actually derived from – 'primordial' *ethnie*. Nevertheless, the forms in which ethnicity is expressed and mobilized are subject to particular historical ('situational') processes. Such developments are illustrated by the case of the Mon.

The one million-plus Mon-speaking people today living in Burma and neighbouring Thailand constitute an 'ethnic minority'. However, this has not always been the case. From early in the first millennium, for a period of more than a thousand years, Mon and Khmer kings ruled over much of mainland Southeast Asia. Across northern and central Thailand until six or seven hundred years ago, and in central and lower Burma for another three hundred years, the bulk of the population were ethnic Mons. The classical period of Mon history came to an end in 1757, when the great Burman warrior-king Alaungphaya defeated the last Mon ruler of Pegu. Thousands of his followers were driven into exile in Ayuthaiya (Thailand), where they settled in the border areas adjoining Burma. At times over the two-and-a-half centuries since the fall of Pegu, it has been supposed that Mon was a dying language and the people in the twilight of their history. The Mons' very success has threatened to be their undoing.

Mon civilization was among the most influential in pre-colonial Southeast Asia. Significant aspects of the language, art and architecture, political and legal arrangements, and above all the religion of the great Thai and Burman civilizations were derived from the earlier Mon society, which acted as a vector in the transmission of Theravada Buddhism and Indianized political culture to the region. This civilizing role helps to explain the enduring prestige attached to the Mon heritage across mainland Southeast Asia. Mon nationalists have looked back to the classical era as a golden age – a source of inspiration and legitimacy. They have struggled to defend the historical Mon identity from assimilation into that of the Burman and Thai majorities.

However, ethnicity was only one factor among several in determining identity in pre-modern Southeast Asia. Victor Lieberman states that the 'Mon' kingdoms of lower Burma were in fact expressions of something more complex, and that 'the correlation between cultural, i.e. ethnic, identity and political loyalty was necessarily very imperfect, because groups enjoying the same language and culture were fragmented by regional ties'.[7] He argues that religion, culture, region and position in the tributary-status hierarchy all helped to determine personal, group and regime identity in pre-colonial times. As authority was vested in the person of the monarch, it was he,[8] rather than any abstract idea of ethnic community, that commanded primary loyalty. A Burman king could act as the patron of Mon princely clients, and vice versa.

Lieberman concedes, however, that the edicts of King Alaungphaya made a clear ethnic distinction between his own (Burman) followers and those of the 'Talaing (Mon) renegades'.[9] Indeed, ethnic polarization accelerated rapidly under Alaungphaya, who played the 'race card' to his advantage.[10]

Certainly, Mon and Burman identities were already well established before the arrival in Southeast Asia of the first Europeans, and since no later than the mid-eighteenth century, individuals and communities have represented themselves as either 'Mon' or 'Burman', depending on the political situation. Kings and modern politicians have used such ethnic labels to create and control power bases, which since the colonial period have tended to become ossified as ethnic communities.[11]

The colonial era

Before the British annexation of Burma, the Mon had already become a subject people. Their ancient culture and language persisted, but the era of Mon political dominion was at an end. Although the advent of British rule was to remove the immediate fact of Burman domination, this was replaced by another, in many ways more insidious regime, under which Burmese demographics underwent a significant shift.

Following the first two Anglo-Burmese wars (1824–26 and 1852), large numbers of ethnic Burmans moved south into lower Burma, taking advantage of new opportunities in agriculture and business. The Mon and other minority groups also changed their patterns of residence, livelihood and education. Indeed, so great was the erosion of Mon culture and language under the British that, by the time the colonialists finally departed, there were very few Mon speakers still living in the Irrawaddy Delta or Pegu, the ancient Mon homelands. According to the last colonial census, by 1931 all but 3 per cent of the Mon population of Burma were confined to Amherst District, in what is today central Mon State.[12] The previous 1921 census had recorded 324,000 Mons 'by race', but only 189,000 'speakers of Mon'.[13] The descendants of these non-Mon speakers would today be classified as ethnic Burmans – i.e. as Burmese-speaking citizens of a relatively new entity: the state of Burma.

In 1886, following th the Third Anglo-Burmese War, Burma was fully incorporated into the Empire, as a province of British India. The British divided the colony into the central lowlands of 'Burma Proper' (where the great majority of Mon speakers lived) and a horseshoe of ethnic minority-populated 'Frontier Areas', on the periphery of the state. In the former, the British governed by direct rule, thereby ensuring the destruction of the traditional Burmese polity. In the Frontier Areas, they followed the more common British colonial model of indirect rule (also adopted by the French in Laos and Cambodia), governing via local potentates. Crucially, the two zones were never integrated administratively. This tended to reduce the scope of those 'colonial pilgrimages' which might have fostered a stronger sense of pan-Burmese identity among the colonized, at least within elite circles.[14] Unlike the diverse peoples of Indonesia (all of whom ruled by the Dutch from Java, thus helping to forge the idea of a unified Indonesian nation) – but like those in Vietnam, Cambodia and Laos – the separate identities of *Bama* and non-Burmans were reinforced by the colonial experience.

Notwithstanding the lack of colonial administrative integration, the adoption of Burmese as the language of state helped to accelerate processes of assimilation. As noted above, over the course of the nineteenth century, large numbers of Mon speakers came to adopt the Burmese language, and associated forms of political culture.[15] Although the colonial authorities instigated optional civil service examinations in Mon, and between 1937–42 funded a Mon literacy and population survey, the British administration generally treated the ancient Mon culture and history with benign neglect. The bulk of official attention focused on potentially restive 'hilltribes', such as the Karen and Kachin, who were more amenable to the colonialists' self-imposed civilizing mission.[16] Nevertheless, Mon elites were able to assert themselves through the patronage of religious works: Mon-language schools were established by monks, and by 1847 the Baptists were publishing Mon tracts in Moulmein. Later, a Mon Buddhist press was set up on Bilu Kyun Island, and the Hanthawaddy Press was established in Rangoon, which printed Mon-language history texts, as well as a regular journal.[17]

The British introduced capitalist economic measures, which over time led to a degree of social mobility and the breakdown of traditional bonds. This 'rationalization of the state' involved the replacement of patron–client relations with an administration based on modern, objective definitions of the role of state agents.[18] As an indirect result of the realignment of traditional power structures, increasingly large numbers of people ceased to identify with a particular region or ethnicity, but came to regard themselves as 'Burmese' – i.e. as citizens of a new entity: the colony (and potential state) of Burma.

Thant Myint-U has described how the British Empire's extended assault on the peripheries of the once poly-ethnic Konbaung Empire reduced the latter to an ethnic Burman, 'relatively homogenous core which ... made easier a stronger sense of local patriotism'.[19] The traditional social, economic and political structures of upper Burma were overthrown, and replaced by an administration geared to the needs of British India. (Although the *sangha* did survive the colonial period, its traditional educational role and close identity with the state were both undermined.) Thus, members of the Burman majority found themselves marginalized within the colonial state, with little reason to identify with its ethos or structures, but considerable reason to resent those who did. Colonial state policy resulted in the creation of a large pool of disenfranchised and disaffected people, available for mobilization by educated elites.

Meanwhile, the colonial authorities attempted to establish a 'level playing field' among the various ethnic peoples of Burma.[20] They were quite successful in ensuring equality of opportunity for different groups in the country, and large numbers of minority people received an education, and went on to types of employment that would not have been open to their ancestors. The British thus fostered the emergence of self-consciously distinct 'ethnic minority' groups, who were encouraged to identify themselves in opposition to the Burman majority. Second- and -third-generation elites from within these 'imagined communities' went on to lead Burma's ethnic nationalist movements in the turbulent years directly preceding and following the Japanese invasion of 1941.[21]

The Second World War and since

Unlike the hill Karen, the Mon did not play a significant role in assisting British officers operating behind enemy lines in Burma during the war. However, large numbers did join the Burma Independence Army (BIA), and a Mon Youth Organization (MYO) was formed in 1941, several members of which later fought with the BIA against the departing Japanese forces.[22]

The wartime regime in Burma outlawed the teaching of minority languages, espousing a quasi-National Socialist ideology of 'one voice, one blood, one nation'.[23] Although, by late 1945, Dr Ba Maw's administration had been thoroughly discredited, non-Burman groups were alarmed by the racial chauvinism inherent in the wartime government's pronouncements. As Taylor observes, by the end of the war, 'ethnicity, religion or Communism inspired more loyalty than did the state'.[24]

Within a year of independence, Arakanese, Karen, Mon and other ethnic nationalists had taken up arms against the state, as had the powerful Communist Party of Burma. Over the following decade and a half, several more groups were to join the insurrections; many articulated some kind of ethnic nationalist agenda.

In this militarized context of rebellion and counter-insurgency, the Tatmadaw moved to capture the state, in order to defend a particular idea of the nation, the origins of which lie in the colonial era and the Second World War. This conflation of state and nation – in the form of a politicized army – has profoundly influenced the development of Burmese political culture.[25] Despite ostensible changes in ideology and political programme, the key concept of an independent nation (identified with the Burman cultural centre) and strong state, with the capacity to shape state–society relations, has remained a constant, with the Tatmadaw regarding itself as the principal agent of implementing policy upon – and defending the state from – the complexities of Burmese society.

Mary Callahan demonstrates how the army developed and projected the idea of an independent Burma, centred on a highly politicized Tatmadaw, dominated by ethnic Burman officers.[26] These veterans of the chaotic war years were influenced by memories of the divisive colonial regime, and were determined to prevent the disintegration of the union. When the Tatmadaw assumed state power, its leaders identified the interests of this – the most 'patriotic' institution in Burma – with those of the state. The young officers who assumed control, first of the Tatmadaw and then of state, had been exposed to competing versions of what an army might be, and how it might relate to the state and wider society (as had the leaders of various ethnic nationalist and Communist armed groups opposed to them).[27]

THE SUPPRESSION OF BURMESE CIVIL SOCIETY

1958–1988

According to Callahan, having experienced the ultimate authority of military over civilian administration under both the British and Japanese, in the 1950s leaders of both the Tatmadaw and civilian government began 'institutionalising the primacy of coercion in state-society relations'.[28] At a Tatmadaw conference (held following the first Ne Win coup), the Psychological Warfare Directorate distributed a detailed critique of civilian-constitutional politics in October 1958. This document attacked the citizen's right 'to express his views and desires upon all subjects in whatever way he wishes'.[29] A blueprint for later military pronouncements, it proposed replacing the 1947 constitution with one written by those 'who have more specialised knowledge', rather than 'unscrupulous politicians and deceitful Communist rebels and their allies' (including recently surrendered Mon and other ex-insurgents: see below). Callahan claims that 'the significance of this paper cannot be overstated... the constitution was no longer sacred'.[30] It laid the basis for the suppression of Burmese civil society in the 1960s.

As the state extended its control over previously autonomous aspects of social life, civil society networks – which were not yet well established – could no longer operate independently. Meanwhile, opposition to the regime was either eliminated, driven underground or forced into open revolt. After 1962–63, the existence of renewed armed opposition to the military government provided a pretext for the further extension of state control, and suppression of diverse social groups deemed antipathetic to the modernizing state-socialist project. The Ne Win regime's suppression of non-Burman cultural and political identities, epitomized by the banning of minority languages from state schools, drove a new wave of disaffected ethnic minority citizens into rebellion.[31]

According to Steinberg, 'civil society died under the BSPP (Burma Socialist Programme Party); perhaps, more accurately, it was murdered'.[32] Under the 1974 constitution, all political activity beyond the strict control of the state was outlawed.[33] By 1980, even the previously independent *sangah* had been brought under at least partial state control.[34] (Nevertheless, Burma's 250,000 monks and novices retained a prestige and influence which extended across all strata of society. Among the few institutions in Burma not directly controlled by the state, the *sangha* – and Christian churches – remained among the potentially most powerful sectors of civil society.)

1988–2002

Since the early years of independence, control over state power has been contested by a variety of identity groups, while its structures have profoundly affected perceptions and modes of social organization. Popular participation may be mobilized either for or against an authoritarian regime, and it seemed for a few weeks in the summer of 1988 that 'people's power' might prevail in Burma, as it had two years previously in the Philippines. The failure of the 1988 'Democracy Uprising' in Burma – like that of the May–June 1989 'Democracy Spring' in China – was in large part due to the underdeveloped nature of civil society in these states.

A lack of democratic culture prevented powerful gestures of political theatre from initiating sustained political change. Unlike those in Eastern Europe in the late 1980s, in the Philippines in 1986, or in Thailand in 1992, the Burmese and Chinese democracy activists had little social space within which to operate, or to build upon the people's evident desire for fundamental change. In particular, Burma and China had no counterpart to the Catholic Church or trades unions, which played important roles in the Polish and Filipino democracy movements.[35] The BSPP regime had succeeded in denying social groups a foothold in mainstream politics or the economy, except under strict state control. Potential opposition was thereby marginalized, and could emerge only in times of crisis and upheaval, presenting the military with a pretext to clamp-down on 'anarchy' and 'chaos' (thus the State *Law and Order* Restoration Council, SLORC).

Under the SLORC, state–society relations were further centralized. Particularly following the ascension of Senior General Than Shwe in 1992, social control was reinforced by the reformation of local militias and mass organizations, and the indoctrination of civil servants. The police, and even the fire brigade were brought under military control, and the SLORC established a number of government-controlled non-government organizations (GONGOs!). By 2002, the Union Solidarity and Development Association (USDA) – established in September 1993, along the lines of the pro-military GOLKAR party in Indonesia – had a membership of some 16 million people, many of whom were reportedly pressurized into joining. Its objectives included upholding the regime's 'Three National Causes' and the 'promotion of national pride'. Beyond this highly circumscribed sector, 'civil society' and the operation of independent political parties, such as the National League for Democracy (NLD), were severely restricted, as were freedoms of expression and association, and access to information and independent media.

In May 1999 the Ministry of Information published a *Declaration of Defence Policy*, which outlined the regime's largely successful attempts to modernize and expand the Tatmadaw. In classic SLORC-style (influenced by the formulaic structure of traditional Buddhist doctrine), this document underlined the leadership role of the Tatmadaw, and outlined 'Twelve Objectives' and 'Four Desires' of state policy. These included opposition to 'those relying on external elements, acting as stooges, holding negative views', and 'the preservation and safeguard of culture and national character'. The regime exhorted patriotic Burmese to 'crush all destructive elements as the common enemy' (a motto emblazoned on billboards across the country in the 1990s).[36] As Andrew Selth noted the same year, 'the armed forces now see themselves as embodying the state'. Clearly, the SLORC–SPDC did not accept the notion of a 'loyal opposition'.[37]

Nevertheless, one consequence of the ceasefire process (discussed in more detail below), and the partial 'opening up' of the Burmese economy in the early 1990s – in an attempt to attract more resources, and modify the military regime's poor international image – has been the gradual re-emergence of civil society in parts of Burma. Since the early-mid 1990s, the NGO sector in particular has undergone a significant regeneration. It currently includes some 40 international and more-or-less officially registered local agencies, as well as various Burmese religious, cultural, social, professional and educational associations.

Among these are a number of organizations working in ethnic minority-populated areas, including both indigenous NGOs and some international agencies working through local staff. Although their access to the most needy rural populations (including internally displaced persons) is highly restricted, and the political aspects of their programmes are usually obscured by a humanitarian welfare gloss, these pioneer NGOs have played an important role in the development of civil society networks, under the most difficult and repressive of conditions.[38] In some cases, they have been assisted by enlightened state employees, who may work surreptitiously towards non-SPDC sanctioned ends. Such elements of the state sector may bridge the public–private gap; although civil society has been repressed in Burma, it can re-emerge in the most unlikely places.[39]

THE ETHNIC DIMENSION

The distinction between 'Burmese' and 'Burman' nationalism has not always been clear; indeed, the former has often been subsumed under the latter. According to D. R. SarDesai, nationalism in Southeast Asia 'has been in most cases a response to imperialism and the political and economic exploitation of the governed. In a certain sense, nationalist revolutions were the creation of Western colonial powers themselves.'[40] This has also been true of ethnic nationalism in Burma, *vis-à-vis* the Burman-dominated central government, which has been accused of practising 'internal colonialism'.

Tatmadaw ideologues have viewed their task as one of 'national salvation': the army has sought to defend the unitary, socialist state, which emerged from the heroic struggle for independence. As the Tatmadaw assumed control of key institutions, it sought to impose a model of state–society relations, in which the (ethnic minority) periphery was dominated by a strong (Burman-orientated) centre. As pluralism was suppressed, it was replaced with a state-sponsored nationalism. The process of 'Burmanisation' saw diverse (and according to the military, divisive) minority cultures, histories and socio-political aspirations subsumed under a homogenizing 'national' identity, derived from the Burman historical tradition.

On the subject of state building, Clifford Geertz has cautioned that communal 'primordialism' (defined by reference to 'blood ties', race, language, region, religion and custom) threatens to overwhelm and fragment many least-developed countries, unless ethnic groups can be persuaded to integrate with the state, recognizing its authority over certain key aspects of political life. However, in *The Integrative Revolution* he is alert to the possibility of a particular ethnic group coming to dominate the state. Indeed, Geertz cites Burma as an example, in which 'peripheral groups ... are naturally inclined to see (the state) as alien ... vigorously assimilationist ... [and prone to a] "Burmanisation" ... which traces back to the very beginnings of the nationalist movement'. He characterizes ethnic conflict in modern Burma as a struggle between 'one central ... group and several ... opposed peripheral groups ... the Irrawaddy Valley Burmese versus the various hill tribes'.[41]

Writing about Burma, David Brown describes a

> situation where the state acts as the agency of the dominant ethnic community ... in which recruitment to the state elite ... and government is disproportionately and overwhelmingly from the majority ethnic group... The ethnocratic state is one which employs the cultural attributes and values of the dominant ethnic segment as the core elements for the elaboration of the national ideology .... and its political structures serve to maintain and reinforce the monopolization of power by the ethnic segment.[42]

Similarly, Gustaaf Houtman calls Burma a 'culture state', where the military government is bent on consolidating the 'Myanmafication' of culture and history, and suppressing Burma's diverse social identities.[43] In its appeal to a monolithic national identity, 'Myanmafication' displays aspects of fascist ideology. Furthermore, the emphasis on Burmese (read Burman) purity, and the denial of minority cultures, has led to a characteristically totalitarian rewriting of history.

In a rare public justification of such policies, shortly after seizing power in 1962, General Ne Win denied the need for a separate Mon culture and ethnicity. According to Ne Win (who apparently claimed to be of mixed Mon ancestry),[44] the Mon tradition had been fully incorporated into Burmese national culture, and thus required no distinct expression. In August 1991 the then-SLORC chairman, General Saw Maung, made a similar speech, in which he denied the need for a separate Mon identity.[45]

The process of Burmanization – or 'Myanmafication' – has been illustrated, since the early 1990s, by the construction of a series of museums across the country, which are intended to institutionalize and reproduce 'Myanmar national culture'.[46] A particularly striking example is the reconstruction of the Kambawzathadi Palace at Pegu, on the supposed site of the mid-sixteenth-century capital of King Tabinshwehti and his successor, Bayinnaung. Since 1990, the royal apartments and audience hall have been excavated and rebuilt in concrete. As historians have little idea what the original palace looked like, the new buildings are modelled on nineteenth-century palace designs from Mandalay.

The Kambawzathadi Palace project received a major boost in September 1999, when it was visited by Lt.-General Khin Nyunt – an event which made the front page of *The New Light of Myanmar*.[47] However, what the government-sponsored literature on Kambawzathadi mentions only in passing is that the new palace was in fact built upon the much older remains of the sixteenth-century Mon capital of Pegu. In fact, parts of these largely unexcavated ruins are still visible as a series of grassy mounds and depressions, between the newly-'rebuilt' royal chambers and the foot of the great Shwemawdaw Pagoda (Mon: Kyaik Mawdaw). If properly examined, this archaeological site might yield important information regarding the historical development of mainland Southeast Asian polity and religion. As it is however, the neglected remains of Hongsawaddy are a symbolic reminder of the balance of power in modern Burma.[48]

THE ETHNIC NATIONALIST REACTION

In the chaotic years between 1945 and independence, elites within the Mon community articulated claims to social and political autonomy, on the basis of ethnicity.[49] As Mikael Gravers puts it, 'identity thus becomes the foundation of political rights'. He calls this process *'ethnicism* the separation or seclusion of ethnic groups from nation states in the name of ethnic freedom ... where cultural differences are classified as primordial and antagonistic'.[50]

By 1950, two Communist factions and a number of ethnic insurgent groups, including the Mon People's Front (MPF), had taken up arms against the government and Tatmadaw, and established 'liberated zones', from where they hoped to achieve independence, or at least substantial autonomy from Rangoon (the Communists of course, sought to overthrow the U Nu regime). Like several other insurgent organizations however, the MPF agreed a ceasefire with Rangoon 1958, and subsequently attempted to pursue its goals from within 'the legal fold'. However, one young MPF cadre, Nai Shwe Kyin, together with a small group of followers, rejected the agreement and, the day after the MPF 'surrender', established the New Mon State Party (NMSP), which was to be in the vanguard of the armed struggle for Monland for the next 40 years. According to its founder, the NMSP aimed 'to establish an independent sovereign state unless the Burmese government is willing to permit a confederation of free nationalities exercising the full right of self-determination inclusive of right of secession'.[51]

Given the traditional importance of education in Mon Buddhist culture, and of language to ascriptions of ethnic identity, it is not surprising that the NMSP organized a school system, soon after re-establishing itself in the mid-1960s. The first of a newly reorganized system of Mon National Schools were opened in 1972–73, and by the mid-1990s the NMSP was running a high school, several middle schools and nearly one hundred primary schools.[52] These offered Mon-language teaching in all subjects at primary level, except for foreign languages (English and Burmese). However, due to a shortage of Mon-speaking teachers, middle school history was taught in Mon, with other subjects in Burmese, while the medium of high school instruction was usually Burmese.[53] The Mon National Schools played an important role in the NMSP's projection of a distinctly Mon national culture, underpinning the party's secessionist – and later, federalist – policies. However, in purging the curriculum of the Burmanization of history and culture, the Mon education system tended to overcompensate, and perhaps over-emphasize the glorious history of the Mon.[54]

The Thailand-based Human Rights Foundation of Monland (HRFM) observes that the state and NMSP education systems' objectives 'are opposite. The government education system aims to implement the government's protracted assimilationist policy by pushing the non-Burman ethnic students to learn and speak Burmese... The main objectives of the Mon education system are to preserve and promote Mon literature ... Mon culture and history, to not forget the Mon identity.'[55]

Somewhat ironically, the Tatmadaw has played a part in this affirmation of Mon identity. As Hobsbawm notes, 'we know too little about what ... goes on, in the minds of most relatively inarticulate men and women, to speak with any confidence about their thoughts and feelings towards the nationalities and nation-states which claim their loyalties'.[56] The manner in which 'ordinary' Mon people have responded to the nationalist agenda is often unclear. The great majority are poor rice farmers, and day-to-day survival is the prime consideration. Nevertheless, Mon villagers have routinely been persecuted *because* of their ethnicity, and as a result many have had little choice but to flee to insurgent-controlled territory. It is a truism of cultural studies that differentiation reinforces identity. Despite the government's avowal that a separate Mon ethnic and national identity is redundant, its oppressive policies have ensured that – at least among the displaced populations along the border with Thailand – the notion of a distinct Mon identity lives on. If nothing else, the displacement and flight of villagers to border areas where they are dependant on the NMSP for basic security (and often food), is likely to have reinforced their public identification with Mon ethnicity.[57]

Since the 1970s, many thousands of displaced Mon villagers have 'voted with their feet', seeking refuge in the insurgent-controlled 'liberated zones' (and later, refugee camps) along the Thailand–Burma border. However, state–society relations in the Mon and other 'liberated zones' have tended to mirror those in 'Burma proper', in reaction against which the insurgents first took up arms.

Joseph Silverstein argues that the political language and concepts of the Burmese opposition are at least partly derived from those of the military government.[58] Similarly, in her study of Burmese political culture, Christina Fink notes that 'the military's propaganda and ways of operating have profoundly shaped even those opposed to military rule'.[59] Like its military opponents, the NLD has often been intolerant of internal dissent. The importance of unity in Burmese political culture is no doubt a legacy of the liberation struggle, and the fractious early years of independence. Its centrality to Burmese politics attests to the degree to which the military, with its paranoia regarding foreign-sponsored disintegration of the union, has imposed its narratives of power on society. This observation recalls Skocpol's analysis of the effects of state structures on social groups' formation and political awareness, and is relevant also to the armed ethnic opposition.

Both sides in the civil war in Burma have long defined themselves in opposition to each other. For many insurgent groups, identity and the claim to legitimacy have come to reside in the act of rebellion itself. By the 1970s, the civil war had become institutionalized, and in many cases the revolutionaries began to resemble warlords. The political culture of the 'liberated zones' reflected the largely extractive nature of many insurgent groups' relations to natural resources and the peasantry (their ethnic minority brethren, in whose name the revolution was being fought). Life in the 'liberated zones' thus became characterized by a top-down tributary political system, similar to that in government-controlled areas, aspects of which recalled pre-colonial forms of socio-political organization.[60]

Although (especially after 1988) most ethnic insurgent groups claimed to be fighting for 'democracy', this ideal was not always reflected in their practices. Rebel leaders tended to discourage the expression of diverse opinions, and socio-political initiatives beyond the direct control of the militarized insurgent hierarchies were generally suppressed. One consequence was the endemic factionalism of Burmese opposition politics, with most groups unable to accommodate socio-political (or personality) differences among their members;[61] another was the suppression of pluralism in ethnic opposition circles, and the development of rigid political cultures in non-state controlled areas.

Thus, aspects of resistance to the forces of assimilation themselves took on the characteristics of 'cultural corporatism'. Ethnic minority opposition (in this case, Mon) civil society became prone to a homogenizing concept of identity, which was in some respects profoundly undemocratic. The Mon and other ethnic nationalist movements had to contend with a contradiction between their message of democracy and national liberation, and a patriarchal tradition. The challenge – and opportunity – facing such movements in the post-ceasefire era is how to combine the struggle for ethnic rights with an appreciation of democracy as a process, rather than a distant end state.[62]

The NMSP leadership seems genuinely committed to a vision of a democratic Burma, based on respect for individual and group rights. However, the party has limited experience of fostering democratic practice in the areas and sectors under its control. The NMSP–SLORC ceasefire has at least created the military-political 'space' within such efforts may be promoted.

THE SIGNIFICANCE OF THE CEASEFIRES

As a result of the series of ceasefires negotiated between the military government and insurgents since 1989, the security situation in much of rural Burma has improved significantly. However, villagers in many areas remain subject to a wide range of human and civil rights abuses, perpetrated by the Tatmadaw and – to a lesser extent – by various armed ethnic groups.

Between 1995 and 2001, five small ex-NMSP splinter groups resumed armed conflict with the Tatmadaw (and sometimes with the NMSP also); in late 2001 another, militarily more significant anti-ceasefire Mon armed group emerged, and proceeded to undermine security across much of Mon State. However, by late 2003, the Hongsawatoi Restoration Party (HRP) had dwindled in support and capacity.

Among other, more self-interested reasons, these Mon anti-ceasefire factions were motivated by complaints of continued Tatmadaw human rights abuses, and in particular, by a campaign of uncompensated land confiscation initiated in 2001.[63] One predictable consequence of the renewed instability in Mon State was the revival of the Tatmadaw's notorious counter-insurgency policy.[64]

The nature of the ceasefire process and 'ceasefire groups' in Burma is not uniform, although in nearly all cases the ex-insurgents have retained their arms, and still control sometimes extensive blocks of territory. (However, the Mon ceasefire zone consists of little more than the Ye River watershed and a few isolated outposts further to the north.) In many quarters, the ceasefire agreements are regarded as little more than a cynical exercise in *real politik*, benefiting only vested interests in the military regime and insurgent hierarchies. However, to other observers and participants, they represent the best opportunity in decades to work towards the rehabilitation of deeply troubled ethnic minority-populated areas. For the NMSP and other ceasefire groups, the truces also represent opportunities to mobilize among their constituencies in government-controlled areas – activities which were previously only possible on fear of arrest.

The ceasefires are not peace treaties. These agreements generally lack all but the most rudimentary accommodation of the ex-insurgents' political and developmental demands. Nevertheless, they have created some military and political 'space', within which community-level associational networks may re-emerge. Other factors behind the tentative revival of Burmese civil society over the past decade include the partial opening up of the economy in the early 1990s, and the cover and the limited support given by the international community.

Many of Burma's fledgling civil society networks are associated with progressive elements among the country's International NGO community. This phenomenon reflects a trend among donors towards supporting local NGOs, which are considered to implement relief and development programmes more effectively than government departments. (Furthermore, in the case of Burma, many INGOs and UN agencies have been reluctant to enter into partnership with the military-dominated state.) The presence of INGOs in Burma – especially in ethnic minority-populated areas – has to some extent, and in some places, helped to create an environment conducive to the development of local counterpart NGOs.[65]

In the case of the Mon, several Thailand-based INGOs had previously supported projects in the NMSP 'liberated zones', including aid to the Mon refugees, the last of whom was repatriated by the Thai authorities in 1996.[66] A few Thailand-based INGOs remain in contact with the party, and with local groups working under its umbrella. In general, these organizations have encouraged their Mon partners to retain an oppositionist stance *vis-à-vis* the Burmese military government. Since the 1995 ceasefire, to which it agreed with considerable reluctance, there have been extensive debates within the NMSP – and the wider Mon nationalist community – regarding the wisdom of engaging with the SPDC and integrating the remaining NMSP-controlled zones with those controlled by the government.

Until 2003, the party had generally been wary of pursuing contacts with the international community via Rangoon, choosing instead to distance itself from the SPDC, while continuing to receive limited cross-border international support. However, in recent years the NMSP has taken tentative steps to engage more constructively with Rangoon-based international agencies.

Nevertheless, since the ceasefire, the party's women's and education departments have succeeded in extending their activities beyond the NMSP-controlled zones, to Mon communities across lower Burma. The Mon Women's Organization (MWO) has implemented community development, income generation, adult literacy and capacity development programmes in a number of areas, and has developed a strategic partnership with the Metta Development Foundation. (Established in 1998, and one of the few legally registered local NGOs in Burma, Metta has projects in Shan, Karenni, Karen and Mon State, and in the Irrawaddy Delta).

Meanwhile, despite some serious setbacks, during the 2003–04 school year the NMSP managed to run 187 Mon National Schools and 186 'mixed' schools (buildings shared with the state system, where the use of minority languages is still banned). The Mon National Schools taught more than 50,000 pupils, approximately 70 per cent of whom lived in government-controlled areas, and would not previously have had access to an indigenous (Mon) language education. Illustrating an important aspect of the post-ceasefire educational environment, a handful of graduates of the two Mon high schools have had the opportunity to continue their studies at state further education colleges.

However, although the NMSP and other ceasefire groups have generally provided the political and military cover within which ethnic minority networks may develop, the key civil society players have often not been the (ex-)insurgents. Those who have taken the lead in community initiatives over the past decade include members of semi-dormant religious and social welfare networks, as well as those who campaigned for ethnic minority parties in the May 1990 general election. In the case of the Mon, the latter include individuals associated with the Mon National Democratic Front (MNDF), which won five seats in the 1990 polls, but was outlawed in 1992.[67]

A number of ethnic nationality social and welfare organizations – in particular, literature and culture promotion groups – were established well before the 1990s, but in recent years have become more active, and concerned with a wider range of issues. As in other parts of Burma, the re-emergence of such networks in Mon areas has been particularly notable in the field of education. As the state school and higher education systems have continued to deteriorate, alternative models have emerged, such as the Mon *sangha* and Mon Literature and Culture Committee's (MLCC) Summer Mon Literature and Buddhist Teachings Training.

A successor to the All Ramanya Mon Association (ARMA) and other cultural and youth groups of the 1930s and 1940s, the MLCC pioneered Mon literacy training in the 1950s, seeking to expand and consolidate the Mon language skills, and thereby the cultural and historical awareness, of the Mon community in Burma. Although it was largely dormant during the repressive Ne Win era, monasteries across lower Burma continued to teach Mon throughout 1960s–80s and, since 1996, the MLCC has re-emerged as a leading player in this field, organizing a series of successful Mon language and literacy training courses, taught by Mon educationalists and monks. Like the Karen and other Literature and Culture Committees, the MLCC is among the handful of specifically 'ethnic' organizations tolerated by the military regime. It maintains branches in Rangoon and at Moulmein University, and in village monasteries across Mon State and in Pegu and Tenasserim Divisions.[68] Supported by local donations and international funds, in 2004 some 55,000 school students (70 per cent of them girls) attended summer holiday courses in Mon language and culture-history, conducted in over one hundred monasteries and schools, in 16 townships across lower Burma. Most of these were situated in government-controlled areas. Although the NMSP was limited to an indirect fund-raising role, this programme would not have been allowed by the regime before the 1995 ceasefire.

However, patterns of development – and stagnation – among Burma's ethnic minority communities are mixed. As Martin Smith has observed, the situation on the ground varies from district to district.[69] While some aspects of the situation in Kachin State (exemplified by the formation of the Kachin Consultative Assembly in October 2002), northern Shan State, and Mon and Karen States are quite encouraging, others are much less so.

This fact is illustrated by an important anomaly: civil society networks may re-emerge among war-torn communities without insurgent groups associated with that population necessarily renouncing armed struggle. For example, the number of religious (Christian and Buddhist) and other Karen groups participating in community development activities has increased markedly over the past five years. These developments have occurred despite the on-going and chronic Karen insurgency (and intra-Karen factional fighting), and continued government restrictions on travel and organization. However, the opposite is also true: not all ceasefires result in the emergence of functioning civil society networks. Those parts of Shan State controlled by the United Wa State Army (UWSA) since its

1989 ceasefire agreement with the SLORC are still characterized by a very circumscribed civil society. The UWSA's 'top-down' command style, and associated distrust of autonomous community organizations, owes much to Burmese – and Wa – political culture, and to ideas of the 'leading role of the party' inherited from the Communist Party of Burma (of which the UWSA was an element until 1989). These factors are exacerbated by the limited social and economic opportunities in the Wa sub-state, the minimal quantity and poor quality of education and health services, the degraded natural environment, and the pervasive corruption, political violence and 'warlordism' associated with the booming drugs trade in the region.[70]

The re-emergence of civil society networks in some parts of Burma raises a number of important issues. These are addressed at the levels of local, national and international analysis.

LOCAL DEMOCRACY

One consequence of Burma's 50-year civil war has been the erosion of pluralism and democratic practices, in both non-state and (especially) state-controlled regions. Emergent civil society networks in ethnic minority areas, beyond the direct control of either the militarized state or often authoritarian (ex-)insurgent groups, represent alternative forms of social and political organization, and opportunities for local democratization (or at least, liberalization). This type of 'small d' democratization (or 'democracy from below') will be essential if any elite-led political transition in Burma is to be sustained, and positively affect the lives of people living in inaccessible, minority-populated border areas.

It is possible that, by participating in such community development programmes, activists may be diverted into 'safer' and less challenging activities, thus depoliticizing the struggle for ethnic rights in Burma. However, many of those involved in 'above ground' social networks – including members of the MNDF, an (outlawed) political party – are in fact still closely involved in politics. Implicitly, they are also challenging NMSP commissars for leadership of the Mon community, obliging the latter to reassess their strategies, decision-making processes and policies.

As a political party, the NMSP is not part of civil society. Could it – or the social welfare, youth and women's departments under its control – be reinvented as a development agency? At present, having given up their largely symbolic armed opposition to Rangoon, the NMSP and other ceasefire groups are in danger of becoming marginalized within their own communities, unless they can reinvent themselves as *post*-ceasefire organizations. Such re-positioning must be accompanied by a reconceptualization of political ideals and processes, reflected in the party's policy and practice. The aging NMSP leaders have to determine where they stand on the big issues of Burmese politics. In particular, they must adopt a consistent policy towards the mainstream democracy movement (i.e. the NLD, but also the MNDF), and explain this position to constituencies inside Burma, in the border areas and overseas.

The on-going realignment of Mon society in Burma is mirrored in developments over the past decade within opposition circles along the Thailand border. Mon exile groups across the border, and in the remaining 'liberated zones', tend to operate under the umbrella – but often beyond the direct control – of the NMSP. The democratization and increasingly sophisticated political analysis of such activist groups bodes well for the future.[71]

POLITICAL TRANSITION

A functioning civil society is a prerequisite of democratic transition. It is essential that groups and networks representative of Burma's broad, plural society equip themselves to fill any power vacuum that may emerge, either as a result of radical shifts in national politics, or of a more gradual realignment, and accompanying withdrawal of the Tatmadaw from state power. The ability of Burma's diverse social groups to reassume control over aspects of their lives, which since the 1960s have been abrogated by the military, will depend on the strength of civil society.

Although grass-roots mobilization often takes place under the guise of 'apolitical', local self-help, welfare and community development activities, it nevertheless represents a challenge to the military regime's authoritarian policies. The creation of locally rooted associational networks undermines the ideological and practical basis of centralized military rule, creating spaces for the development of community autonomy, at least in limited spheres (e.g. language use). As Steinberg states in a recent article, the development of civil society in Burma 'widens the space between the state and society, giving people greater freedom from government control. Such pluralism is an important base on which more responsive and responsible governments can be built'.[72]

However, although it may be necessary to build democracy 'from the base up', the re-emergence of civil society networks is not in itself sufficient to affect political transition. This will require a concerted, explicitly political act of will on behalf of Burmese politicians. Members of the predominantly urban-Burman political elite in Rangoon, represented by the NLD, have proved that they are ready to take these risks, as have a number of ethnic leaders, who in July 2002 formed the United Nationalities Alliance (UNA), representing parties which participated in the 1990 elections (including the MNDF).[73] Recent developments indicate that the NMSP is also attempting to make its presence felt in the national political arena, although with limited success.

INTERNATIONAL RESPONSES

Post-ceasefire politics in Burma's ethnic minority areas have generally been under-reported, in comparison with the 'national level' struggle between Daw Aung San Su Kyi's NLD and the SPDC. The situation of a number of well-armed ceasefire groups in northern Burma has attracted some international attention, as many have been active in narcotics and amphetamines trafficking, the social effects of which are felt in Thailand and the West. However, the international community has been slow to recognize the significance of other ceasefire groups, such as the NMSP and the Kachin Independence Organization (KIO), which remain politically engaged – although their influence on events from 'within the legal' fold has been limited.

Nevertheless, since the ceasefire, Mon nationalists – including those who never took up arms, or had long ago renounced armed conflict – have found some limited space and funds with which to work towards the re-emergence of civil society within their community. If the international community is serious in its desire to support political transition in Burma, it can play an important role in encouraging the development of such networks in ethnic minority areas.

As Steinberg suggests, donors should 'encourage local elements of civil society that can act as points for eventual political pluralism'.[74] However, these groups' capacity to absorb funds and implement effective projects is limited, and may remain so for some time. Therefore, donors wishing to help develop local civil-society networks – and thus secure the fragile ceasefire process across much of rural Burma – must be prepared to commit to long-term partnerships, and to ensure that their interventions are made in consultation with local communities and their representatives.[75]

CONCLUSION

Changes in state structure have profoundly affected the historical formation and mobilization of ethnic identities in Burma. Since 1962, the 'ethnocratic state' has suppressed non-Burman political identities and the operation of civil society, with profound consequences for the conceptualization and expressions of ethnicity.

The altered relationship between the central government (and Burmese military) and some minority groups (and ethnic insurgents), as a result of the ceasefire process, constitutes a significant realignment of state–society relations. As a result, new forms of social and political organization have begun to emerge within the Mon and other minority communities that have the potential to affect state structures, including those of the 'liberated zones'. Whether the realignment of ethnic minority politics ultimately feeds back into the loop, and contributes towards transition at the national level, will depend on how politicians react to political opportunities – and attendant risks.

Meanwhile, the NMSP is in danger of becoming marginalized, unless it can respond to the new environment with a new strategic vision. The ceasefire groups are uniquely positioned to take the lead in redefining the nature of civil-military relations in Burma. Ultimately, for both the *Tatmadaw* and the armed ethnic groups, the transition from insurgency to relative peace and stability – of which the present military regime is so proud – is less difficult than that from dictatorship to democracy. The first phase (peace-making) is a prerequisite of the second phase (peace-building), but the latter addresses more fundamental issues.

After decades of conflict, and amid on-going repression, opportunities exist for conflict resolution and political transition in Burma. To varying degrees, the SPDC, the NLD and ethnic minority leaders have all expressed their desire for peaceful social and political development. Although the scope and mechanics of any transition will be negotiated among elites, in order for recovery to be effective, members of the country's diverse social and ethnic groups must enjoy participation and a sense of 'ownership' in the process. Post-conflict transformation thus requires the rehabilitation of Burmese civil society. This difficult and uneven process is already underway, and is worthy of support.

Foreign governments, UN agencies and INGOs should work to empower those non-regime groups attempting to work inside Burma, under the most challenging circumstances. They should also continue to bring pressure on the SPDC to initiate political reform and enter into dialogue with representatives of Burma's ethnic minority and opposition groups.

Although the international community can play an important role in facilitating political transition, the success of this process will depend on the Burmese state and social groups. Based on a reading of British and French history, Skocpol suggests that 'states not only conduct decision-making, coercive, and adjudicative activities in different ways, but also give rise to various conceptions of the meaning and methods of "politics" itself, conceptions that influence the behaviour of all groups and classes in national societies'.[76] The field of political culture – attitudes to and valuations of power and politics – is often stubbornly resistant to change. As Alan Smith and Khin Maung Win observe, the absence of consensus and 'accumulated distrust and unwillingness to compromise between and centre- and Burman-dominated state ... and non-Burman ethnic groups' is the most serious obstacle to political transition.[77]

In a recent report for the Minority Rights Group, Martin Smith concludes that 'conflict resolution, demilitarization and the building of civil society will be vital bridges in achieving reconciliation in the country and supporting the creation of conditions in which democracy can take root and minority rights be enjoyed'.[78] However, as he – and many ethnic minority leaders – recognize, if it is to be sustained, peace and reconciliation must be accompanied by a just settlement of state–society issues.

AUTHOR'S NOTE

This chapter represents the author's analysis as of late 2002. As far as possible, the facts cited were up-dated in September 2004. In general, the situation on the ground had not changed greatly in the interim. However, the case study does not take account of the government-organized National Convention in Burma (re-convened in May 2004) On the National Convention, and for a discussion of 'top-down' and 'bottom-up' political transition in Burma, see South (2004 a).

NOTES

[1] McLean (1996).

[2] Ethnic nationalist organizations which take on state-like characteristics do not constitute civil society. However, like other state structures, they may either encourage or suppress the development of civil society.

[3] Steinberg, in Burma Centre Netherlands and Transnational Institute (1999, pp. 2–3).

[4] Steinberg (2002, p. 102); for an extended discussion of civil society in the Burmese context, see ibid. pp. 101–20.

[5] Skocpol (1985, p. 21).

[6] Anthony Smith (1988, p. 11).

[7] Lieberman (1978, p. 480).

[8] Or – in the case of the Mon – very occasionally, she: see Guillon (1999) and South (2003).

[9] Lieberman (1978, p. 480).

[10] Ibid. p. 472.

[11] See Aung-Thwin (1998, p. 147). Mikael Gravers also warns against adopting ethnicity as the sole criterion of identity, arguing that religion (or cosmology) is at least as important (Gravers 1999, pp. 19–35).

[12] South (2003), p. 22.

[13] Quoted in ibid. This was almost unchanged from the 1911 census, which had recorded 320,629 Mon, of whom not more than half spoke the language. The 1881 census had recorded 154,553 'pure' Mon and 177,939 'mixed' Mon-Burmans. Thus over a period of 40 years, while the population of Burma increased, the number of Mons apparently remained static. Interestingly, the 1891 census had recorded a population of 466,324 Mon (including 226,304 Mon speakers), an increase of 46 per cent over the figure for 1881. This may be explained by the demise of the Burman monarchy, and subsequent decline of fears associated with being identified as Mon.

[14] On integrative/ exclusive patterns of nation-building in Indonesia and Vietnam, see Anderson (1991, pp. 114–119).

[15] South (2003, pp. 18–25).

[16] See Chapter 2 in this volume by Mandy Sadan, who examines the construction of Kachin identity during the colonial era.

[17] South (2003, pp. 90–94).

[18] R. Taylor (1987) and Furnivall (1991).

[19] Thant Myint-U (2001, p. 253).

[20] R. Taylor (1987, pp. 66–67).

[21] Robert Taylor has demonstrated how modern forms of ethnic nationalism in Burma are partly derived from the racial theories, ascriptions and administrative procedures of the colonial period: ibid. p. 286, and see Taylor (1982). As with other minority groups in Southeast Asia, Karen (but rarely Mon) ethnic identity has been labelled an artificial construction, derived from speculative missionary ethnography and politically expedient colonial classification. However, such assertions fail to appreciate the complexity and agency involved in articulations of ethnic identity. Although this 'imagined' identity may be constructed from disparate (including non-indigenous) elements, it is nonetheless authentic for that.

[22] South (2003, p. 95).

[23] Taylor (1987, p. 284).

[24] Ibid. p. 285.

[25] For an account of these factors from the perspective of the Tatmadaw, see Maung Aung Myoe (1998).

[26] Callahan (1996).

[27] As with the different 'imagined communities' of the nation, these were essentially modular concepts, constructed by Burmese actors according to their understanding and experience of the British colonial, Japanese and other armies. Again, it is important to stress that this 'pirating' of modular forms (Anderson's phrase) constituted a dynamic reinterpretation of the colonial legacy. Anderson implies that an 'imagined' community is 'fabricated', a view which effects its perceived legitimacy (Anderson 1991, p. 6). Gravers employs Chatterjee's critique of Anderson to question whether national identity in developing countries must be passively, 'trapped within the imaginations of state and nation inculcated by their former colonial masters, or are they able to create models based on their own cultural imaginations and their own genuine practices'? (Gravers, in Tønnesson and Antlöv 1996, p. 242).

[28] Callahan (1996, p. 128).

[29] Quoted in ibid. p. 478.

[30] Ibid. p. 479.

[31] On the Burmanization of the civil service and education, see Brown (1994, pp. 48–49).

[32] Steinberg, in Burma Centre Netherlands and Transnational Institute (1999, p. 8). See also Steinberg (2002, pp. 105–108), and in Pederson et al. (2000, pp. 106–112).

[33] R. Taylor (1987, pp. 303–309).

[34] Ibid. p. 112.

[35] Furthermore, capital markets and outside forces (e.g. US pressure) played more important roles in determining the course of events in the Philippines and Thailand than they did in isolated Burma and China, with their relatively 'closed' societies.

[36] Quoted in Maung Aung Myoe (1999, p. 18). The 'Three National Causes' were announced as the basis of SLORC rule in September 1988: ibid. pp. 3–14.

[37] Selth (1999, p. 2). According to another recent report, 'the *Tatmadaw* believes that it exclusively embodies the nation's destiny and goals, and it is intolerant of political pluralism which is viewed as damaging to national unity and therefore to national security' (International Crisis Group 2000, p. 9).

[38] See Steinberg (2002, pp. 115–120). However, the discussion here ignores the activities of local NGOs which may be working towards both community development *and* political goals. Steinberg diagnoses the Burmanization of the state, and the marginalization of ethnic groups, but does not acknowledge that the latter may nevertheless engage in community mobilization.

[39] See ibid. p. 104. In his study of the 1989 democracy movement in China, Craig Calhoun makes an important point regarding state institutions and civil society: '[I]t is important to separate the questions of whether the particular organizational bases are internal to the state and whether they are able to resist the exercise of central power' (Calhoun 1994, p. 168).

[40] D. R. SarDesai (1994, p.135). David Brown makes a similar point (Brown 1994, p. 2).

[41] Geertz (1963, pp. 136–137) (parenthesis added). Anthony Smith claims that 'in order to forge a "nation" today, it is vital to create and crystallise ethnic components' (A. Smith (1988. p. 17). However, echoing Geertz's warning, he notes that 'the result of turning nationalism into an "official" state ideology is to deny the validity of claims by any community which cannot be equated with an existing state ... If the state does not itself possess long and inclusive traditions, its dominant ethnic community is liable to seek to impose its traditions on the rest of the state's population, and this usually ignites the fires of separatism' (ibid. pp. 222–223).

[42] Brown (1994, pp. 36–37).

[43] Houtman (1999, pp. 142–47). Mikael Gravers refers to a process of 'cultural corporatism', in which an 'imagined Myanmar has one singular cultural essence, which is embodied in all individual citizens' (Gravers 1996, p. 240).

[44] Guillon (1999, p. 213).

[45] An extract from this speech is quoted in Gravers 1996, p. 240.

[46] See Houtman (1999). Although such museums represent the state's definition of ethnicity, institutions such as the Mon museum in Moulmein, the Karen

museum in Pa'an and the (private) PaO museum in Taunggyi may nevertheless help to create a space for the examination of minority history and culture.

[47] *The New Light of Myanmar* (20 September 1999).

[48] See South (2003, pp. 33–34).

[49] See Nai Tun Thein (1999) and South (2003, pp. 100–108).

[50] Gravers (1999, p. 145); see also, Brown (1994, pp. 3–4).

[51] NMSP (1967), p. 1.

[52] NMSP (15December 1994, p. 27). In December 1994, the party's Fundamental Political Policy and Fundamental Constitution of Administration stated that the following were the 'basic enemy of the Mons: colonialism, bureaucracy policy (capitalism), dictatorship, majority Burmanisation'. The NMSP constitution reflects longstanding commitments to both Mon national liberation and leftist political analysis.

[53] Thein Lwin (3 March 2000).

[54] Ibid.

[55] *The Mon Forum* (August 1998).

[56] Hobsbawm (1990, p. 78).

[57] See Hazel Lang (2002).

[58] Silverstein (Rotberg 1998, pp. 12–27).

[59] Fink (2001, p. 5). According to Taylor, the philosophy of the NLD – in its early years at least – was influenced by the left-wing ideology of the Tatmadaw and BSPP.

[60] See South (2003, pp. 129–130; 341–342).

[61] According to this reading, the 1994 Democratic Karen Buddhist Army (DKBA) rebellion among the KNU ranks may be seen as subaltern reaction against an unrepresentative and unresponsive elite, which became problematized in religious terms, but was as much an expression political (class-based) grievances.

[62] See David Tegenfeldt 2002 which examines – and outlines an approach to the transformation of – ethnic conflicts in Burma, through the lens of identity construction (focusing on the case of the Kachin).

[63] The Human Rights Foundation of Monland (HURFOM) has documented the confiscation of at least 7,780 acres of farmland from Mon farmers, between 1998 and 2002. Adding insult to injury, farmers have sometimes been forced to work on the confiscated lands, building barracks etc. on behalf of the Tatmadaw. The problem is felt particularly acutely in areas previously contested between the NMSP and the Tatmadaw, from which the MNLA pulled-out following the ceasefire – thus withdrawing a minimal level of protection to villagers, and allowing the Tatmadaw to more easily access areas it could previously only enter at risk of attack (HURFOM, October 2003.

[64] See South (2003), Part Six, and *The Mon Forum* (2002–04 *passim*).

[65] International agencies working inside Burma (and along the Thailand border) may be divided between donors – which are often able to support the development of local groups' capacities, and may not be operational in the field – and implementing agencies. The latter, although they may address urgent humanitarian needs, can sometimes divert talented individuals away from indigenous organizations, towards their own programmes. Agencies may adopt aspects of both roles, as when an implementing organization also funds local partner groups. For a detailed analysis of the relationship between international agencies and Burmese civil society, see South (2004).

[66] See South (2002), Part Five.

[67] South (2003, pp. 328–329).

[68] Ibid. p. 37.

[69] Martin Smith, in Burma Centre Netherlands and Transnational Institute (1999, pp. 46–48).

[70] However, the UWSA is not a monolithic organization. Some Wa leaders are attempting to promote a community-based approach to development, as part of a Wa state-building exercise.

[71] See South (2003, pp. 284–287).

[72] Steinberg, in the *International Herald Tribune* (28 August 2002).

[73] The UNA is a successor the United Nationalities League for Democracy (UNLD), an umbrella group of ethnic nationality political parties elected in the May 1990.

[74] Steinberg (2002, p. 120).

[75] For a detailed discussion of civil society and democracy promotion in Burma, see South (2004 a).

[76] Skocpol (1985, p. 22).

[77] Khin Maung Win and Alan Smith, in Sachsenroder and Frings (1998, p. 132).

[78] Martin Smith (2002, p. 34).

Chapter 7

WHO ARE THE SHAN?
AN ETHNOLOGICAL PERSPECTIVE

Takatani Michio

INTRODUCTION

At the beginning of 2002, a Shan acquaintance of 20 years' standing gave the author a pamphlet containing an appeal for co-operation in preserving the traditional Shan culture, written in both Bamar (Myanmar or Burmese) and Shan scripts. In the Shan version, the Shan people, land and culture are referred to not as 'Shan' but as 'Tai', which is what they call themselves. Tai-speaking people living in Burma have traditionally been called 'Shan' in Bamar, but this term is only used by people who are not 'Shan' themselves. This pamphlet symbolizes the situation which surrounds the Shan people and culture in Burma. Bamar is the language of the majority and is the language officially used in school education and administrative offices. Any cultural activity conducted by an ethnic group in this country must therefore also be presented in Bamar.

This chapter is an attempt to present an ethnological analysis of the Shan people living in Burma.zThe process whereby the Bamar have politically and culturally influenced the Shan will be referred to as the Burmanization (Myanmarization)[1] of the Shan. Today we can see several different stages of Burmanization. In parallel with this phenomenon, the Shan must have experienced a kind of 'Shanization' of their own people that may have raised their own self-consciousness. So 'Shanization' as used here does not signify the assimilation of their hill neighbours in the pre-modern period (Leach 1977 [1954]: 40–41) but various phenomena of cultural dynamics such as the preservation and revitalization of their own culture and the formation of a collective identity under the political and cultural pressure of Burmanization.[2] The discourse of 'Shanization' relates to two-way construction of Shan ethnicity: internally by some common modes of acquiring, maintaining and extending knowledge of ethnicity; externally by political negotiation in an effort to co-exist with the Bamar. It hypothetically continues from the nineteenth century to present time through the influx of 'scientific' ethnic differentiation from the West.

The author's field research for this chapter was conducted intermittently from 1997 to 2003 in Shan State and Kachin State.

MOGAUNG (MÖNG KAWNG) IN KACHIN STATE

Mogaung is an old town located in Kachin State. Shan historical documents and legends often refer to this town, especially when dealing with the founding of the Shan.

The terms *'mo'* and *'maing'* in Bamar are *möng/muang/mäng* in Shan,[3] which was and is their common political unit for subsistence during the emigration and settlement process. Mogaung is Möng Kawng in Shan. Most of towns on Bamar maps which begin with *mo* are found among 'Burmanized' Shan in Kachin State or in the western area of Shan State, for example Mogaung, Mohnyin, Momeik and Mogok, where the lords kept intimate contacts with the Bamar palace before British annexation.

E. R. Leach's monograph entitled *Political Systems of Highland Burma* first published in 1954 is essential reading for any ethnologist planning to study the Shan people and this area. He emphasized in his conclusion that the ordinary ethnographic conventions as to what constitutes *a* culture or *a* tribe are hopelessly inappropriate and expressed a message which sounded alarm bells for all ethnological and cultural anthropological studies (Leach 1977 [1954]: 281–285). His research field was located on the border of the Kachin Hills Area and the Shan States (presently Kachin State and Shan State), near the China–Burma border. It is important to understand that his field-research was done during the Second World War and the areas that foreign researchers could legally visit are currently in a different political situation. Let us look at this in more detail. He classifies the Shan into Burmese Shans (*Shan B'mah*), Chinese Shans (*Shan Tayok*) and Hkamti Shans as follows:

The Burmese make a distinction between Burmese Shans (*Shan B'mah*), Chinese Shans (*Shan Tayok*) and Hkamti Shans. Roughly Speaking, Burmese Shans comprise the Shans of the Burmese Shan states, where Buddhism is more or less of the Burmese type and where the princes (*saopha*) have long been nominally subordinate to the Burmese King. Chinese Shans are the Shans of the Shan states in Yunnan, the most important of which lie in the area south of Tengyueh and west of Salween. Many of the Shans now resident in Burma in the Bhamo and Myitkyina districts are recent immigrants from Yunnan and are classed by the Burmese as Chinese Shans. Hkamti Shans are looked upon as a sub-type of the Burmese Shans. They may be defined as Shans who, on historical grounds, might be regarded as having had some political allegiance to the former state of Mogaung (Möng Kawng). (Leach 1977 [1954]: 32–34)

Leach says that the term 'Burmese Shans. (*Shan B'mah*) is apparently only current in the Bhamo and Myitkyina districts (Leach 1977 [1954]: 32 footnote). It is obvious that Leach was considering Shan *saopha* not only in present Kachin State but also Shan State when he classified *Shan B'mah* (Shan-Bamar). At present the Bamar call the Shan people who come from Shan State merely 'Shan'. Culturally speaking, as mentioned above, the Shan people there have experienced Burmanization from the dynastic period to the present time. But now references to *Shan B'mah* in the same context are heard not in Shan State but in Kachin State. The only exception is for children whose parents are a Bamar and a Shan, who may be called *Shan B'mah*. How they are now legally registered is another matter.

Another term 'Shan-Ni' (Red Shan) in Bamar refers to the Shan residents near Mogaung and Mohnyin. They call themselves 'Tai-Lieng' in Shan and recognize their culture as partly Burmanized, but are proud of their Shan origin, and their ancestors belonged to Mogaung *saopha*. In the report of the Frontier Areas Committee of Enquiry in 1947 just before independence, 'Burmanized Shan' refers to the people who lived in Homalin Subdivision, an area along the Chindwin River in present Sagaing Division. At that time, the committee chairman asked two persons who came from the area 'Are you originally of the Shan race?' One of them answered, 'Our ancestors came from Hkamti Long, but, on account of the dangers from the Kachins, they had to migrate down the valley of the Chindwin. Nowadays though we are Shan by descent, we are Burmanized, and, in fact, Burmese.' (FACE 1947: 1–21, 2–104).

Not only 'Shan-Ni' but also another term, 'Tai-Shaun', is sometimes heard near Bhamo for 'Burmanized' Shan. Tai-Shaun means 'Tai at the riverside'.

Both terms are dependent on context of utterance and signify not ethnic groups but cultural and geographical categories.

Shan Tayok group has a close relationship with a group that call themselves 'Tai-Nuea', living near the border between China and Burma. The Bamar call them 'Tai-Lei'[*4] and tend to view their culture as influenced by Chinese on politico-geographical grounds. 'Lei' is another form of 'Nuea.' Hkamti Shan is a cultural unit in an area near Putao in present Kachin State and Sagaing Division. Both terms, 'Shan Tayok' and 'Hkamti Shan', which Leach mentions may be more appropriate as ethnic categorizations than *Shan B'mah*, because they seem to preserve their own identity in spite of changes in the political environment.

Leach's classification had an influence on following ethnological studies. For example, *Ethnic Groups of Mainland Southeast Asia* edited by F. K. Lebar and others and published in 1964 adopts Leach's classification as if such ethnic groups really exist.[5] Leach's information is only a kind of categorization by the Bamar of the Shan people, especially *Shan B'mah*. An aged Kachin who was born in Bhamo and studies Shan culture says that *Shan B'mah* or Shan-Ni is the same as Tai-Lieng who use it as self-reference, and adds that they have forgotten the native language and mastered Bamar and have became *Shan B'mah*. He adds that their origin dates back to the China expedition by the king of Anawrahta during the Pagan period: they descend from the people who remained there and mixed with the Shan, or from the Bamar who came to the present Kachin State as railway workers during the colonial period (personal communication). Legends such as this show how the term *Shan B'mah* is a relative social indicator of the degree of Burmanization.

Therefore it is evident that *Shan B'mah* is not the name of a particular ethnic group but a kind of categorization through inter-ethnic negotiation. Though the Shan living in present Shan State were and are culturally influenced by the Bamar, they never call themselves '*Shan B'mah*'. After independence in 1948, Mogaung was located not in Shan State but in Kachin State and is currently merely a historical site of the Shan in the pre-modern period. No archaeological survey has ever been done. Under the pressure of Burmanization at the present time, the Shan have no choice but to submit to being a cultural minority against the background of national culture preservation, and Mogaung cannot be more than a centre of an 'imagined community' for the Shan. Today most of the Shan people residing in Kachin State have forgotten the Shan language, and they use the Bamar language as their native tongue. These form the group that I shall refer to as 'Burmanized' Shan.

Though Leach uses *saopha* (prince) to refer to a traditional Shan chief, this word needs re-examination on historical grounds. 'Sawbwa' in Bamar – a Burmanization for *saopha* in Shan – seems to have been a title denoting subordination to a Bamar king. It is more exact to consider 'Sawbwa' as a sign of negotiations with a Bamar king. After the Konbaung dynasty came to an end and all upper Burma was colonized in 1886, the British government simply continued the Sawbwa system. This meant that Shan Sawbwa switched allegiance from the king of Burma to the king of Britain.

KO SHAN PYI

When we study the inter-ethnic relationship between the Shan and the Bamar, 'Ko Shan Pyi' (Nine Shan States) or 'Kawsampi' emerge as key terms. Both sides have records of nine legendary chiefdoms, or *möng*, of the Shan, and Mogaung was the leader among the chiefdoms, having been founded by a legendary hero who came from Möng Mao. Möng Mao is thought to be the earliest site of the Shan in Burma.

Tai-speaking people began to migrate to the mainland of Southeast Asia before the eighth century as an anchor. Most historians say that the last big wave of immigration was in the thirteenth century and their living area can be called a Shan (Tai) cultural area. They have kept their cultural similarity and communicate more easily among each other than those whose mother tongue belongs to the Tibeto-Burman linguistic family or others. The 1983 population census of Burma said that the number of the Shan population was about 2.8 million and 90.6 per cent of them were Buddhists. Their cultural area extends across the borders with Thailand, Laos, the Assam region of India and the Yunnan Province of China.

In a sense, European colonial elites recognized 'racial' or ethnic minorities in the eighteenth and nineteenth centuries during the period of colonial conquest (Renard 1987: 257) as recorded in *Gazetteers of Upper Burma and Shan States* (GUBSS) published in 1900–1901. Many Shan sub-groups were 'scientifically' discovered in that period where Shan *saopha* (Sawbwa on the Bamar side) were recognized as lords by the British colonial government.

Though Leach argues that the uniformity of Shan culture is correlated with the uniformity of Shan political organization (Leach 1977[1954]: 40), it was not until 1922 that the Shan States were officially federated. Most *möng* kept political uniformity in the pre-modern period and were never known by an 'ethnic' name (Rujaya 2000: 196), but were not able to found a nation state encompassing the Shan States in the modern sense. The term 'Tai-Long' (Greater Tai) is so evocative that it has become a symbolical imagined category including almost all Shan people in Burma. The feudal Sawbwa system of the present Shan State continued until the latter half of 1950s. Such a political situation explains why Shan culture may not have been homogeneous enough to be a unit but possessed a collective consciousness of identity.

A historical document (Thant Sin 1935: 1–3) records that Hsipaw Sawbwa, who was one of the lords of the present Shan State, held great Buddhist propagation and donation ceremonies (*thathana pyu pwe daw gyi* in Bamar) at least three times in 1914, 1924 and 1934. Many monks were invited from all over Burma and the Shan States. The main purpose of the first was to reunite Thudharma, Shwegyin, Yun and Zawti Buddhist sects as was done during some Bamar kings' reigns. The Maha Myat Muni pagoda in Hsipaw, modelled after that of Mandalay, was enshrined and dedicated by the Sawbwa's family. He grew up in the Bamar palace like other Sawbwas. Leach writes that the Shan ideal of a Sawbwa was best achieved by the kings of Burma (Leach 1977[1954]: 215–216), and the above-mentioned Buddhist events show how often the Bamar and the Shan had political and religious contact and how similar their cultural basis was and is in spite of the difference of language.

Dr Toe Hla, who in 2002 became deputy director-general of Universities Historical Research Centre, that has served as a national centre for research on Myanmar history since 1991, says that Shan Pyi [land] called 'Kambawza' was composed of nine cities (*kyaing* or *chiang*), nine towns (*maing* or *möng)* and nine swords (*da*), and ruled by nine Sawbwas (Toe Hla 1982: 13). Sao Saimong Mangrai, who was a historian and dedicated himself to the invention and promotion of new Shan scripts, writes that the Shan States were known collectively as 'Kambawza', and this is still the practice (Saimong Mangrai 1965: 43). 'Kambawza' is often used to mean Shan Pyi, especially the western area of the Salween River, as Than Tun mentions (1990: 12). Some of the more prominent Shan States of the Konbaung period were known not only by their Shan names but also by Bamar royal names and titles. Some of Sawbwa were given royal titles including 'Kambawza': for example Möng Nai, Yawnghwe, Möng Pai, Möng Pan, Lai Hka and Hsipaw. The title of

Hsipaw Sawbwa was Kambawza Maha Wanda (San Aung 1973: 5–7; Naw Mong 1997: 170–171).

In Chapter 139 of *Hmannan Maha Yazawin Daw Gyi* (HMYD, Glass Palace Chronicle of the Kings of Burma), edited in the palace from the former half of the nineteenth century, the story of a couple is mentioned. They were King Anawrahta, founder of the Pagan dynasty, and Saw Mon Hla, the daughter of a Sawbwa who ruled 'Mo Ko Pyi Taung (Mo Nine Land)'. They met when the king made an expedition to China to search for Buddha's ashes and got married, but parted in the end (HMYD 1993: 254–256; Tin and Luce 1923: 83–84). Most historians interpret 'Mo' as 'Mao' Shan, thought to be the earliest Tai-speaking people who lived in the Bamar area, probably near the present Muse and Namkham.

The above-mentioned chronicle does not give the nine names. Though the number of nine seems to refer to a collective image for the Shan land, the main versions of nine *möng* are as follows (the former in Shan, the latter in Bamar):

Version 1: Möng Kawng (Mogaung), Möng Yang (Mohnyin), Möng Mit (Momeik), Möng Nai (Mone), Möng Maü (Bhamo), Hsenwi (Theinni), Yawnghwe (Nyaungshwe), Hsipaw (Thibaw) and Möng Pai (Mobye) (Mi Mi Lwin 1992:1).

Version 2: Hsenwi (Theinni), Hsipaw (Thibaw), Möng Nai (Mone), Yawnghwe (Nyaungshwe), Möng Mit (Momeik), Möng Kawng (Mogaung), Möng Maü (Bhamo), Möng Yang (Mohnyin) and Kale (Kalei).

Version 3: Möng Kawng (Mogaung), Möng Yang (Mohnyin), Möng Mit (Momeik), Kale (Kalei), Hsenwi (Theinni), Hsipaw (Thibaw), Yawnghwe (Nyaungshwe), Möng Pai (Mobye) and Möng Nai (Mone).

Version 4: Möng Kawng (Mogaung), Möng Yang (Mohnyin), Hsawng Hsup (Thaung Thut), Möng Mit (Momeik), Hsenwi (Theinni), Hsipaw (Thibaw), Möng Nai (Mone), Yawnghwe (Nyaungshwe) and Möng Pai (Mobye) (Khä Sën 1996: 250).

Version 5: Möng Kawng (Mogaung), Möng Mit (Momeik), Möng Yang (Mohnyin), Kale (Kalei), Hsipaw (Thibaw), Hsenwi (Theinni), Yawnghwe (Nyaungshwe), Möng Nai (Mone), and Möng Pai (Mobye) (Sao King Tung 1954: 9). [6] (See Map 7.1)

The last two versions are found in Shan historiography. Möng Mit (Momeik), Hsenwi (Theinni) and Hsipaw (Thibaw) are located in northern Shan State, Yawnghwe (Nyaungshwe), Möng Nai (Mone) and Möng Pai (Mobye) in southern Shan State, Möng Kawng (Mogaung), Möng Yang

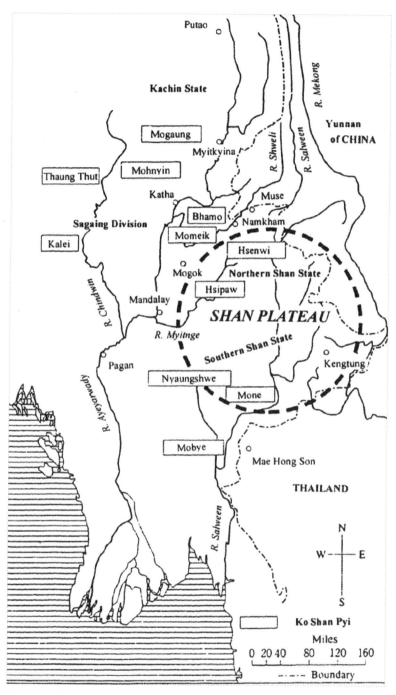

Map 7.1. The geographic distribution of Shan möng

(Mohnyin) and Möng Maü (Bhamo) in Kachin State, Kale (Kalei) and Hsawng Hsup (Thaung Thut) in Sagaing Division. Every version mentions Möng Kawng (Mogaung). N. Elias who was an attaché of the British Foreign department in the late nineteenth century said that the most important province or section of the Mau (Mao) kingdom under the central state of Mung-mau (Möng Mao) or 'Kusambi' was known as Mogaung (Elias 1876: 39).

Historians say that the lords of Mogaung, Mohnyin and Bhamo were not recognized as Sawbwa by Bamar palace in King Thibaw's reign (San Shwe 1992: 4–5). This did not mean that Shan political power in Mogaung became independent from Bamar palace, but it exerted less influence than previously from the historical viewpoint that Mogaung had leadership among Shan Sawbwa as Shan chronicles and the above-mentioned nine *möng*.

Such a trend continued after British annexation when the Kachin Hills Area became a different administrative unit from the Shan States. The lords of the Shan States officially became subordinate to British supervision in 1895. The former six states, Hsenwi, Hsipaw, Möng Nai, Yawnghwe, Möng Pai and Möng Mit, were included in the list. Möng Kawng and Möng Yang were not included (*Burma Gazette* 1895: 262).

However, many Shan people lived in Kachin State at that time. According to the 1931 Census of India published in 1933, the population of Shan people ('Tai group') was as follows: 408,758 (47.0 per cent) in southern Shan States, 288,659 (46.8 per cent in Northern Shan States, 62,622 (36.5 per cent) in Myitkyina District. In each area Shan people were the most populous. In Bhamo District, the Tai group was 34,569 (28.5 per cent) in second position following the Kachin group (38.6 per cent. In Upper Chindwin District in present Sagaing Division, the Tai group was 86,546 (42.2 per cent) in second position, after the Burma group (47.7 per cent) (Census of India 1933: 243–244). By the time of the 1983 census, it is reported that there were about 200,000 Shan people residing in Kachin State, next largest after the Kachin group (300,000) and the Bamar group (240,000) (Immigration and Manpower Department 1987). A population report on Mogaung township in 1996 says that there were 21,142 Kachin, 47,057 Bamar, 28,062 Shan, totalling about 100,000 persons. Thus the Shan population in Kachin State was and still is a considerable proportion. Such ethnic circumstances may have been the factor that continued to make Mogaung the centre of the 'imagined community' of Shan historiography.

Concerning 'Kawsampi', GUBSS says:

The term of Ko-shan-pyi or nine Shan States is more easily explained. The various Shan chronicles which so far have been consulted, while they give their own local name as that of the paramount kingdom, unite in adding the classical or Buddhistical name of Kawsampi. This may very probably have been borrowed from Kaw-sambi, one of the most celebrated cities of ancient India, but the Burman official, with the ear of a hippopotamus and the arrogance of a self-made man, could not bring himself to admit that a Shan Kingdom had any right to a classical title, if indeed he knew that Kawsampi was classical. He therefore transformed Kawsampi into Ko-shan-pyi. Scott and Hardiman 1900–01:189).(

Sao Saimong Mangrai writes about the above-mentioned paragraph as follows:

The term *Koshanpyi* seems to have had a definite geographical application. If the term is synonymous with anything, it is so only with the phrase *Kopyidaung* (nine states) and this latter term makes it even less possible for Koshanpyi to be confused with Kawsampi. In Burmese, Kawsampi is written to read as Kaw-tham-bi and is never mistaken for Koshanpyi, because both existed side by side. (Sao Saimong 1965: 42)

Many Europeans writers, including Yule and Sladen, subsequently referred to the nine Chinese Shan States as the Koshanpyi, and I am convinced they were right. (Saimong Mangrai 1965: 43)

On the other hand, Cit Phumisak, who was a Thai national and published a book about the history of Tai groups, says that the Tai borrowed Ko Shan Pyi from the Bamar and changed it into Kawsambi (Cit Phumisak 1992: 129–130). One probable reason for these various interpretations is that 'nine' in Shan is *kaw*, which is phonetically similar to *ko* in Bamar. Another is that the term 'Shan' has had a long appearance since the twelfth century in inscriptions. It is not certain who borrowed the terms 'Ko Shan Pyi' and 'Kawsambi' from whom, but the symbolic number nine is a key to ethnic identification of the Shan and Shan Pyi for both the Bamar and the Shan.[7]

SHAN PEOPLE IN KACHIN STATE

There have been no intensive ethnological or sociological reports on the Shan States and other Shan areas since the time of GUBSS. During the period of the Revolutionary Council, on the basis of the 1955 census, 27 main ethnic groups and 32 minor ethnic groups were reported in Shan State. The list of the former includes the Li near Kengtung (Kyaington in Bamar) (BSLP 1968: 44–50). This group is the same as the Tai-Lue who live in Sipsonpanna Dai Prefecture, where they are in the majority. But this ethnic group is not included in the 135 national races (*tainyindha*) or ethnic groups in the 1983 census. Shan categories among the 135 names comprise 33 ethnic names.[8] Though the categorization of the census reflects administration divisions, the contents do not. Today the total number of national races, 135, is used by every political leader to refer to Burma's status as a multi-ethnic nation state. From an ethnological point of view, however, the number 135 has not been supported by any intensive survey.

It was difficult for the young government just after independence to guard the border with China owing to the Kuomintang invasion, conflicts with the Communist Party and other factors. So even now there is constant strife due to regional power politics, and it is almost impossible for anyone to accomplish ethnological research in much width and depth.

The diversity of Shan methods of ethnic identification may be another reason for the lack ethnological reports since the GUBSS period. According to the ethno-historian Hasegawa Kiyoshi, the Shan people tend to have two methods of identification. One is through *möng* of birth, the other is geographical: for example, Tai-Nuea (upper course of the Salween River) and Tai-Tau (lower course of the Salween River) (Hasegawa 1996: 84–86). The latter indicates Shan people living in Shan State and both usages can be heard near the border between Burma and China.

On the other hand there is much more consistency about Shan people residing in Kachin State, as the following notice board at Kachin State Museum illustrates:

Tai-Long	116, 197
Tai-Lei	3,524
Tai-Lieng	138, 176
Tai-Hkamti	3,679
Tai-Hsa	556
Total (1973 census)	**262,132**

Figure 7.1. Announcement at Kachin State museum noticeboard

Assuming that the data is reliable, it seems that Tai-Long and Tai-Lieng are the majority groups. No other groups of Shan people are mentioned.

So these five ethnic labels seem to have become culturally patterned in the present Kachin State.

The 1931 Census of India includes some interesting data on 'Races in Myitkyina and Katha districts' (see Table 7.1). The number of the Shan Bama(r) (*Shan B'mah* in Leach's monograph), who seem to occur for the first time in the 1921 Census, has increased from 6,000 to 23,293. As the editor of the census surmises, it is apparent that many of the Hkamti Shan and Shan-Tayoks listed themselves as 'Shans', while a very large number of Shans must have listed themselves as 'Shan-Bama(r)' and they are possibly Shans who had become 'Burmanized' (Census of India 1933: 189).

Table 7.1: Races in Myitkyina and Katha Districts

Race-group/ Race	1921	1931	Increase
Tai group			
Shan	109,325	94, 421	-14,904
Shan-Tayok	6,926	5,537	-1,389
Shan-Bama(r)	6	23,293	23,287
Hkamti	4,851	1,121	-3,730
Others	1	...	-1
Total	121,109	124,372	3,263

Source: Census of India 1933: 181.

Interesting data is also given on the percentage of persons whose mother tongue is in the Shan (Tai) group but who speak a subsidiary language in the Burma group. A large proportion of the Shans in Myitkyina (61.6 per cent), Katha (81.6 per cent) and upper Chindwin (76.2 per cent) Districts speak a language in the Burma group as a subsidiary language,[9] whereas very few do so in the northern Shan States (7.2 per cent) or in the southern Shan States (3.8 per cent). Conversely the percentage of persons whose mother tongue is in the Burma group and who speak a subsidiary language in the Shan group is too few to mention (Census of India 1933: 196, 238–239). Though it is not clear how reliable the above-mentioned data is, it seems that a Bamar language was largely used for communication in areas corresponding to the present Kachin State and a part of Sagaing Division. We can thus see that a cultural environment promoting Burmanization had been formed during the colonial period to the degree that lots of Shan people became Shan-Bamar by identification. Since then this tendency has been modified relatively little.

SHANIZATION AND SHAN ETHNICITY

During my stay I repeatedly asked the question 'How many ethnic groups exist among the Shan people?', in order to gauge their knowledge of themselves. 'Ethnic group' is generally translated as *lumyo* in Bamar. Though the Shan have similar expressions like *tai* or *khä/khü*, these are less general than the Bamar words among the Shan, and the prefix of *tai* represents the imagined big group, 'Tai'. As may be expected, most of the respondents were aged Shan intellectuals. Almost all answered that the Shan people comprise about 30 sub-groups. However the list they mentioned included not only hill tribes like Kachin, Kayin (Karen) and Chin but also the Chinese Tayok, though not Bamar. An essay titled 'Thirty Tai names', which was edited in the latter half of the 1960s lists, names such as Tai-Pao, Tai-Yang, Tai-Lisu, and Tai-Lawa (SPYS 1966: 46). 'Yang' has a direct relationship with Karen, and 'Lawa' belongs to the Mon-Khmer linguistic unit. It is as if the word *tai* is a general term for a social unit within the area where the Shan language is used as a lingua franca. Ronald D. Renard's description reinforces this interpretation. He regards *tai* and *kha* (*khä/khü*) as social indicators showing that traditional groups identified themselves in a way quite different from present-day ethnological and linguistic standards (Renard 1997: 177). Thus the number 30 connotes a collective image for both the Shan people and their hill neighbours. Though there is a general tendency for the term 'Shan' to signify all Tai-speaking people in Burma, it is sometimes used for most of the people living in Shan State (including non-Tai). Therefore, Shan ethnicity must be treated with ethnological care.

The 1931 Census of India reports that the Shan call mountain tribes in the surrounding areas 'Tai-Loi' or 'Hkun (Kun)-Loi,' i.e. Shan in the mountains (Census of India 1933: 245). Tai-Lwe is one of the 135 national races included, but Tai-Lwe and Tai-Loi refer to the same tribe.

The author has reported some oral founding-legends of the Shan (Takatani 1996). These stories have a common motif that their ancestors were brothers, of whom Shan-Gyi (Tai-Long) was the older and Tai-Noi, also called Yodaya Shan, was the youngerO. The word 'Yodaya' derives from Ayuttaya. The memories of the narrators seem to reflect their consciousness of their historical background, because the Siamese who founded Ayuttaya in the fourteenth century fought with the Bamar in the sixteenth and eighteenth centuries. In other words, the Shan in contact with the Bamar and others viewed their human and ecological environment in the light of

Figure 7.2. Shan people at Bawgyo Pagoda festival in Northern Shan State, March 2000. Bawgyo pagoda festival is one of the biggest ones in Shan cultural area. (Photo: Takatani Michio)

Shanization. Though the term 'Tai-Long' is used to describe a national race, it can include all Shan people living in the State in contrast with Tai-Noi who are Tai-speaking people in Thailand. The latter call themselves not 'Tai-Noi' but 'Tai-national' or 'Tai-Thai', and call the Shan in Burma not 'Tai-Long' but 'Tai-Yai'. Some of them migrated to Mae Hong Son Province in northern Thailand in the nineteenth century. Therefore some people regard Tai-Long as the national race, as the 1983 census reports; others use it as collective image of all Shan in Burma including 'Burmanized' Shan and others. The usage of the latter, which in a sense denies Burmanization, is surely indicative of one phase of Shanization.

Lung Tang Ke, who was a member of the new Shan script project that began in 1940 and is a famous scholar of Shan cultural tradition, says that it was not until the 1950s that the term 'Tai-Long' was used. This project was first led by Sao Saimong Mangrai with the intention of making the Shan writing system easier for students to read and write. If his memory is correct, it means that the term 'Tai-Long' has been invented through the process of promotion of Shan common scripts as a phase of Shanization.

Though it may be guessed that Leach's description 'a Kachin became a Shan' is another phase of Shanization that signifies that the Shan accepted different mother tongue groups like the Kachin who learned Shan ways of action and thought, 'Shanization' in this chapter refers to the hypothetical formation of collective identity in contrast with other groups like Bamar, Kachin and others who are 'ethnically' different in modern terms after British rule.

Though the word '*lumyo*' in Bamar has a general significance of race or lineage, '*tainyindha*', or '*tainyindha-lumyo*' in official contexts, means a group that composes the nation state together with other groups. This term is also found in Burma Citizenship Law, issued in 1982. The third article of the law is as follows: 'Nationals [*naingandha*] such as the Kachin, Kayah, Karen, Chin, Bamar, Mon, Rahkine or Shan and ethnic groups [*tainyindha*] as have settled in any of the territories included within the State as their permanent home before 1185 B.E. (1823 A.D.) are Burma citizens,' (1823 AD was the previous year of the beginning of the First Burmese–British War).

The way the Bamar see the Shan is expressed by their ethnic identification. The Bamar tend to use the Shan suffix for only three groups: Hkamti Shan, Mao Shan and Goun Shan who live near Kengtung. Each group has maintained its identity and is usually recognized by others as an ethnic group. In contrast, when the Bamar use the Shan prefix as in Shan-Ni, Shan-Tayok, such identification reflects so much consciousness of Burmanized or Sinicized acculturation that the government does not register such groups as *tainyindha*. Otherwise relative standard names of native *möng* are used for identification. In this way a clear classification method seems to have been adopted by the Bamar for ethnic identification. In case of the Shan, the border between the Shan and the non-Shan was indistinct, at least until British annexation.

For a geographical perspective on Shan Pyi, two rivers are important: one is the Ayeyarwady and in particular its branches, the Shweli, the Chindwin and Myitnge, and the other is the Salween. Mao Shan, Hkamti Shan and Shan-Ni are connected through the Ayeyarwady and the Chindwin. Northern Shan State connects through the Myitnge diverging to the south of Mandalay. These river basins are connected to Mao Shan by foundation legends. Mogaung *saopha* has a genealogical relationship with Mao Shan, and Mohnyin and Momeik have similar legends. In contrast, the origin of *saopha* of the southern Shan States is said to be from Momeik in the northern states (Scott and Hardiman 1900–01: 203, 280–281). The Tai-Yai or Ngiaw in Mae Hong Son Province in Thailand live along a branch of the Salween.

Goun Shan or Tai-Khün residents in the east of Salween are said to have more intimate connection with northern Thailand and the Sipsonpanna of Yunnan Province of China. In Buddhist affairs, monks in the region recite the Pali traditional formula that begins *namo tassa*, as opposed to the *namo tatta* of the Bamar (Sai Kham Mong 2001: 36–37). It seems that the background is different from the cultural transfiguration that the people in the western area of Salween experienced.[10] Between these two rivers, there is the wide Shan Plateau, which was the centre of Shan Sawbwa in the British colonial period and has a more diverse ethnic population than other areas.

As mentioned before, the western area of the Salween has been called 'Kambawza' historically. It is probable that Shanization advanced mainly in this area through inter-ethnic negotiations. On the other hand, the Shan who migrated to Kachin State have been more Burmanized than those in Shan State. Therefore, the Shan in Shan State seem to have preserved their own culture. They must have adjusted to the environmental conditions of the Shan Plateau, through which the two rivers pass, as shown by the following episode. At the time of Union Day in 1972, a cultural troop of Tai-Mao from Kachin State was invited to dance, and they wore Bamar-style *phaso*. In 1974 another group from Myitkyina came to Hsipaw for friendship among the Shan, and they wore *phaso*, not Shan-styled trousers. An aged lady in Hsipaw remembered these and expressed her surprise at how different they were. It thus seems that not only language but also cultural customs had been changed by Burmanization.

It may be said that Burmanization was promoted in 'Kambawza' after independence and the end of the Sawbwa system in 1959. Since then central-ized Burmanization continues under the military regime.

NATIONAL CULTURE AND SHAN CULTURE

Nowadays not only the Shan but also other national races have begun to try to research, perform and preserve their own culture with permission from the government. As can be seen in the following official speech that was reported in a national newspaper, such activities must coincide with governmental policy. 'Not only the State, but also the national races themselves have permitted all the ethnic races to freely preserve their traditions and culture, religion and race, contributing to perpetual existence of the national solidarity and the Union' (*The New Light of Myanmar*, 19 December 2002).

On the other hand, Bamar culture is at the centre of the national culture conservation policy. 'Culture' translates into Bamar as '*yinkhiehmu*' and into Shan as '*fingngë*' or '*phingngë*', which are derived from the same origin. We often see the phrase 'Myanmar traditional culture' (*Myanmar yoya yinkheihmu*) in mass media under the authorities. A member of the Myanmar literature and language commission (*Myanmarsa Aphwe*) says that the term '*yinkheihmu*' was first translated from 'civilization' in the period of British rule. So the difference between 'culture' and 'civilization' expressed by *yinkheihmu* is obscure. The usage of *Myanmar yoya yinkheihmu* began after the independence and represents an enhancement of national heritage.

In 1962, *Amyodha Yinkheihmu Sazaung* [Magazine of national culture] was published. In it, U E Maung, Professor of the department of Bamar, University of Rangoon (Yangon), wrote an essay about national culture. His definition of it was *Myanmar ta-myolon Amyodha Yinkheihmu Mya*. '*Mya*' is a suffix that indicates plural. Thus, at least at that period, national culture seems to have been composed of multi-ethnic cultures. This definition was repeated in school textbooks until the 1980s. In the latter half of the 1980s, national culture appeared in the singular form in Bamar in parallel with the change of the state name from Burma to Myanmar. A traditional culture contest has been held once a year since 1993, but all the contestants have appeared to be well advised in the Bamar tradition Other ethnic groups have to research and preserve 'their own culture' under pressure from Burmanization.

Since 1970s, a festival concerned with Shan cultural heritage has taken place in northern Shan State. It is called '*pöy khu mö tai*' in Shan, or '*shan sahsodaw nei pwe*' in Bamar, meaning 'celebration of great Shan men of letters.' '*Pöy*' means festival and is derived from *pwe* of Bamar. '*Khu mö*' means a very learned person. The first *pöy khu mö tai* was planned at a meeting of the Taunggyi literary association in March 1968 and held in December of the same year in Taunggyi. In Bamar tradition, one of the annual rituals is *sahsodaw nei*, which means 'great men-of-letters' day'. That tradition can be historically traced to the latter half of the Konbaung dynasty, when U Ponnya Day was celebrated in memory of that great literary master (Aye Naing: 1980: 347). The modern *sahsodaw nei* took place in November 1944, for the first time, in honour of great men of letters in both

Figure 7.3. Opening ceremony of Shan New Year Festival celebrated in Hsipaw (Thibaw), December 2001. Shan people celebrated Shan New Year 2096 by Shan calendar (Photo: Takatani Michio)

ancient and modern periods. In April 1980 the first national conference of men of letters was held, and they formed their own association. On the day of *sahsodaw nei* the association paid respect to ten literary masters. Since then, this ceremony has become an annual one and national literary prizes are presented to great literary contributors.

Since the Shan people have their own 'great men of letters' on historical grounds, they adopted the idea in 1968. Nowadays the festivals are held more prosperously in northern Shan State, especially Kyaukme and Hsipaw located along the Burma–China Road, rather than in Taunggyi.

In the 1990s, Shan literary and cultural committees in some parts of Shan State began to act to preserve the Shan traditions and language with permission from the authorities concerned. That action means that schools for studying the Shan written language can be opened in the summer. Members of such associations are collecting Shan 'authentic' traditions and standardizing them. Though such associations had existed before at various social levels, it seems that a more organized one than before was needed to affirm the collective consciousness of Shan culture at that time.

For example, the committee in Kyaukme in northern Shan State has the following seven aims as follows:

(1) The continuation of various beliefs

(2) The preservation of old literary culture

(3) The fostering of Shan and other ethnic cultural heritage

(4) The safeguarding of each ethnic literary culture

(5) The promotion of friendship among ethnic groups, and mutual understanding of literary culture and customs

(6) The dissemination of Buddhist culture by national integration

(7) The education of outstanding students of the nation who will preserve both sacred Buddhist and secular wisdom.[11]

This association has standardized Shan annual rituals according to the Buddhist rites, though not all of them are held in every Shan village every year. A similar association in Shan State supports all Shan cultural heritage. In particular *pöy khu mö tai* is highlighted together with *pi maü tai* – Shan New Year. The latter combines with Shan cultural performance and has a shorter history than the former in Kyaukme and Hsipaw, but in Muse near the border with China, *pi maü tai* with Shan cultural activity has a longer history.[12]

For the Shan, 'religious' identity and 'ethnic' identity are inseparable. *Pöy khu mö tai* is a symbolic activity that represents both identities. Their literary tradition is regarded as essential and valuable, just like other ethnic groups', who have their own writing systems. Any association working for the preservation of ethnic cultural heritage is usually called a 'literary and cultural committee', *sapei hnin yinkhehmu comiti* in Bamar or *kö liklaay lë fingngë* in Shan. This shows how literary tradition is perceived as an important component of culture[13]. How the Shan view their written language relates to how they view their tradition. The continuity from their ancestors can be experienced through the medium of Buddhist written scriptures. Thus being Buddhist signifies not only an affirmation of Buddhist belief but also joining in Buddhist traditions.

CONCLUDING REMARKS

What is the future of Shanization under Myanmar centralization? The nation state is the dominating political form of our times. It implies a well-defined territory, a more or less homogenous population and some kind of representative government (Rothermund 1997: 13). Any national group that comprises a nation state usually learns the national language for the purpose of building a more modern nation state together with other ethnic groups. Once registration of an ethnic group is officially recognized by the government, any change of ethnic identity will meet with much more difficulty, and any performance of ethnic culture will tend to be planned according to ethnic boundaries at the time of registration. Though the movement for the preservation of Shan culture at the present time is trying to mobilize as many collaborators as possible, only sub-groups of Tai-speaking people are included, and non-Tai-speaking people influenced by Shan culture may not be invited: no cases where 'a Kachin becomes a Shan', as mentioned in Leach's ethnography, will occur. However, other cases where 'a Shan formally becomes a Bamar or Myanmar by national registration' may appear because of political reasons in spite of ethnic background.

Burmanization and Shanization seem to be as closely related to each other as the two sides of a coin. In a sense the Shan have been forced to preserve their 'authentic' culture, otherwise it will be seen only in written records. This may be called a crystallization of culture, for such a process tends to be done retrospectively and invent traditions. The Shan in Shan State have shouldered most of the responsibility. Recently a similarly motivated process has been taking place in Yangon, but almost all of those who have participated have a common lineage with the Shan in Shan State. These movements to preserve traditional Shan culture deserve careful analysis, and every ethnologist must take Shan construction and reconstruction of ethnic identity and discourse of Shan ethnicity into consideration.[14]

NOTES

[1] J. L. Lewis analysed 'Burmanization' of the Karen as his Ph.D. dissertation in 1924. He writes as follows: '[I]n general a Ka-ren (Karen) is considered Burmanized, when he uses the Burmese dress, speaks, more or less fluently the Burmese language, adopts Burmese customs, assumes many of the characteristic Burmese attitudes, and accepts the Burmese religion, Buddhism' (Lewis 1924: 2).

[2] Chao Tzang Yawnghwe regards a project to have Burmese Pali texts translated into Shan led by his father, Chao Shwe Thaike, who was the first president of the Union of Burma, as the move which 'Shan-ized' Buddhism (Tzang Yawnghwe 1987: 7, 230–232).

[3] In this chapter Shan scripts are basically romanized by Shintani's system except place names and some words like *saopha,, tai and möng* because of customary

usage (Shintani and Caw Caay Hän Maü 2000). Marks of tones are omitted. Bamar scripts are basically romanized by customary usage.

[4] 'Tai-Lei' is a different term from 'Tai-Lue' for the people living in Sipsonpanna, Yunan Province, China, and northern Thailand.

[5] Hkamti Shans, Chinese Shans and Burmese Shans are mentioned (Lebar *et al.* 1964). Such a classification can be misleading.

[6] The author does not so much intend to research the identification of 'nine *möng*', but rather wishes to clarify what 'nine *möng*' signified and signifies for Burmanization and Shanization of the Shan.

[7] Shan historian, U Sai Aung Tun says that the name of 'Kokang' who are registered as a national race, is derived from their nine lands, and that they were subordinate to Hsenwi *saopha*.

[8] They are Shan, Yun/Lao, Kwi, Phyin, Thao, Sanaw, Palei, In, Soun/Hsan, Hkamu, Kaw/Ahka/Ikaw, Kokang, Hkamti-Shan, Goun/Hkun, Taungyou, Danu, Palaung, Myaungyi, Yinkya, Yinnek, Shan-Kalei, Shan-Gyi, Lahu, Lwela, Intha, Aiktwe, Pao/Taungthu, Tai-Lwe, Tai-Lieng, Tai-Long, Tai-Lei, Maing-tha- and Mao-Shan. U Min Naing, who is a famous ethnologist there, explains that these 33 names were self-declared, so we can see some contradictions: for example Shan-Gyi and Tai-Long are inter-changeable but classified separately.

[9] In the case of Bhamo District, 32.2 per cent of the Tai group speak a language of the Burma group and 18.9 per cent of the Burma group speak a language of the Tai group. Bhamo is near the border between present Kachin State and Shan State.

[10] Whether the Tai-Khün belong to Tai-Long or not is controversial. It is a historical fact that they decided to remain in the federation of Shan States in 1947 (FACE 1947: 2–22) and have been incorporated into Shan State. Rujaya writes that it was in the interest of the British to keep the two categories, Shan (in Burma) and Tai (Tai-language-speaking people except Shan), completely separate (Rujaya 2000: 197). If the term 'Tai-Long' came to be used among the Shan in the process of invention and promotion of the new Shan scripts in the 1950s, Tai-Khün's position cannot but be ambiguous, for they have their own scripts that are similar to those of northern Thailand and Sipsonpanna, and Tai-Khün tend to identify themselves with them.

[11] The Lashio Shan literary and cultural committee has five aims: (1) friendship and intimate relationship among the members, (2) continuation and preservation of literature and culture, (3) fostering of literary and cultural heritage, (4) mutual assistance in happiness and unhappiness and (5) non-political activity. The last one shows the situation such an organization faces.

[12] See Takatani 2003.

[13] In 1985 the People's Council of Shan State legally recognized that the new Shan scripts could be used in schools and administrative offices. However, its practice always needs political negotiation in order not to conflict with governmental policy.

[14] The author has requested that some Shan academics comment on this paper. The discussion and exchange of viewpoints about 'Who are the Shan?' is on-going.

Chapter 8

CHRISTIANITY AND CHIN IDENTITY

Lian H. Sakhong

INTRODUCTION

In 1999 when the Chin people in Burma celebrated the centennial anniversary of the arrival of Christianity, more than 80 per cent of the Chin population proclaimed their faith in Jesus Christ. In West Chinram of Mizoram State in India, the church growth has been even faster and Christian life was more vigorous than in the Chin State of Burma. This means that within the time span of mere a century, almost the entire Chin population has accepted the Christian faith, and the church is deeply rooted in the socio-cultural tradition of the people.[1] Such unusually fast growth of Christianity on both sides of Chinram during the twentieth century and the vitality of its practice, or what Chin theologian Mangkhosat Kipgen called 'a uniquely *Chin* form of Christianity', and a link between indigenization of Christianity and the rapid growth of the church in Chinram are the factors that I intend to explain theoretically in this chapter. In doing this, I shall argue that a link between indigenization and the growth of Christianity was one of the reasons why Christianity could provide the Chin people with a means of preserving their identity and promoting their interests in the face of the powerful forces of change.

Christianity was brought to East Chinram largely by the American Baptist Mission. There have also been significant indigenous Chin missions, more notably the Chins for Christ in One Century (CCOC). I have argued elsewhere that the growth of Christianity in East Chinram during the first five decades of the twentieth century was based on the contribution of at

200

least three factors: (1) the socio-political change represented by the British colonial power, (2) the missionary factor (both foreign and indigenous), and (3) the theological similarity between Christianity and traditional Chin religion, which meant that conversion was not a radical change but a religious transformation from *Khua-hrum*-oriented ritual practices to a *Khua-zing*oriented worship service within the same conceptual pattern of belief system.[2]

This chapter is divided into three parts. The first part deals with the search for *Chin Ethnicity,* and the second part explains the links of socio-cultural change with the formation of a new ethnic identity, and in the third part, I shall to explore the theological continuity between the traditional Chin religion and Christianity, which served as a means of preserving the Chin ethnic identity in the midst of multi-ethnic, multi-religious, and multi-cultural contexts of the modern nation state of the Union of Burma.

THE CHIN ETHNICITY: DEFINING THE COLLECTIVE NAME OF 'CHIN'

First, by applying a comprehensive approach of ethno-symbolic theory, Ishall investigate who the Chins are. Why can they be described as a separate ethnic group? What are the main features that distinguish the Chin as separate ethnic nationality from other human collectives or ethnic groups? And what criteria make it possible for them to be recognized as a distinctive people and nationality in Burma? I shall not limit myself to any single theory of either 'primordialism' or 'circumstantialism' but apply both theories when they are deemed to be appropriate as I explain the ethnicity of the Chin.

Anthropologists such as A. D. Smith suggest that there are six main features, which serve to define 'ethnic nationality'. These are:

(1)   a common proper name
(2)   a myth of common descent
(3)   a link with a homeland
(4)   collective historical memories
(5)   one or more elements of common culture, and
(6)   a sense of solidarity.[3]

A causal link between 'ethnicity' and the formation of an 'independent homeland' or 'Autonomous State within the Union', which the Chin and other non-Burman nationalities in the Union of Burma today are fighting so hard for, is the search for what Clifford Geertz called 'primordial identities', that is, the search in the past to find evidence of the existence of 'collective memories, symbols, values and myths, which so often define and differentiate' the Chin as a distinctive people and nationality throughout history.[4]

My first argument, therefore, will be that the word 'Chin' is not a foreign acquisition but Chin in its origin, coming from the root word '*Chin-lung*'. According to the myth of origin, the Chin people emerged into this world from the bowels of the earth or a cave or a rock called '*Chin-lung*'[5], which is spelled slightly differently by different scholars using various Chin dialects and local traditions: e.g. '*Chhinlung*', '*Chinn-lung*', '*Chie'nlung*', '*Chinglung*', '*Ciinlung*', '*Jinlung*', '*Sinlung*', '*Shinlung*', '*Tsinlung*', and so on.

The tradition of *Chin-lung* as the origin of the Chin has been kept by all tribes of the Chin in various ways, such as folksongs, folklore and legends known in Chin as *Tuanbia*. For people who had no writing system of their own, a rich oral tradition consisting of folksong and folklore was the most reliable means of transmitting past events and collective memories through time. The songs were sung repeatedly during all kinds of feasts and festivals, and the tales that made up Chin folklore were told and retold over the generations. In this way, such collective memories as the myth of origin and the myth of common ancestors were handed down from one generation to the next.

Different tribes and groups of Chin kept the tradition of '*Chin-lung*' in several versions; the Ralte clan/group of the Mizo tribe, also known as the Lushai, who are now living in the Mizoram State in India, have had a tradition of what is now generally known as 'Chinlung tradition' that brings their progenitors from the bowels of the earth. The story was translated into English and recorded by Lt Col. J. Shakespeare in 1912 as follows:

[Once upon a time when the great darkness (Thimzing) fell upon the world,] many awful things happened. Everything except the skulls of animals killed in the chase became alive, dry wood revived, even stones become alive and produced leaves, so men had nothing to burn. The successful hunters who had accumulated large stocks of trophies of their skill were able to live using them as fuel.

After this terrible catastrophe [called] *Thimzing*, the world was again re-peopled by men and women issuing from the hole of the earth called *Chin-lung.*[6]

Shakespeare described another similar story:

> The place whence all people sprang is called *Chin-lung*. All the clans came out of that place. The two Ralte came out together, and began at once chattering, and this made Pathian [The Supreme God] think there were too many men, and so he shut down the stone.[7]

Modern scholars generally agree with the traditional account of the origin of the name '*Chin*' and that the word comes from '*Chin-lung*'. Hrang Nawl, one of the most prominent scholars and politicians among the Chin, confirms that the term 'Chin ... come(s) from Ciinlung, Chhinlung or Tsinlung, the cave or the rock where, according to legend, the *Chin* people emerged into this world as humans'.[8] The 'Chinlung' tradition of the origin of the Chin was also corroborated by such Chin scholars from the Indian side of Chinram as T. S. Gangte, K. Zawla and Mangkhosat Kipgen. They all reiterate that the Chin 'came out of the bowels of the earth or a cave called *Chinlung* or *Sinlung*'.[9] Vumson also confirmed the tradition that the Chin 'were originally from a cave called *Chinnlung*, which is given different locations by different clans'.[10]

The literal meaning of *Chin-lung* is 'the cave or the hole of the Chin', and this has the same meaning as the Burmese word for *Chindwin* as in the 'Chindwin River', that also is – 'the hole of the Chin' or 'the river of the Chin'.[11] However, the word *Chin-lung* can also be translated as 'the cave or the hole where our people originally lived' or 'the place from which our ancestors originated'.[12] Thus, the word *Chin* without the suffix *lung* is translated simply as 'people' or 'a community of people'. A Chin scholar, Lian Uk, therefore defines the term *Chin* as follows: 'The Chin and several of its synonymous names generally means 'People' and the name Chinram is generally translated as 'Our Land' reflecting the strong fundamental relationship they maintain with their land.'[13]

Similarly, Carey and Tuck, who were the first to bring the Chin people under the system of British administration, defined the word 'Chin' as 'man or people'. They recorded that the term 'Chin' is 'the Burmese corruption of the Chinese "Jin" or "Jen" meaning "man or people"'.[14]

Evidently, the word 'Chin' had been used from the very beginning not only by the Chin themselves but also by their neighbouring peoples, such as Kachin, Shan and Burman, to denote the people who occupied the valley of the Chindwin River. While the Kachin and the Shan still called the Chin 'Khyan', 'Khiang' or 'Chiang', the Burmese usage seems to have changed dramatically from 'Khyan' (cᵗif;) to 'Chin' (csif;).[15] In a couple of stone inscriptions, erected by King Kyanzittha (1084–1113), the name 'Chin' is spelled 'Khyan' (cᵗif;).[16] As far as historical and linguistic records are concerned, these stone inscriptions are the strongest evidence indicating that the name *Chin* was in use before the eleventh century AD.

Prior to the British annexation in 1896, there were 17 written records in English regarding research on what was then called the 'Chin-Kuki linguistic people'. These early writings variously referred to what is now called and spelled, 'Chin', as 'Khycng', 'Khang', 'Khlang', 'Khyang', 'Khyan', 'Kiayn', 'Chiang', 'Chi'en', 'Chien', and so on. One of the earliest Western writers to note the existence of the hill tribes of Chin in the western mountains of Burma was Father Sangermano, who lived in Burma as a Catholic missionary from 1783 to 1796. In his now classic book *The Burmese Empire* – published one hundred years after his death in1833 – he spelled the name Chin as 'Chie' and the Chin Hills as the 'Chein Mountains'. He thus recorded: 'To the east of Chein Mountain between 20"30' and 21"30' latitude is a petty nation called 'Jo' [Yaw]. They are supposed to have been Chien, who in the progress of time, have become Burmanized, speaking their language, although corruptly, and adopting their customs'.[17]

In Assam and Bengal, the Chin tribes – particularly the Zomi tribe who live close to that area – were known as 'Kuki'. The Bengali word for *Kuki* means 'hill-people or highlanders', which was, as Reid described in 1893:

> [O]riginally applied to the tribe or tribes occupying the tracks immediately to the south of Cachar[,i]t is now employed in a comprehensive sense, to indicate those living to the west of the Kaladyne River, while to the west they are designated as Shendus. On the other hand, to anyone approaching them from Burma side, the Shendus would be known as Chiang, synonymous with Khyen, and pronounced as 'Chin'.[18]

Shakespeare, who was one of the authorities on the Chin, said in 1912:

> The term Kuki has come to have a fairly definite meaning, and we now understand by it certain ... clans, with all marked characteristics, belonging to the Tibeto-Burman stock. On the Chittagong border, the term is loosely applied to most of the inhabitants of the interior hills beyond the Chittagong Hills Tracks; in the Cachar its generally means some families of the Thado and Khuathlang clans, locally distinguished as new Kuki and old Kuki. Now-a-days, the term is hardly employed, having been superseded by Lushai in Chin Hills, and generally on the Burma border all these clans are called Chin.

These Kuki are more closely allied to the Chakmas, and the Lushai are more closely to their eastern neighbours who are known as Chin.

And he concluded: 'Nevertheless, there is no doubt that the Kukis, Lushais and Chins are all of the same race.'[19]

In 1826, almost one hundred years before Shakespeare published his book, Major Snodgrass, who contacted the Chin people from the Burma side, had already confirmed that Kukis and Lushai are of the Chin nation, but he spelled Chin as 'Kiayn'. He also mentioned Chinram as 'Independent Kiayn Country',[20] in his *The Burmese War*, in which he described a detailed account of the First Anglo–Burmese War in 1824–26. Sir Author Phayer still spelt Chindwin as 'Khyendweng' in his *History of Burma*, first published in 1883.[21] It was in 1891 that the term 'Chin', written as 'CHIN', was first used by Major W.G. Hughes in his military report, and then by A.G.E. Newland in his book *The Images of War*[22] and the conventional spelling for the name became legalized as the official term by The Chin Hills Regulation in 1896.

As far as historical evidence is concerned, the Chin were known by no other name than CHIN, before they made their settlement in the present hilly region in Chinram. However, after they were expelled from their original homeland, the Kale Valley in Upper Chindwin, by a flood as oral traditions recount it – or conquered by the Shan as modern scholars have suggested – the Chin split into different tribal groups speaking different dialects, with different tribal names.[23]

According to the *Linguistic Survey of India* in 1904, the Chin dialects are linguistically divided into four major groups as the northern, the central, the old Kuki, and the southern.

(1) The northern group: Thado, Kamhau, Sokte (Sukte), Siyin (Sizang), Ralte, and Paite.

(2) The central group: Tashon (Tlaisun), Lai, Lakher (Mara), Lushai (Mizo), Bangjogi (Bawmzo), and Pankhu.

(3) The old-Kuki group: Rangkhol, Kolren, Kom, Purum, Hmar, Cha (Chakma).

(4) The southern group: Chin-me, Chin-bok, Chin-pun, Khyang (Asho), M'ro (Khuami), Shendus (Yindu), and Welaung.[24]

Scholars generally agree that there are six major tribal groups of the Chin, namely the (1) Asho, (2) Chó or Sho, (3) Khuami or M'ro, (4) Laimi, (5) Mizo (Lushai) and (6) Zomi.[25]

SOCIO-CULTURAL CHANGE

Prior to British annexation in 1896, the Chins were independent people ruled by their own traditional tribal and local chiefs called '*Ram-uk*' and '*Khua-bawi*', respectively. Surrounding kingdoms like Burman or Myanmar, Bengal and Assam (India) never conquered the Chin people and their land, Chinram. As a result, Buddhism, Muslim and Hinduism never reached the Chin. The Chin traditional religion was the only social manifestation of people's faith, which bound the community together. Although all the tribes and villages followed the same pattern of belief systems, the ritual practices in traditional Chin religion – called '*Khua-hrum*' worship – were very much mutually exclusive, and could not serve to unite the entire Chin people under a single religious institution. Thus, until the British occupation, the Chin society remained a tribal society and the people's identification with each other was tribally exclusive; the formation of a common national identity remained to be researched.

By the turn of the twentieth century, however, Chin society was abruptly transformed by powerful outside forces of change. The British conquered Chinram, and the Christian missionaries followed the colonial powers and converted the people. Within this process of change, the Chin people found themselves in the midst of multi-ethnic and multi-religious environments, which they did not welcome. They also realized that their country was not the central of the universe but a very small part of a very big British Empire. After the colonial period, they found themselves again being separated into three different countries – India, Burma, and Bangladesh – without their consent. While west Chinram of present Mizoram State became part of India, east Chinram of present Chin State joined the Union of Burma according to the Panglong Agreement signed in 1947. The smaller part of Chinram became part of what was then called East Pakistan, i.e., present Bangladesh.

The primary agent of change, in my hypothesis, were the modern political systems represented by British colonial power and its successors – i.e., independent India and Burma. The political development, of course, was the only agent with the necessary power to force change. In tribal society, 'distinction cannot easily be made between religious, social, cultural and political elements'.[26] Anything that affects one aspect of life can strongly affect every aspect of life. In fact, 'tribal society can only be maintained through traditional instruments of integration, if they remain in fundamental isolation from other societies'.[27] When centuries-old isolationism in Chinram was broken up by the British colonial power, the traditional way of maintaining the tribal group's identity was no longer effective, and the process of de-tribalization had begun.

This could be a dangerous moment because it could either become what Frederick Downs called the process of 'dehumanization',[28] or a process of what Swedish scholar Eric Ringmar called a 'formative moment'.[29] If it became that of dehumanization, i.e., 'to rob them of their essential life' of the 'people's soul', as Down puts it, then the existence of tribal peoples could really be endangered. There are many examples, according to Dawns, in the Americas, Africa, other parts of Asia and India where many tribal peoples have ceased to exist.[30] On the other hand, the process of detribalization could become a 'formative moment' if the people could find any other alternative, instead of seeking "to revitalize the old culture".[31]

In my hypothesis, the process of detribalization in Chin society became a process of 'formative moment', that is – at a time in which new meaning became available and people suddenly were able to identify themselves with something meaningful. It was Christianity, which provided the Chin people with the new meanings and symbols within this process of 'formative moment', but without 'a complete break with the past'.[32] I shall, therefore, explore how Christianity helped the Chin people – no longer as divided tribal groups, but as the entire nationality of Chin ethnicity – to maintain their identity, and how Christianity itself became a new creative force of national identity for the Chin people within this 'formative' process of powerful changes.

THE GOSPEL AND A NEW SOCIETY

Conversion to Christianity was not a single event but a long and gradual process of adjustment to the demands of the new faith as opposed to the old ritual habits, and also for the necessities of life. These adjustments to the new life always began with the abandonment of all the ritual systems connected with their traditional religion of *Khua-hrum* worship. The abandonment of old ritual systems included not only the sacrificial ceremonies but also many kinds of feasts and festivals which were regarded as practices of the 'old life', what the Chin called *Lai phung*. Moreover, all the converts were expected to stop the practice of polygamy and the consumption of intoxicants, *Zu le Zuhui*.

The missionaries also encouraged the early Chin Christians to separate the 'new ways of life', i.e., *Krifa Phung* (Christian ways of life), from the 'old ways of life', *Lai Phung* (the traditional Chin ways of life), and they portrayed the 'old life' as sinful in nature and full of unhappiness and permanent unrest, while the 'new life' was brightly coloured and full of happiness and peace. Thus, when people converted to Christianity they located themselves in the 'new life' and conceived their identity in terms opposing the old *Lai Phung* to the new *Krifa Phung*. It was due to the fact that nineteenth-century evangelicalism represented by nearly all the Protestant missionaries, including the American Baptist Chin mission, 'placed emphasis upon Christianity as a way of life, a lifestyle'. For them, 'doctrine was important but meaningless if not associated with a transformed life'. Thus, as Frederick Downs observes, 'the idea of becoming a Christian meant adopting a new mode of life'.[33] In this way, conversion to Christianity and the adoption of new ways of life were inseparably linked to each other.

Within this long process of adjustment, at least three new forms of imagining the social world appeared – Sunday worship services, singing from the same hymnbooks, and reading the Holy Bible.[34] In fact, these three characteristics of the social world were related to their new ritual systems in Christianity and the expectation of salvation in Christ's life after death in *Mithi-khua*. The observation of the Sabbath, Sunday, was the very first step the Chin Christians took to 'imagine' themselves as 'living lives simultaneous with other lives in an homogenous time', measured not only by Biblical teaching about the Holy Sabbath (Gen. 2: 2, and Exod. 20: 8), but also by modern clocks and calendars. It was novel yet effective and meaningful for the Chin Christians to create an 'imaginary community' beyond their clan and tribal boundaries. As they observed Sunday, they also practised the same rituals of singing from the same hymn- books and reading the same Bible everywhere in Chinram. Whether they sung hymns or read the Holy Bible, congregations at the Sunday service knew that they were singing and reading what many other believers were singing and reading at the same time with the same hope and faith they had in one God. Thus, the observation of Sunday services, singing from the same hymnbooks, and reading the same Holy Bible gradually became the most powerful sources for the creation of an 'imaginary community', and thereby the creation of a common national identity for all the Chin Christians.[35]

NEW RITUALS AND PHENOMENA IN CHIN SOCIETY

The moment of conversion was not the end of the story but the beginning of a long process of adjustment to the demands of a new faith in relation to the ritual habits of traditional religion it supplanted. In this long process of adjustment, the adoption of a new faith and new identity was marked by some sort of ritual. The most observable phenomenon for the converts among the Chin was what we call in Chin '*inn-thianh*', that is, 'cleansing the house'. The *inn-thianh* ritual was the first observable phenomenon of conversion and was usually followed by baptism.

The procedure of the *inn-thianh* ritual is almost the same everywhere in Chinram. I shall quote from the eyewitness account of Dr East, reported in 1910. He described 'cleansing house' in the Tiddim area as follows:

Mr. Cope and I were now in Tang Nu Kwa [Thangnuai village] by invitation. We were called there by people, as seven families have accepted 'the new way' and have asked us to help them break down the altars and all emblems of evil spirit worship, to remove all heads of animals sacrificed and all bamboo resting places for evil spirits. This is quite a job as there are many altars and many skulls, sometimes numbering fifty to a hundred, and as we have to take the initiative in order to embolden the people to touch things formerly held sacred and to help us in this most destructive breaking down of spiritualism and building up of Christianity. It took us from about 2 P.M. until the lengthening of the shadows.

The last house we sanctified to God belonged to an old couple, and when all emblems had been taken out and readied to be burned, the old man asked, 'Will I dare to sleep in this house tonight since the spirits are not here to protect us and they have no resting place?' We then knelt and I placed my hands upon their heads and prayed that Jehovah God should now and thereafter dwell with them to protect them against sickness and all harms. Now they were ready to go back into the house and were not afraid, as God was greater than the evil sprits.

Dr East concluded his letter to his wife:

209

My dear, it is not an easy thing to break loose from an age-old custom and imprinted beliefs. Man's heart is hungry for atonement. Man's heart is seeking a resting place. Man's heart is only satisfied when it knows that it is protected by one stronger than himself. And so a tremendous struggle takes place in the hearts and minds of these people when they awaken from age-long ignorance and face God.[36]

When the Chin converted to Christianity, they wanted to abandon their traditional ways of life. This was also encouraged by missionaries. Their traditional religion, after all, was inseparably linked with every aspect of life. In Chin traditional concept, a house was not just a home for people; it was also an abode for the household god called '*chung-um*'. Thus, when they wanted to become Christians, the first thing the Chins needed to do was to let their guardian god leave the house. In order to do this, they needed to clean their houses and destroy the altars called '*Kho le Kheng*'. That was the reason people used to say '*Kho le Kheng kan thlak cang*' when they became Christians.

For many able-bodied people, destroying *kho le kheng* was not enough. They even rebuilt their houses completely and usually changed the architectural style as well. Thus, most of the Christian houses are not in the traditional long-house style, but resemble the house Dr East built in Haka. They also usually shifted away from their old house sites when they became Christians for they knew that the sites themselves were associated too much with their guardian god. When a whole village became Christian, they even moved off their old village site, which was inseparably linked with the village guardian god, *Tual Khua-hrum*. In the new village, the church was at the heart of the community instead of the *Tual* or *Tlenlai Lung* that had been the communal sacrificial stone or altar.

From the traditionalist point of view, this new phenomenon of the *inn-thianh* ritual was a painful memory of the destruction of centuries-old institutions of Chin society. Today the Chin people view this painful memory from a different perspective. They now remember those stories as a symbolic departure from the 'old ways' (in Chin *Laiphung* or *chan hlun*) and portray the epoch as an abrupt juncture, a fold in the course of social history marked by sharp changes in the ethos of everyday life. In a nutshell, these new phenomena or rituals such as *inn-thianh* and baptism, which are part of the conversion process, are the key social and ritual activities through which the transformation of identities and communities are accomplished.

FINDING COMMON GROUND AND COMMON KNOWLEDGE

The views of the first missionary couple, Arthur and Laura Carson, on traditional Chin religion, culture, and custom were completely negative. Thus, Arthur Carson would write bluntly that 'the Chin had no word for God, grace, mercy, forgiveness', or even 'love'. Mrs Carson also wrote that 'sacrificing to evil spirits' was 'their only religion and system of medicine'.[37] They passed, as Johnson points out, 'this attitude along to young Dr East' and other missionaries. The reason, according to Johnson, is that 'when Laura and Arthur Carson first came to the Chin Hills, they were so struck by the backwardness of the people that they overreacted'.[38]

Dr East seemed to have changed his view after staying nine years in Chinram and travelling widely among many tribes of the Chin. In 1909, he met 'a man over one hundred years old' at Roshi in the Falam area. He mentioned this old man in his letter, and that he would not be surprised 'if he was even older' than one hundred years. This old man told him about the origin of the Chin and also the story of *Pa Lo Tuanbia*, which Dr East translated as 'The Story of Fatherless', and other myths and legends. Here I would like to relate the story of *Pa Lo Tuanbia*, which was recorded by Pu Sakhong of Aibur.

> Once upon a time, a young lady who was still a virgin was collecting firewood far away from her village. On her way home, she found a fruit called *Khuhlu* on the village sacrificial stone called *Tlenlailung*. Without thinking much about the consequences, she just picked up the fruit and ate it because she was so thirsty from working the whole day under the hot sun. However, the fruit was not just ordinary fruit, since it had been left there by *Khua-zing*, the Supreme God. Moreover, *Khua-zing* had mixed His own fluid with the juice of the fruit, for *Khuhlu* was a very juicy fruit. So the young lady conceived without knowing a man and gave birth to a baby boy. Since she was unmarried, the baby was simply named Pa Lo, meaning 'Fatherless'. Pa Lo was extraordinarily strong and handsome. When he grew old enough, he asked his mother who his father was, where he lived, and so on. His mother told him that his father lived in heaven without mentioning His name. Their conversation was overheard by God from heaven. God had another son in heaven. So he sent his son in heaven to visit his younger brother on earth. Pa Lo's brother from heaven did not stay long on earth, but during his short stay he made all kinds of domestic animals out of clay, and then he turned them all to living animals. In this way, Pa Lo became the richest man in the world and performed all kinds of feasts and festivals such as *Bawite-bawi* and *Khuang-cawi*.[39]

Dr East was also told the story of Theizam, which is similar to the biblical story of the Tower of Babel and the story of Ngun Nu, a parallel to the biblical story of the Flood. Thus, he wrote on 4 February, 1909:

> To me it seems that the easiest way of getting into their hearts is to meet them where we have common ground and common knowledge. I was led to believe that these people had no knowledge of God, no word for love, and no word for heaven. However, I could not accept that idea as I very thoroughly believe in racial unity and that 'God made all men out of one blood', and it is therefore unreasonable to believe that any part of that race should be absolutely destitute of all knowledge of the Creator. It is a certainty that the wild Chins believe in the God of Heaven as Creator. This knowledge is universal among them.[40]

From the Chin's point of view, however, the most attractive common ground and common knowledge between their own traditional religion and Christianity consisted not only of stories such as the ones about the Tower of Babel, the Flood, the Virgin Mary and Pa Lo, as Dr East pointed out, but also the theological similarity between the traditional Chin religious teaching of life after death in *Mithi-khua* and the biblical teaching of heaven or paradise. Among missionaries, however, only Dr Strait applied this similar theological concept of eschatology in his ministry after Dr East left the field. As a matter of fact, Dr Strait did the first scholarly work on traditional Chin religion for his doctoral dissertation, *A History and Interpretation of Chin Sacrifice*, in 1933. His knowledge of traditional Chin religion helped not only in his ministry of preaching the Gospel but also when he translated the Bible and hymns. He could apply the idioms and concepts of the Supreme God and life after death in *Mithi-khua* to help the Chin find common ground.

In the Chin traditional religious concept, there was no problem in reaching heaven after death, for their religion taught them that one must surely reach heaven if one died an ordinary death. The problems concerning heaven, which bothered the Chin most, were: 'Are we going to be rich or poor? What kind of house are we are going to live in?' According to traditional Chin religious teaching, the house they built here on earth was the image of the house in their future life in *Mithi-khua*. If one could build a very big and good house here on earth, then one would surely have a very big and good house in the future life. But now the Chins were told by Christian missionaries that if they became Christians they would have a very big and good house glittering with silver and gold, a house prepared for them by God Himself. They did not need to build homes on earth for life in heaven, they were told, but they must abandon their own traditional way of life to become Christian! And they were told that if they did become Christians, their homes in heaven would be like the missionary house in Haka built by Dr East in 1907. Such concrete examples and promises were most attractive to the first generation of Chin Christians. Thus, for the first and second generation Chin Christians, one of the most popular hymns translated by Dr Strait was:

> *Ni nak in a ceu khua a um ko,*
> *Zumnak in a hnu ah kan hmuh lai,*
> *Khi khin kanmah kanpa hngak len ko,*
> *Kannih umnak a ser lio dah ngai.*
>
> (There is a place brighter than the sun,
> And we will reach it by faith,
> Our Father is preparing a house for us,
> That is glittering as silver and gold).[41]

Second, the most attractive Christian teaching for the Chin was the substitute death of Christ. According to traditional Chin religious teaching, if one died an accidental or violent death, their soul must go to *Sarthi-khua*. No soul can be redeemed from *Sarthi-khua* except with a substitute violent death, that is, revenge for his or her death. To illustrate my point here, I would like to relate a story of an accident that took place in the early 1950s, in Leitak in the Zophei area.

Leitak was the principal village of the Zophei area and used to be ruled by a very powerful chief, Mang Hnin of the Hlawn Ceu clan. When Mang Hnin died, he had only one son by his principal wife, *Nutak.* This son was to inherit his power and wealth although he had many more sons from his minor wives, called *Nuchun.* Unfortunately, a son of a former slave of Mang Hnin accidentally killed Lian Hei, the heir of Mang Hnin's house. According to the traditional Chin religious belief of *Laiphung*, Lian Hei would become the slave of his slayer, no matter who he was. For his mother, Pi Khuang Cin, it was completely unacceptable that her beloved son, the heir of Mang Hnin, would become the slave of her own former household slave. Thus, Pi Khuang Cin, Regent of Mang Hnin's house, gathered together all her relatives from far and near and ordered them to take revenge on her son's death. At that time the government strongly prohibited such action, but Pi Khuang Cin was determined to take revenge no matter what. She was ready to make war if the government of newly-independent Burma intervened in any way.

On that occasion, Pu Sa Khawng, who was married to Lian Hei's elder sister, convinced Pi Khuang Cin that revenge had already been taken for Lian Hei, for he was a Christian. Lian Hei had converted when he was in mission high school at Insein near Rangoon where his uncle, Lt Tial Khuai, served in the Chin Hills Battalion of the British-turned-Burmese army. Pi Khuang Cin asked who had taken that revenge for his son, and she was then told about the substitute death of Jesus Christ on the cross. Pi Khuang Cin was convinced because Jesus was crucified but she would not have been convinced if Jesus had died an ordinary death, for she knew according to her religious teaching that only a violent death could substitute for her son's death. Thus, she was converted and baptized by Rev. Heng Cin, who was once expelled from Leitak by Pi Khuang Cin's late husband.[42] In this way, the theological similarity between traditional Chin religion and Christianity, especially the substitute death of Christ, opened the doors for the conversion of the Chin people – even for people who were the heads of the Chins' religious and political institutions like Pi Khuang Cin.

GRADUAL ADJUSTMENT TO THE NEW WAYS OF LIFE

In this section, I shall discuss how Christianity helped the Chin people not only to adjust to the change thrust upon them, but to create a new society based on the Gospel, and how Christianity provided a means of promoting the self-awareness of the Chin through its ideology and ecclesiastical structures.

The formation of a new ecclesiastical structure

Although the Chin professed the same religious doctrine and belief system before they became Christians, their ritual practices, which centred upon the sacrificial worship of *Khua-hrum*, divided them into many groups of clans and tribes. When they gradually became Christians, however, the Chin people were not only provided with the same religious doctrine and belief system but also with a single ecclesiastical structure where all the tribes and clans of the Chin could join as members of a single community of believers. Thus, one of the most significant things that the new religion provided was the formation of the 'Chin Hills Baptist Association' (CHBA) at Haka in March 1907. Officially, the CHBA was formed by the election of its executive committee during a meeting of the representatives of the young churches and individual Christians, most of them new converts who attended the meeting in order to receive baptism. 'From a worldly standpoint', Johnson observes, 'it was not a very important matter – just thirty-four people gathered to effect a little organization to bind scattered believers' in Chinram. But 'this was the tiny seed that later grew into today's Chin Baptist Convention, one of the largest church groups in Burma.'[43]

In 'Baptist polity', Johnson explains, 'an association brings together Baptist churches, not individuals, into an organization for fellowship. It is not an authority over churches, but provides a forum for the discussion of issues, for encouragement in the faith and acts as a body to advise churches on ordination.'[44] At that time in Chinram, however, there were very few organized churches and only a group of believers scattered in six or seven villages. Thus, the significance of the formation of the CHBA was that it was a 'binding medium' for these new and often weak Christians. Since the CHBA functioned as a binding medium throughout East Chinram, it could hold and unite all the Chin Christians who came from many different tribes and clans within a single community of faith. It meant that, unlike their old religious institution of *Khua-hrum*, the CHBA could accept people from different tribes and clans as believers of the same faith within a single ecclesiastical structure. In joining the CHBA, the Chin people were therefore encouraged to seek their self-awareness and national identity of Chin-ness through membership in a new Christian community. To put it another way, when they became Christians and joined the CHBA, the meanings and values of tribal and clan affiliation based on their traditional religion of *Khua-hrum* worship, which had been so effective in the Chin's resistance against the British, lost its strength. Thus, the national identity of Chin-ness gradually surpassed the meaning and effectiveness of clan and tribal identity.

From the very moment of its formation, the CHBA even challenged the notion of tribal identity, and 'racism begins to break down', as Johnson put it. As mentioned, no Chin would allow the presence of a stranger from another tribe at any kind of traditional religious ceremony. But the Christians in Haka now welcomed strangers from other tribes – especially the Zomi tribe from the Sizang and Kamhau groups in the Tiddim area – to take part in their new religious ceremonies as their own brothers and sisterst. This event was very significant in Chin history. Johnson observes:

The Hakas were used to calling the Sizang and Kamhau by the appellation 'Thaute', a derogatory term, and could not understand how Christians could accept these Thautes as brothers. The superstition that the Tiddim area people possessed the power of the 'evil eye' was still strong, and so the Hakas tended to shun them.[45]

Recognizing the effect of this event, the missionaries and Chin Christians not only held an Association Meeting as a recurring annual religious ceremony and festival; they also routinely shifted it from one place to another. In this way, the Association Meeting, also known in Chin as *Civui*, eventually became one of the most important religious activities for the Chin Christians and the best-known religious festival in Chinram. At the *Civui*, different tribes and clans of Chins who formerly had never shared any kind of religious ceremony could now freely share their inner feelings and experiences in one faith, and also the same ritual practices, such as attending the same worship service, singing from the same hymn book, reading the same Bible, etc. And the *Civui* itself therefore constituted one of the identity-shaping sources which not only provided for the individuals' epistemological characteristics, i.e. their beliefs and basic values, but also catered to interpersonal relationships and brought about a sense of total solidarity between an individual and a fellow Christians who, in turn, shared the same ethnic nationality. Thus, the formation of the CHBA gradually provided the Chin people not only with a single ecclesiastical structure but also its related religious festival called *Civui*, both constituting sources for the creation of their national identity in a new society, Christian Chinram. Moreover, these new religious institutions also transformed Chin society gradually from a 'tribal and clan-oriented society' to the 'community of faith' in Jesus Christ.

The feast as worship

According to traditional Chin belief systems and ritual practices, there was no worship without a feast. Moreover, the feast was not just the sharing and partaking of food, but sharing the source of life (*zing-dangh*), and therefore a communion between god and man as well as between men. Since the Chin viewed the feast as sharing the source of life, there was no feast without animal sacrifice, known in Chin as *Sathi luan lo cun Do a si lo* (literally, 'there is no feast without pouring blood'). The concept of pouring blood is very important because blood, according to traditional

Chin religion, was the source of life, which must be shared as communion not only between the family, clan, and tribe, but also between them and their guardian god *khua-hrum*. In other words, pouring sacrificial animal blood was a symbol of communion between the guardian god *Khua-hrum* and man, and the sharing and partaking of the flesh and blood of sacrificial animals at the feast was a communion between men which united not only members of the community with each other but also with their god, *Khua-hrum*. The idea of animal sacrifice in the worship of *Khua-hrum* could be compared with the idea of animal sacrifice in the Hebrew Bible. According to W. Robertson Smith: 'The leading idea of animal sacrifices of the Semite was not that of a gift made over to the god, but an act of communion in which the god and his worshipers united by partaking together of the flesh and blood of a sacred victim'.[46]

When they became Christians, the Chin concept of communion as sharing the 'source of life' (*zing-dangh*) was gradually transformed into the concept of communion with the 'giver of life' (*Khua-zing*), that is, the Supreme God. Together with such a transition in belief, missionaries introduced a new ritual practice of 'Holy' Communion between the Supreme God and man, which was simply a symbol without any animal sacrifice or real feast. Since there was no sharing and partaking of a real meal at Christian Holy Communion, it was only a communion between man and the giver of life, the Supreme God *Khua-zing*, and not a communion between men. In traditional Chin religious concept, there was no communion between men without sharing and partaking of 'the flesh and blood of a sacred victim' because the Chin considered it a source of life that must be shared between men so that the members of a family, clan, and tribe who shared the same source of life could be united as one. By contrast, the Christian 'Holy Communion', which was usually held on the first Sunday of the month, did not bond people together as the same family or clan or tribe but rather as a community of believers. Moreover, the missionaries discouraged almost all traditional Chin feasts and festivals, which, of course, were in one way or another related to traditional ritual practices and belief systems. Thus, to become Christian during the missionary era was to abandon the traditional Chin way of life, *Lai-phung*.

However, how could life be possible without feasts and festivals for the people who viewed the feast as worship to god? The spiritual life of the Chin people could not survive without feasts and festivals, even in Christian churches. Traditional Chin religion received 'its own rhythm through the regular changes of the agrarian year', and people had to renew their spiritual life through the rhythm of seasonal changes which were usually marked by many feasts and festivals. Feasts and festivals are the ancient rhythm through which people can renew their spiritual life without ceasing. Thus, the Chin church, as in Africa, 'has adapted itself to this ancient rhythm but also has created new festivals and given the year a new meaning'.[47] In this way, Christmas (*Krismas*), New Year (*Kumthar*), and Easter (*Tho*) became the most important social feasts and festivals for the new Chin Christian community. They also created a new festival called *Civui*. Although Christmas, New Year and Easter are seasonal festivals, the Chin celebrate them rather like feasts, and a single family usually hosts the festival for the entire community.

Krismas, Kumthar and Tho

Although there was a transition from the Chin traditional ways of life to the new community of faith, the conversion to Christianity did not break down the ties of family, clan, and tribe in Chin society overnight. Instead, a good relationship between members of the family, clan, and tribe was somehow strengthened by the teaching of Christian love. The only thing that was needed for the new converts among the Chin was to create a new ethos of how to express such love and good feelings among themselves.

In their old culture, love and good feelings were expressed in feasts and festivals, which tied family, clan, and tribe strongly together. Since Christian teaching encouraged good relationships and strong ties among members of the family, clan and tribe, feasts and festivals were also needed for newly converted Chin Christians so that they could express their love and ties not only between members of the family, clan and tribe but also among members of the church who shared the same faith. The only difference between the two – the old and the new – was that in the old culture, feasts and festivals were centred upon family, clan and tribe, emphasizing the difference between one family and another, one clan and another, one tribe and another, and so on. Hence, it reinforced clan and tribal identities, which in the long run resulted in deep separation between different tribes of the same people. In the new Christian society, however, feasts and festivals were centred upon a love that transcended the boundary of family, clan, and tribe; they emphasized the love of God and humanity, which everybody could share and enjoy freely. Thus, the celebrations of Christmas, New Year, and Easter Sunday in the new Chin society were not just the celebrations of seasonal feasts and festivals but the transformation of Chin society from 'clan and tribal groups' to 'the religious community of the Church' with no boundaries. In this way, the Chin society was gradually transformed from a 'clan and tribal oriented society' to 'the community of faith in Christ'.

In present Chin society, *Krismas, Kumthar* and *Tho* are celebrated like many other feasts and festivals in the old culture. Normally, a family who has a harvest as good as expected declares that they will host *Krismas* or *Kumthar* or *Tho*, whichever is most appropriate for them. Most families prefer to host *Krismas* and *Kumthar* because *Tho* usually occurs during the farmers' busiest time, when they need to prepare their fields for sowing before the monsoon rains come in the middle of May. Even when the harvest is not as good as expected, a Christian family still offers a portion of money or food to the church and the church arranges to make the feast as best as they can. Thus, *Krismas, Kumthar* and *Tho* are really community events for the new Chin society, and also a time for community fellowship and reunion. Even today, when things are changing rapidly, the Chin people still prefer to celebrate those feasts, especially *Krismas,* in their birthplace.

During the feast, the host family has to prepare meals for the entire community, but cooking and preparing food are the responsibility of the community as a whole, especially the youth, as it was in their old culture. As long as the feast lasts, there are many activities in which almost all of the community or church members have to participate, such as song contests for both solo and choir, dramas, speeches and sermons, etc. Villagers and the community commonly employ these events not only to recall the past but also to share their faith and the rituals that define the new Chin society. In this way, those feasts and festivals gradually continue to help to create a new identity for a new society.

Civui and the religious festival

If *Krismas, Kumthar* and *Tho* are feasts and fellowship events for a single village or a single town, *Civui* is a festival for a larger community in which at least three villages participate. This is not just a religious festival but an expression of how the ecclesiastical structure of the Baptist Church in Chinram created 'new festivals and has given the season a new meaning'. Moreover, this is about how Christianity helped the Chin people overcome 'clan and tribal barriers' – which confined them separately in their history – and created a new tie and a new national identity for the whole Chin people. In other words, it is how Christianity has helped Chin society make the transition from a 'clan and tribal oriented society' to a church-oriented community, which transcends the old tribal identity.

As mentioned already, *Civui* means 'meeting', but it implies 'any Church administrative meeting which is larger than the local Church meeting'.[48] Thus, based on the ecclesiastical structure of the Baptist Church in Chinram, there are three levels of *Civui*: (1) Area Civui, (2) Association Civui, and (3) Convention Civui. Area Civui is held annually but Association and Convention Civvies are held tri-annually. (In some areas, especially in the Mizoram State in India, *Civui* is known as *Khwam-pui*, meaning 'big gathering'.)

Indeed, *Civui* is a good combination of a Church administrative meeting and a religious festival for the new society in Chinram. For Area Civui, the church business meeting usually starts on Thursday, but at the Association and Convention levels, where much more business has to be done, the meeting usually starts on Monday. In both cases, however, ordinary pilgrims (*Civui a zawh mi*) must arrive on Friday when the church administrative business is over. In fact, Friday is the real beginning of *Civui*. Usually, there are at least seven worship services during the *Civui*: one on Friday night, three on Saturday and three on Sunday. The intervals between worship services are used for fellowship and games. During the services, there are many speeches, sermons and choirs, and services, even dramas at night. The churches send their choir groups to highlight this special event, and the host village is responsible for providing room and board throughout the *Civui*. Nowadays, an Area Civui is mainly held in rural areas, while Association and Convention Civuis are usually held in more urban areas – in towns such as Haka, Falam, Tiddim, etc. For the new Chin society, *Civui* has become a religious festival from which people can receive both spiritual and social benefits.

Civui is also a time when villagers and communities commonly recall their past, discuss their present and share visions for their future together in one hope and one faith. This is a time when people do not identify each other as members of family, clan, or tribe but only as members of the community of faith. This is a time when people share not only their experiences both past and present, but even their emotions and faith. When people can freely share their experiences, emotions and faith, these are remembered not only as personal memories but also as common memories or socially reconstructed narrative events. And when personal memory becomes common memory, this is called social history, a factor that holds 'history and identity together'. In this way, the Chin people do 'identity work' together, especially during such events as the *Civui*.

CONCLUSION

In this chapter, I have argued that conversion to Christianity in Chin society was the product of a long-term process of change, resulting from the pressures of external forces. Scholars from various disciplines have already affirmed the fact that there is a connection between religious change and social pressure in society. Social anthropologist Raymond Firth, for instance, writes: 'Religious change has often been a result of social pressures upon guardians of the doctrine and ritual.' He continues: 'Religion, like other social institutions, is continually in a process of change, due partly to external pressures of an economic or political kind, or to internal pressures of doctrinal debate or personal ambition.'[49]

Second, I have tried to analyse the paradoxical continuity between traditional Chin religion and Christianity. Doing this, I am mindful of the fact that if 'change is a lawful fact of social life', as scholars like Geertz have argued, how do we account for continuity? Scholars from various disciplines have tried to grapple with the problems of continuity within the process of change. In my hypothesis, continuity between traditional Chin religion and Christianity was possible because of the two religions' similar theological concepts and belief systems, especially the traditional Chin concept of a Supreme Being, *Khua-zing*, and the Christian understanding of a Supreme God, the creator of all things in this universe. Traditionally, the Chin had a clear concept of the Supreme God, *Khua-zing*, but they did not worship Him because He was good and did not require any sacrificial appeasement like *Khua-hrum* and *Khua-chia* did. Thus, traditional Chin religion was centred upon the worship of *Khua-hrum* (guardian gods) and *Khua-chia* (evil spirits), not upon *Khua-zing*, the Supreme God.

When the Chin converted to Christianity, they inevitably passed through a long-term process of adjustment between the demands of a new faith and the ritual habits of their traditional religion. In this long-term process of change and adjustment, the Chin people completely abandoned almost all their traditional ritual practices of sacrificial ceremonies and their related value systems. This process of change also made deep inroads into the original patterns and structures of traditional religion, and thereby society itself. The belief system, however, was transformed from *Khua-hrum*-centric to *Khua-zing*-centric within the same conceptual pattern of belief system. In other words, the worship of *Khua-hrum* was transformed into the worship of *Khua-zing*, or the worship of the lesser god to the Supreme God.

In order to highlight the Chin response to the new religious challenge and how they did become Christians, I have approached my study from the Chin local perspective. Thus, instead of investigating purely institutional development of the Chin churches, I investigated the gradual shift from traditional Chin religion to Christianity as an integrating factor in the development of Chin self-awareness. In this way, I analysed the local stories that people tell about their society and about the past, especially events personified in ancestors and other historic figures. Through such stories, both small and large, personal and collective, the Chin people do much of their 'identity work' together. In other words, such 'stories hold history and identity together.'[50]

The most prominent and frequently repeated local stories are, of course, about the moment of first confrontation with colonial power and the Christian mission, and subsequent conversion to Christianity. The stories of conversion are repeatedly told and retold, often in narrative accounts as writings, songs, sermons, and speeches passed on during such occasions as religious feasts, celebrations and worship services. These are times when people engage in exchange practices that define social and political relations. Although the wars against British annexation (1872–1896), the Anglo–Chin War (1917–1919), the Second World War and Japanese invasion (1939–1945) and the Independence of Burma (1948) are also significant junctures in temporal consciousness, the events of Christian conversion are uniquely important in the organization of a socio-historical memory.

In present Chin society, telling dramatic versions of the conversion stories has become almost a ritual practice during Sunday services and the annual Local and Association Meetings called *Civui*, where villages and communities commonly gather to recall the past. Narratives of shared experience and history do not simply represent identity and emotion, they even constitute them. In other words, histories told and remembered by those who inherit them are discourses of identity, just as identity is inevitably a discourse of history. Thus, 'history teaching', as Appleby claims, 'is identity formation.'[51] Especially for the people who live in communities transformed by powerful outside forces, the common perception of a threat to their existence as well as the narrative accounts of socio-religio-cultural contact with the outside world had created identity through the idiom of shared history. However, just as history is never finished, nor is identity. It is continually refashioned as people make cultural meaning out of shifting social and political circumstances. I have analysed how the old tribal and clan identities were gradually replaced, and how Christianity provided a means of preserving and promoting the self-awareness of Chin identity through its theological concepts and ideology and its ecclesiastical structure; and how the Chin people gradually adjusted to Christianity through an accelerated religious change in their society.

In addition to theoretical framework which I have applied; another dimension which is needed to take into account is political developments after independence that made strong impacts on the Christian movement in Chinram was the promulgation of Buddhism as a state religion of the Union of Burma in 1961 by the U Nu's government. This state religion issue provoked the Chin's religiously motivated liberation movement led by the 'Chin Independence Army' in the 1960s. Observing that Christian missionaries were the ones who kept 'imperialism alive' and agitated separatist movements among the Chin and other ethnic nationalities in Burma, General Ne Win, who came to power in 1962 through a military coup, not only expelled foreign missionaries but also intensified his military campaign against the Chin and other ethnic nationalist movements.

Ironically, when the military aspects of the Chin nationalist movement were suppressed from both India and Burma, the *indigenous form of Christianity*, that is, the church without foreign missionaries, became a more valid expression of ethnic identity of the Chin in Burma. Moreover, the Christian movements under dictatorship, especially 'Chins for Christ in One Century', which was launched during the peak of Ne Win's era in 1980s, became symbolic expression of the Chin national identity. Knowing that Christianity and the Chin identity are inseparably intertwined with each other, the present military junta in Burma notoriously practises religious persecution as a means of eliminating a distinctive Chin identity. The Burma Army destroys churches, removes Christian symbols of the cross – which also is a Chin national symbol – from mountain tops and holy places, convert Christian Chin to Buddhism by force, and use forced labour to construct pagodas. The military junta arrested and even killed a number pastors and Church leaders, who boldly protested for freedom of their belief.[52] The Christian Chin view the religious persecution that they are suffering as 'part of the plan of providence of God, and an integral consequence of following Jesus Christ', and they proclaim that 'the blood of the martyrs are the seeds of the Church and the Chin nation.'[53] In this ironical ways, the Chin Baptist Churches have shown spiritual vitality against of the revolutionary change under General Ne Win's regime and religious persecution under the current military junta, and the Christian Chin are manifested their own true character of an indigenous Chin church in the midst of a multi-ethnic, multi-religious cultural environments in the Union of Burma.

NOTES

[1]   During the first three decades of the twentieth century, 'the great majority of' the Chin people in Mizoram State of present India had become Christian already. See Mangkhosat Kipgen (1996). For the church growth in East Chinram of Chin State in Burma, see H Sakhong (2000, 2003), and Pum Suan Pau (1998).

[2]   See Sakhong (2000).

[3]   A.D. Smith (1986, p. 6).

[4]   Ibid.

[5]   See J. Shakespeare (1912, p. 93–94); Carey and H. N. Tuck (1983, p. 142); Parry (1976, p. 4).

[6]   Shakespeare (1912, pp. 93–94) (the sentence within bracket is added).

[7]   Ibid. p. 94 (emphasis added).

[8]   Cited by Vumson (1986, p. 3).

[9]   Gangte (1993, p. 14); see also K. Zawla (1976, p. 2) and Kipgen (1996, pp. 31–35). (Brackets within italic are mine.)

[10] Vumson (1986, p. 26). Vumson cannot accept the traditional account of the legend 'as fact, because', for him, 'it is contradictory to known facts of how man originated' (p. 26). He therefore proposed that the word 'Zo' (meaning; 'hill people or highlander') be used for the national name of the Chin.

[11] F. K. Lehman (1963, p. 20).

[12] Za Peng Sakhong (1983, p. 7).

[13] Lian Uk (1968, p. 2).

[14] Carey and Tuck (1983, p. 3).

[15] It has to be noted that in Burmese the combination of letters 'KH' is pronounced as 'CH'.

[16] Luce (1959, pp. 75–109).

[17] Sangermano (1995, p. 43). Explanation within brackets is provided by John Jardine, who wrote an introduction and notes when the book was first published in 1833, some one hundred years after Father Sangermano died. As John Jardine had explained quite clearly, what Sangermano described as 'Jo' is not the 'Jo' group of the Zomi tribe of Chin, but the 'Yaw' people who occupied the Gankaw Valley of upper Chindwin. This particular point had been misinterpreted by many scholars, especially Zomi scholars including Vum Kho Hau and Sing Kho Khai, sometimes quite intentionally. Vum Kho Hau (1963, p. 238), for instance, writes in his book: *Profile of Burma Frontier Man*, 'From time immemorial we call ourselves Zo (Jo, Yaw). This fact had been admirably recorded by Father V. Sangermano since the year 1783 when he made his headquarter at Ava.'.

[18] Reid (1983, p. 5).

[19] Shakespeare (1912, p. 8); cited also in G. S. Gangte (1993, p. 21).

[20] Snodgrass (1827, see map on p. 320).

[21] Phayer (1967, p. 7).

[22] Newland (1894).

[23] See further details of the historical development of the Chin settlement in Chindwin Valley to present Chinram, in Chapter One of my dissertation (Sakhong, 2000).

[24] Grierson (1967, p. 67).

[25] Vumson (1986, p. 40).

[26] Downs (1994, p. 4).

[27] Ibid.

[28] Ibid.

[29] Ringmar (1996, p. 145).

[30] Downs (1992, p. 24).

[31] Ibid.

[32] Ibid., p. 29.

[33] Ibid., p. 146.

[34] I borrowed the theme of 'imagining social world' from (1991, especially pp. 9–36).

[35] Cf. Anderson (1991, especially chapter 3).

[36] East 1990: FM-186, and also Johnson, *History of American Baptist Chin Mission*, *Vol. 1* (1988), pp. 259–60.

[37] Laura Carson, *Pioneer Trails, Trails and Triumph* (New York: Baptist Board Publication, 1927), p. 161.

[38] Robert Johnson, *American Baptist Chin Mission* (1988), p. 263.

[39] Pu Sakhong, *Kan Pupa Thawhkehnak Kong* (Aibur: Manuscript, 1971), p. 11.

[40] East, FM-186, 1908–1919.

[41] This hymn is inscribed on the gravestone of Pu Hreng Kio of Aibur who became a Christian in the early 1930s and died as the church leader of Aibur in 1961.

[42] Interview with Pi Men Tang, Lian Hei's sister, on 27 December, 1990.

[43] Johnson, *American Baptist Chin Mission* (1988, p. 145).

[44] Ibid.

[45] Ibid.

[46] W.R. Robertson Smith (1996, pp. 43–64).

[47] Sundkler (1980, p. 181).

[48] Hup (1993, p. 105).

[49] Firth (1996, p. 199).

[50] Cf. White (1995).

[51] Appleby (1998, pp. 1–14).

[52] The Chin Human Rights Organization (CHRO) has compiled hundred of cases of religious persecution in Chin State, committed by the current military junta in Burma. See *Religious Persecution: A Campaign of Ethnocide against Chin Christians in Burma* Ottawa: CHRO, 2004).

[53] See *Religious Persecution*, report by CHRO.

Chapter 9

CONVERSION AND IDENTITY: RELIGION AND THE FORMATION OF KAREN ETHNIC IDENTITY IN BURMA

Mikael Gravers

Through the centuries the Karens had preserved themselves as a race distinct from the Burmese and other people.[1]

This quotation from a memorandum published by the Karen delegation to London in 1946 emphasizes the ethnic difference and the absolute opposition, which are still manifest parts of Karen political identification among the elder generation of Karen, particularly among members of the Karen National Union (KNU). It refers to the historical experience of the Karen as victims of Burmese oppression, sadly confirmed in recent years of violence.

An important element in the making of Karen identity is religion. In 1946, being a Christian Karen, in their own self-identification, signified that the ethnic group had reached a level of civilization qualifying them as a nation in their own right with the right to claim their own state. Christianity became part of an ethnic opposition and confrontation with the Burmese. However, religion is also a source of both internal cohesion and division as well as of conflict among the Karen. This chapter probes into the complex historical relationship between ethnicity, religion and nationalism, although it is by no means an exhaustive or conclusive analysis. Much more research is needed in the form of fieldwork, personal narratives, and archival search for documents.

In 1994, a conflict between the Christian dominated leadership of the KNU and Buddhist soldiers in the Karen National Liberation Army (KNLA), supported by Buddhist Karen monks, developed into a serious split culminating in the formation of the Democratic Karen Buddhist Organization (DKBO) and the Democratic Karen Buddhist Army (DKBA). Although the DKBA developed into a tool of the Burmese army and has seen its support dwindle, this conflict is significant for the understanding of Karen identity which is much more complex than often stated in the literature and media.

A brief and superficial comparison with the Kachin and Chin ethnic groups underlines the role of religion: While an estimated 15–20 per cent of Pwo and Sgaw Karen are Christian, the vast majority of Chin and Kachin seem to have embraced Christianity although in various denominations, probably with a predominance of Baptism.[2] According to Lian H. Sakhong (2000) more than 80 per cent of Chin are Christian, and about 90 per cent of Kachin are believed to be Christian. Moreover, Christianity seems to be the basis of a national identity minimizing the internal ethnic or 'tribal' differences. Chin, Kachin and Karen are ethnic categories and conglomerates of diverse ethnic groups speaking different dialects and with significant cultural differences. Yet, these heterogeneous categories were meaningful entities in the ethnic identification, internally and externally, even before colonization.[3] But their political meaning was transformed during colonial rule in the age of Plural Society, as explained by Furnivall (1956: 304). The categories became an instrumental part of a politics of difference, and were often reduced to simplified models of relations between minorities and the majority population during the colonial period and reproduced in the literature (Lehman 1967a: 105; Gravers 1996a : 239). In the process they became bounded entities with emphasis on incompatible ethnic qualities. In the present political discourse among the democratic opposition the term 'ethnic nationality' has replaced 'ethnic minority' in order to emphasize their status as equal nations.

Internal social and cultural differences in ethnic identification among these ethnic categories have, I believe, often been understated, especially the historical confrontation of Buddhism and Christianity which was a crucial part of the colonial conquest of Burma. This confrontation, which began with Christian conversion in 1830, created an internal opposition among the Karen, that has erupted into violent conflicts several times. It also created an internal boundary between mainly Baptists on one side and Buddhist/Animists on the other. The divide, however, is more than religious. The Buddhist Pwo and Animist Sgaw in some areas are poorer and have had less education than Christian Sgaw, and many Pwo also have a historical sense of being dominated by Sgaw.[4] Thus, we have to look into history in order to uncover the complexities of ethnic and religious diversity and the process of boundary making. But first a brief outline of the concepts applied in the analysis.

Ethnic identity and boundaries have been discussed extensively since the 1960s, as for example F.K. Lehman (1967; F. K. L. Chit Hlaing, this volume) and Barth (1969). Identity – or rather the *process of identification*, which is the object of study in its various historical conjunctures – includes self-identification of sameness as well as differences in relation to others. The external categorization, often used by powerful 'Others', is often internalized as part of an internal self-identification.[5] Categorization and classification are important parts of the process of identification – they may strengthen and essentialize identity in resistance and confrontation with other groups. Another important element of identity formation is the construction of ethnic/national boundaries, that combine geographical and cultural mapping into a political landscape.[6] The outcome is not only a spatial model of ethnic or national boundaries, but also a cognitive model, which, in the case of the Karen, includes general mental and cultural characteristics. Such models tend to homogenize internally while making those outside incompatible and deeply opposed. However, Barth (2002b : 31, 33) has warned that although such cognitive models may appear as hegemonic political representations, the realities of cognition produce different strategies, and models are never shared by all. When ethnic and religious differences erupt into violent actions it is not an outcome of the 'natural' ethnic logic of differences but politically generated. In the politics of ethnic differences, identities are often presented as primordial with a static essence, erasing variation and individual agency as we have seen in so many ethnic/national conflicts. The role of religion in this process is often to provide a fundamental cosmological model, timeless as well as overarching.[7]

In the case of the Karen, ethnic boundaries and the model of a nation (and of the Kawthoolei state) – as of 1946–47– had the double function of erasing the internal differences while depicting the external, i.e. with the Burmese, as a deeply opposed entity and utterly incompatible with the Karen identity. As Saw Po Chit wrote before he and the Karen delegation went to London to negotiate in 1946: '[The nature of Karen and Burman] are in fact different and distinct genuses and it is a dream that Karen and

Burman can ever evolve a common nationality" [8] Then follows an index of the incompatible differences: race, religion, custom, literature, civilization, history, myths and epics, culture heroes, etc. The memorandum quoted above adds the following mental qualities: reserve, unobstructiveness, steadiness and simplicity. More recent KNU publications repeat some of these differences in mentality and culture.[9] The Burmans are generally depicted as aggressive while the Karen are the victims who suffer from their aggression.

In 1946 the expectations among the Karen had reached their highest point. They were convinced that the British would reward their loyalty and sufferings during the Second World War with an autonomous state. Although they were utterly disappointed and perplexed when the state did not materialize, their expectations and the British support seemed to converge into a common *conjuncture of expectations*. This concept is used to describe the immediacy of the historical events – not merely the realization of a symbolic structure, a cultural scheme, as defined by Sahlins (1985: xiv) – but *the conjunction of knowledge, concepts and cognitive models in a specific social and political context*. Such high expectations – and conflicting imaginations – have been in the foreground of Karen history since the 1830s, when conversion to Christianity began. Most Karen share a dramatic vision of the world in their knowledge traditions, a vision of crises, decline and apocalyptic destruction followed by a golden era. This evolution is cognized in conjunctures of expectations identified in specific events and persons. They expect charismatic leaders or a king to appear, followed by prosperity and a new communal morality. However, before these expectations are fulfilled, the Karen anticipate a conjuncture of violence.[10] I have tried to identify and characterize the main conjunctures in order to illustrate the historical process of identity and boundary making. However, this common model based on religious cosmology is not seen as a schema performed as if by choreography. It is a shared knowledge tradition, in different versions, used to reflect upon and act on in a changing world, and this model has been challenged and changed in the process.[11] At moments in the process, the chain of conjunctures may appear to the participants as the realization of the structuring principles of the cosmological model. In this way a transformation is also imagined as a cultural continuation.

Although I focus on the conflict between Buddhists and Christians, I am aware that much co-operation and mutual understanding have been exchanged across boundaries of religious denominations in the past and in

Figure 9.1. A Karen girl playing the harp in Mae La refugee camp, Thailand. (Photo: M. Gravers)

the present. The aim is primarily to elucidate the historical production of differences. It is important to emphasize that the past cannot be applied to explain all present actions, and vice versa; it can, however, illuminate the origin of the present sources of conflict. My point here is that the differences have been politicized in the historical process and that an internal social hierarchy with the poor, mainly Buddhist/Animist Karen at the lower end, has been concealed under descriptions of the Karen as a homogenous culture.

During recent fieldwork in northern Thailand, a Baptist Sgaw Karen explained to me that all Karen share part of a common *ta a lu a la* (custom) – a common Karen knowledge tradition – yet, the local *mo lu pha a la* (mothers' and fathers' customs) differ a lot from community to community – a point actually made in the first missionary journals from Burma.[12] The missionaries later understated the differences in favour of a selected, common tradition in order to promote a Christian Karen culture and secure a proper translation of the Bible. By inventing new words, metaphors and concepts, mainly from Sgaw Karen, the missionaries worked to create a single presentation of Karen custom, knowledge and identity despite the considerable local differences![13] Thus, in order to analyse this historical process, I found that the journals in the *Baptist Missionary Magazine* (hereafter *BMM*) are extremely valuable sources. They are detailed ethnographies and straightforward in their mode of relating problems and conflicts between Christians and Buddhists. If some would argue that they are biased, the reply would be: yes, by honestly exposing success and failure as well as sympathy and antipathy. Conversion and the making of a new knowledge tradition entered the process of ethnic categorization and boundary construction in a powerful way. It is important, however, to reconsider the process of conversion and see it from a Karen point of view as a new ritual practice (in Sgaw *nei ta ge a sau*) or a new worship (*ta bu ta ba*), but not as a change of culture or custom. Christianity and Buddhism have actually been converted into genuine Karen traditions replacing former rituals and prayers. Thus, Christianity and Buddhism are not seen as a non-Karen religious traditions.[14]

1830–1850: CONJUNCTURE OF EXPECTATIONS – CONVERSION AND KNOWLEDGE

'I have learned one thing' – explained a Christian Karen assistant – 'the most valuable of all knowledge, – to pray and obtain.'[15]

In this conjuncture many Karen were searching for new knowledge, power and a leadership, which could unite the various scattered groups – often described metaphorically as being orphans. Since mid-1700s when the last Mon kingdom of Pegu was annexed by the Burmese king, a line of *min laùng* [imminent king, pretender] appeared among the Karen. They used a mixture of Buddhist cosmology and Karen customs to announce prophecies of a new era, when the Karen would obtain knowledge and prosperity and become like those living in towns and cities. I have described the Buddhist Karen cosmology, the historical events and the line of *min laùng* rebels in detail in Gravers (2001c). Here the space only allows me to focus on the role of Christian conversion in conjunction with these largely Buddhist oriented expectations of a *bodhisattva*.

An important element of the Karen expectations around 1830 was that they would be liberated from the menace of evil spirits – a reason often given by Karen today when they convert to Christianity or become Buddhists. In order to be liberated from evil spirits, the complicated rituals and expensive sacrifices of animals, a new powerful knowledge had to be obtained. One of the first missionaries to contact the Karen was George Boardman, to whom a Karen religious leader (a *bu kho*) from the Tavoy area showed a book that he and his supporters treasured and worshipped. It turned out to be the *Oxford Book of Psalms and Common Prayers*. A prophet had told them not to eat pork and chicken nor to make offerings to the spirits, indicating that they belonged to one of the Buddhist movements (Stern 1968; Gravers 2001c). The leader offered to build Boardman a *zayat* [a ceremonial building] in the style of these movements. It was indeed a good book, but the most important, explained Boardman, was the Bible. However, this meeting initiated the first conjuncture and the missionaries soon had raised their expectations when they heard a myth about the lost book of knowledge. In the version most often reproduced in missionary texts, God (*Yuah Ga Cha*) gave the book (*le ta gu se*, 'the book of wisdom') to all human kind, the Karen lost his in the field, but his white brother took his across the sea and was expected to bring it back and share its knowledge with the elder Karen brother.

In the early years of conversion this myth generated the theory of the Karen as one of the lost tribes of Israel and of a pristine Christian–Jewish origin. However, another version of the myth refers to Buddha as the source of the book, and I have recorded several different local versions. The other problem with the missionary version is that Yuah has never been an object of religious worship among the Karen. This was even admitted by missionary Cross (1854: 308): 'At the time when Christianity was first introduced among the Karen, no distinct trace of worship of Yuah were found'.[16] Yuah is the creator of the world, of mankind and of the local spirits, which have to be shown respect. The Karen who met the first missionaries were not expecting the return of Yuah but the arrival of the coming Buddha, Ariya Metteya. In a Pwo version given by two Catholic missionaries in 1847, the important figure is a son of Yuah, Ka Cha Klau (Ga Cha Glong) 'the lord of the pagoda', i.e. Ariya. He returns a resurrect humanity from decline and sin (Lacrampe and Plaisany 1849: 179). When he comes, poverty, lack of knowledge, immorality and violence will disappear. Before the arrival of the Baptist missionaries, the name of Yuah was taboo, according to the two Catholic fathers, and Yuah was called Phu Kè Re'. James Low (1850: 417), a British official, wrote that the book of knowledge and writing was given to them by a very sacred personage, *Kachaklong*, dressed somewhat like a Buddhist monk. He left the sacred writing with a holy man. Before Ariya Metteya will arrive to revive Buddhism, a religious and moral decline will end in an apocalyptic destruction by fire, wind and water. Thus, the Karen would anticipate war and destruction before the transformation.[17]

Whenever the Karen recited the verses about the end of Buddha's era, missionary expectations rose: 'The Lord his messages doth send and he himself will quickly come – the priest of Boodh, whose reign is short, must leave the place to make them room.'[18] However, the lord was Ariya Metteya and the many Karen, who joined *mìn laùng* movements, believed that not only was the Buddhist doctrine in decline but that the monks had also lost their moral and symbolic power. Thus, the Karen religious leaders (*bu kho*) had to guide the Karen in the interval before Ariya Metteya's arrival (Gravers 2001c).

Francis Mason and other missionaries gradually realized the content of the Karen expectations, but there was a struggle to define who was the real Lord: God or Buddha/Ariya. Mason wrote:

> The Karen were not agreed in regard to the name to be used for God. I found that according to traditions Yuwah was the omnipotent, omniscient, and omnipresent creator and ruler of the world. I therefore adopted the word Yuwah in prayer and preaching, to the exclusion of the others, which they [the Karen] have done ever since'. (*BMM*) 1856: 131)

In the followings years, Mason and his colleagues met several Karen leaders who worshipped books, mostly Christian tracts, but also a commercial publication from a London firm (*BMM* 1833: 115; 1835: 367). In most cases these Karen never converted, and Mason described the problem in this way: '[T]hey were all ready to worship the Bible, prostrating themselves and knocking their head to the ground, but not one was willing to obey the precepts it enjoined.' (*BMM* 1856: 101). To the missionaries the Animist Karen appeared to make the book into an object of fetish worship, not realizing that the Karen were searching for the power of knowledge.

Mason, Judson and other missionaries were strongly opposed by Karen Buddhist monks and by Karen religious leaders (*bu kho*). They considered Christianity to be the religion of the English government and would only convert if they were forced to do so by the colonial power (*BMM* 1832: 358; 1834: 73). These Karen realized that conversion implied a political identification.

However, other Karen, Animist Sgaw in particular, viewed the missionaries as people with a special power over the spirits.[19] These Karen were more easily persuaded to go through the process of conversion beginning with a confession of sins and a renunciation of traditional rituals including drinking rice liquor and sacrificing animals. In this process the help of the Holy Spirit was emphasized by the missionaries, as well as by Karen converts (*BMM* 1832: 84). The role of the Holy Spirit as an agency before Christ returns seems to have been crucial in appealing to many Karen and it is still emphasized in Christian Karen literature.[20] One Karen told Vinton that 'the smallest portion of the Holy Spirit seemed to him of more value than all in the world' (*BMM*: 1845: 83), and a Karen preacher said that 'many were sick, but they were so intent on obtaining the Holy Spirit' (ibid. 85). The missionaries merely provided the words, while the Holy Spirits revealed the knowledge. To the Karen, however, it was crucial that new supernatural agencies ruled and that they would not risk being punished by the local spirits they abandoned. Thus, the new ritual practice had to prove its power.

After conversion followed the organization and control of the right knowledge and understanding before and after baptism. The candidates often had to prepare for a year and to prove they had stopped their heathen practices. 'Their disposition and ability to converse on religion, and particularly to pray' was examined (*BMM* 1831: 154). And only carefully examined Karen were gradually allowed to minister the baptism since this was the 'passport' of the new identity and thus a very powerful instrument. Whereas the missionaries controlled the mind and morals of the converts, the Karen looked to the power of rituals. Prayers, a strong collective morality and the agency of the Holy Spirit, I believe, appealed to many Karen because they could replace elements in most local traditions and thus control the local spirits. Witnessing and confession is also part of Karen Buddhist/Animist tradition, for example: adultery has to be revealed, otherwise the tiger will bite and misfortune strikes the family. That is why the Karen often consider Christianity as their own religion, the knowledge they lost and retrieved.[21] Even the water of the baptism was translated into a traditional Karen symbolic metaphor: it was 'cold' and not 'hot' as in the past during spirit worship (*BMM* 1837: 116). To cool down with water also means to make the place peaceful (see Gravers 2001c: 16).

In this phase there were disappointments on both sides. Karen families and villages were divided and numerous cases of such conflicts have been described in *Baptist Missionary Magazine*. The first village chief to convert was not followed by his family or the villagers, who then supported his son as a new chief. If a man converted, his wife and relatives would blame him in case of illness in the family (*BMM* 1837: 77; 1841: 36). Ritual offerings to the family guardian spirit, *au hrae* or *au bhga* [to eat the offering], could not be executed in such cases. Missionary Abbot described the hate by non-Christians: '[S]ometimes even in families, there exists the most deadly opposition'; Judson reported of a baptised Karen who was extradited from the village. In another case, a Christian Karen woman left her husband and child.[22] In cases of apostasy the individuals were excommunicated and could end up as outcasts. Cases of apostasy and conflicts mainly occurred among Karen led by a *bu kho* and who expected a total redemptive transformation of their social world here and now and not a distant salvation.[23] Several such cases are reported; these Karen did not feel that the Christians revealed all the expected knowledge.[24]

On the other hand, the converts gained access to Christian schools and Western knowledge. Missionary Wade constructed the Sgaw and Pwo Karen alphabets during the 1830s, and translations of the Bible and other texts followed in 1843. The translation was seen as crucial by both missionaries and Karen converts. Thus, Saw Quala wrote in the Karen journal *Morning Star*, that with an exact translation of the Bible, knowledge would not be lost (again) if the white brothers returned home (*BMM* 1856: 135). The lost book had been returned to some of the Karen, but also became the major symbol of ethnic and religious divide internally and in relation to the Burmans.

1850–1886: CONJUNCTURE OF CONFRONTATION ACROSS RELIGIOUS BOUNDARIES

During the first years of conversion, missionaries often confronted Buddhist monks and initiated theological discussions. Often the missionaries were very negative in their judgements and attacked the worship of 'men in yellow and idols'. Buddhism merely provided individual salvation while Christ provided salvation for all converts and a universal kingdom (*BMM* 1851: 413). The missionaries, argued Mason, must emphasize the differences and not the similarities, for example in ethics, between the two religions (*BMM* 1849: 111). An example of the more serious confrontations is missionary Bullard's attack on a pagoda spire (*hti*) hoisted by Buddhist Karen monks.

He threatened to cut the rope, making the Karen so angry and confused that the spire eventually came down (*BMM* 1845: 314). Moreover, the missionaries considered Buddhism as a part of the Burmese despotic regime (*BMM* 1851: 413), while Christianity represented civilization. In this period the Baptist missionaries challenged the Burman religious identity and Burman political legitimacy and emphasized the differences as a fundamental opposition. They were drawing boundaries, which not only delineated the symbolic differences but also created political boundaries based on symbolic violence. The Burmans responded in the same manner. Their reaction to the missionary efforts was a strong opposition, in particular against 'the Book', and the common feeling that the missionaries not only changed the religion but also the entire social and cultural identity of the converts; they became *kala,* 'foreigners'. King Bagyidaw did not want the new doctrine spread and did not allow the distribution of Christian books (*BMM* 1834: 156). Christian Karen were jailed in Rangoon and persecuted in the kingdom. A Burman official complained to missionary Abbot about the books: 'This is the way you do to get away the hearts an of my subjects, is it? You came and fight us, and get away part of our country, and now you wish to turn away the hearts of the poor, ignorant Karens' (*BMM* 1839: 105). Bigandet, a Catholic bishop wrote that those who converted were merged in a community called *kalas,* 'because in the opinion of the Burmese, they had embraced the religion of the Kalas and had become *bonâfide* strangers, having lost their own nationality' (Bigandet 1887: 4). Clearly, conversion was seen as a threat to both identity and political loyalty. Thus, 'to be a Burman is to be a Buddhist' found its opposite identity in 'to be a Karen is to be Christian', but in the sense that a Christian was loyal to the foreigners. In 1840 the Burmans burnt Christian books and an escalating conflict with the growing number of Christians inside Burma became a part of the overture to the next British annexation after the war in 1852.

In 1851 the Burmese governor in Rangoon and the missionary Kincaid discussed religion. The governor said about Christianity: 'It aimed to destroy every other [religion], and this was uncharitable. They [the Burmese] allowed our religion to be good, but we would not allow theirs to be good; this was his great objection.' Kincaid replied that Christianity gave humanity a love of God and loving kindness among all humans. The governor continued: '[Y]ou are getting all the people to your side, for you make them think well of yourselves, and of your doctrine' (*BMM* 1851: 69). Other officials also objected to missionary maps showing the world as round as an orange and for aiming to destroy Burma. But Kincaid rejected that this scientific knowledge had anything to do with religion or politics – subjects that were not separated in Burman cosmology.

The governor thus continued to prohibit books seen as the major instrument of destruction of the Burmese, Buddhist world. 'Despotism has stamped a value on these books which they would not otherwise have obtained', wrote Kincaid (ibid. 108). He and other missionaries were deeply involved in the preparations for the ensuing war and annexation in 1852 (ibid. 104). Christian Karen were attacked by the Burmese near Bassein and they responded by ambushing and beheading a Burmese chief of 450 armed men on their way to attack a Karen village. (*BMM* 1853: 162). A Karen pastor was fastened to a cross and shot (ibid. 168). The Burmese blamed the Karen for the war because they had received the 'white book' (ibid. 163), and the annexation was seen as victory for Christianity.

In 1856 a widespread *min laùng* rebellion broke out with centres in Papun, north of Moulmein, and near Bassein. The rebels were Buddhists led by Karen but joined by groups from Pa-o, Shan, and Mon and supported by a Kayah *sawbwa*. The rebels often attacked Christian villages and Mason, who worked east of Toungoo, asked the British to arm the Christian Karen. The British hesitated, fearing that rebels would use the arms.[25] The confrontations between Christians and Buddhists escalated in the 1880s, in particular after the final annexation of Burma. Buddhist monks participated in the widespread resistance against the British 'pacification'. Some of the missionaries looked forward to an enlarged mission field and were astonishingly active in the 'pacification': 'we are all belligerent', exclaimed Cross (*BMM* 1886: 237). His Paku congregation attacked rebels, or *dacoits* (gang robbers) in colonial jargon, and killed two Buddhist monks. This time, the British supplied some guns to the Karen. 'This is what American Baptists have been praying for ever since Judson went to Ava. God has now answered these prayers' (ibid. 35). When the king is gone Buddhism will collapse, they believed, and tyranny will disappear. The monks, active as dacoits, were a sign that Buddhism was a 'dying monster' (ibid. 130). Thus, the missionaries shared the vision and expectations among Buddhist Karen of a declining Buddhism – although cognized from opposite knowledge traditions and cosmological models. For both sides war was the sign of imminent change, and in Shwegyin there was serious fighting between rebels and Christian Karen. Missionary Smith participated with his gun: '[T]he heathen Karen villages constitute the base of supplies to the party [of rebels]' (ibid. 132).

The Buddhist Karen were very active with the Burmese rebels and the missionaries feared they would be able to destroy most of the Christian villages. Several were burned, books and chapels destroyed, animals killed and crops burned or looted. Monks were often the leaders, and in Toungoo, Cross blamed the British for being totally unprepared. It was a widespread rebellion – 'a tremendous upheaval' – according to the missionaries, supported by the east Kayah *Sawbwa* and the stated aim of the rebels was to drive Jesus out (ibid. 336). Just as the priests of Buddha were the leaders of the rebellion, the Baptist pastors were leaders against them; and there were rewards of 25 rupees on the monks' heads. Several were brought in (ibid. 151), although most Christians did not participate in these acts. The leader, the Myankhyaung Hpòngyi, escaped Cross's group but was captured by missionary Bunker and his Karen; his captor was said to be a woman. Several Christian Karen were killed. However, they had now shown their loyalty and were supplied with guns (ibid. 152). Around Rangoon the Karen were more effective in 'bush-fighting' than the British troops and missionary Vinton Jr. was delighted: 'It is Buddhism in arms against Christianity', the Christian Karen feeling superior: 'We now know that we have a God fit to be trusted, and infinitely greater than we had supposed' (ibid. 331). In other words, this was the ultimate confirmation of the power they had obtained from the new knowledge and thus partly a fulfilment of their expectations. They now entered a new phase where the key words were 'self-support' and 'self-organization'. This strategy, however, also had its problems: for example in Tavoy where mission work had begun in the 1830s. Many had left the congregation and one fifth was excluded in 1885. The congregation was not supervised and had only its Karen pastors ending in 'disorder and defection' (*BMM* 1885: 208). In order to counter Buddhist influence from schools in local monasteries, missionary Carpenter insisted on giving priority to Christian schools and higher education in order to promote Christian and Western knowledge. However, the more conservative missionaries, Cross and others, considered schools as merely tools to support conversion. This division among the missionaries must have had an impact upon the levels and quality of education in the local congregation with most of the educated elite coming from Bassein and Rangoon. Control of knowledge internally and externally became crucial in the identity process.

Unfortunately, the armed conflict between Buddhists and Christians also created a boundary, which included violence in its symbolic and physical forms. Violent historical events tend to create fearful expectations of future violence when it enters the ethnic identification and the social memory of the groups involved. To the Burmans, the Christian Karen supported the foreign demolition of the kingdom and the humiliation of Buddhism. This historical opposition became a significant ingredient in the ensuing history and its narratives.

1881 AND 1947: CONJUNCTURES OF NATIONALISM – MAPPING NATION AND STATE

These two conjunctures were dominated by nationalism, independence and the prologue to the 54 years of rebellion. It began when the Karen formed the Karen National Association, KNA, (or Karen National Society) in 1881. According to Saw Tha Din, the founder was Than Bya, DD, who obtained his degree in the USA.[26] The KNA was said to be completely secular and independent of the Baptist Mission (*BMM* 1886: 334). Its origin and structure, however, was mostly described very briefly and often metaphorically in a few missionary journals and books (Bunker 1902).[27] It included some non-Christians, notably the Bwe prophet Meh-Tee and his followers. The Karen name of the KNA was Daw Ga Lu ('All the clans', i.e. all Karen groups). The missionaries realized that a future conflict between Buddhists and Christians could be a serious threat. They needed a separate political organization in order to co-operate with the colonial government and as a response to Burmese resistance.[28] Some colonial officials, in particular Donald Smeaton, officiating chief commissioner, whose book (1887) is a main source, supported it. He pronounced that the Karen were a nation thanks to the missionary efforts, but were also successful because, 'the movement has been truly a national one, a genuine uprising of the people themselves' (Smeaton 1887: 195). He quoted a Karen – probably Than Bya: '[T]here is ground wide enough for us all, without distinction of belief to meet on a common platform, united by ties broader even than this of religion' (ibid. 222–223). Christianity had segregated the Karen, he said, and it was time that the Karen helped each other to improved education and agriculture. This is very important because it signifies that they realized that they had to change the hostile boundaries created during the rebellion. Smeaton further emphasized the rights of the Karen as a separate nation: language, their own officials, education, village self-defence and development of a national civilization and religion (ibid. 237). Bunker (1902: 237) called it

Figure 9.2. A young Karen weaver, Thailand. (Photo: M. Gravers)

a spontaneous movement to counter the crisis of the 1880s, and this included preventing the Karen from producing utopian ideas and supporting *mìn laùng* movements. Nationalism was the instrument to unite the Karen and to replace traditional movements. A Karen barrister with an English degree and a former 'prophet' (*bu kho*), sitting side by side at the founding meeting, symbolized tradition within a modern identity. The ethnic-national identity was seen as the means to unite what religion, education and class had separated. The times when the Karen lived divided in separate groups and like orphans without leadership had ended and Smeaton refers to the various Karen myths about Yuah, the lost book and the story about Taw Meh Pha – all the ingredients reproduced as part of a homogeneous 'Karen culture' in numerous publications ever since.[29]

The process of nation-making, however, was slow and only after Sir San C. Po became a member of the Legislative Council in 1916 did Karen nationalism become more visible and outspoken about the possibilities of a future Karen 'homeland'. After 'pacification' many Karen enjoyed relative prosperity. Educated Karen, mostly Christians, became teachers, barristers or officers in the army. Among the Karen leaders were rich farmers and traders. The Karen had their own club in Rangoon, the Rangoon Karen Social and Services Club a significant symbol in colonial times.[30] However, from the club to the poor swidden farmers in the hills above Papun was a considerable social, political and cultural distance. During the Hsaya San rebellion 1931, Christian Karen police participated actively in fighting and killing the rebels thus confirming not only their loyalty to the British but also their opposition to Burmese nationalism and Buddhism.[31]

In the 1935 constitution, the Karen obtained a special representation. At this time, the KNA also began to claim an extension of their land to include Toungoo – 'the cradle of their traditions', while the British excluded 40–45 per cent of Burma's frontier areas as outside of what was later called 'Ministerial Burma'. The 'backward tracts' of this frontier area included the Kayah States and Salween District (see Map 1.1 on p. 15). The mapping of future nations and states had begun. How did the Karen in the KNA imagine a future nation state, and how did they map it – geographically and culturally? As I have argued elsewhere (Gravers 1996a: 265–269), a nation can be imagined by using variations of the same model at a general level as well as at a local village level, often containing serious contradictions, yet still forming an authentic representation. The process of identity formation thus takes place at different levels and is a contradictory process of segmentation – which is not the same as making a Karen national identity a mere fictitious construction; it has been a political reality for more than a century. In order legitimize a claim to a land as a nation, one has to be indigenous and among the first to arrive in the land. The Karen emphasized during the Burma Round Table conference in 1935 as a historical fact that they were the aborigines.[32] They came from China, according to a myth, and crossed the River of Flowing Sand, believed to be the Gobi Desert. This legend, which related to the missionary theory of the Lost Tribe of Israel, has been reproduced ever since and displayed in maps.[33]

In relation to modernity, the KNA imagined that the Karen – by virtue of knowledge, education and civilization – qualified to be a nation as attested to by missionaries and other foreigners. The general model implied an unchanging culture (race) but a changing consciousness. The following are examples of the rhetoric in 1945–47: 'Karens have meticulously preserved their race, creed and culture in spite of all changes. The national consciousness of the Karens has passed its embryonic stage.'[34] The cultural-religious homogeneity was also emphasized: 'No matter whether a Karen lives in the mountains or in the plains, whether Animist, Buddhist, Christian, Sgaw, Pwo ... A Karen is a Karen – one in blood – one in mass of nationhood ... this war [The Second World War] has awakened and aroused nationalism'.[35]

Their experience during the war is mentioned in all documents as decisive for the relative unity in 1945–47. The Burma Independent Army (BIA) and the Japanese Army attacked the Karen in and around Myaungmya, in the Irrawaddy Delta and around Papun. Many Karen had kept their weapons and three British officers stayed in the eastern hills after the British retreat. The tensions turned ugly when Christian Karen were murdered in churches where they had sought sanctuary. An estimated 1,800 Karen lost their lives. In Papun, ten elders were executed, women were raped and Karen taken as hostages in order to capture Major Seagrim, who stayed behind the Japanese lines. The Karen blamed the BIA and took the cruelty displayed as a clear sign that the two groups could never exist peacefully together.[36] Thus, xenophobia was produced and later reproduced on both sides. The remedy was a separate state and the criteria used in the mapping were geographical as well as mental/cultural and published in so called memorials from the KNA as well as booklets such as Saw Po Chit's cited in the introduction of this chapter. The first publication – the *Humble Memorial of the Karens of Burma* – was written in September 1945 by Saw Tha Din 'with the hope of realizing our just and national aspiration at this momentous juncture' – the Karen were 'second to none in loyalty.' The text is a mixture of Karen cosmology, myths and political rhetoric. Saw Tha Din emphazised that the Karen came into Burma before other ethnic groups and 'kept aloof as a race, jealously preserved their national identity'. They suffered mental and physical torture during the war and – the killing of 1,800 Karen in Myaungmya is mentioned in most papers – 'the Burmese treat Karens with contempt', 'The Karen under Christian missionaries helped to suppress crime and petty revolutions' (i.e. *mín laùng* rebellions).[37] This memorial was one of many papers circulated during the negotiations for independence and before a Karen delegation arrived – as the first – in London 1946 – presenting a somewhat confusing flow of arguments and statements. At first, the KNA included Kayah and part of Siam on the other side of Salween District with a Karen population, as well as Tenasserim and admission to the sea after an agreement with the Mon people. But gradually the area of the state was shrinking. Some Kayah supported the KNA insurrection while others did not want to be included in a Karen State.

There also seemed to have been a conflict between the Catholic Church and the Baptists in the Kayah States in 1948 (Smith 1991: 45).

However, there were several problems in the argumentation. The Karen were only in the majority in some areas, which were not connected.[38] There had been no certain figures for the Karen population, or who was included, since the 1931 census of 1.3 million. The KNA used the Japanese figure of 4 million as a reality and further claimed that 33 per cent were Christians.[39] The figure given by missionary sources is only 15–17 per cent. As the process continued, dissenting Karen voices appeared within the Karen Central Organization (KCO) formed to encompass the KNA as well as the Buddhist Karen organizations; the Karen Youth Organization (KYO), founded in 1945 and part of the AFPFL; and the Buddhist-dominated Burma Karen National Association (BKNA), which was against the goodwill mission to London, i.e. against the persons selected. They were all Christian Sgaw. The BKNA also wanted a Karen State, but argued that the discussion about a Karen State should take place at a conference including all Karen organizations. They also claimed to represent all Karen. However, little is written about the BKNA. It was founded in 1929 by Saw Pe Tha, barrister-at-law, Saw Ba Shwe (president in 1945) and U Punna Wuntha, a Buddhist monk, in order to promote unity among the Karen nation, create a national spirit and raise the standard of Karen in politics. It had 22 branches mainly in the plains.[40] The British side argued that the Buddhists normally sided with the Burmese: 'So far as our experience goes, Buddhist Karen have always identified with the Burmese and have never asked to be classified as a separate race.' [41] The last point is important because it is a significant difference in the way ethnicity was defined. Many Christians used race as a criteria. However, the first point is not entirely correct. In early 1946, all Karen organizations (KCO, BBKN, KYO) asked for a separate state and many Buddhist Karen supported the idea of a Karen State, either inside Burma or independently, until Christian leaders formed the Karen National Union (KNU) in January 1947 and began to dominate the political process. However, many later supported Aung San, the AFPFL and a unitary state. The situation is difficult to assess from the documents because the voices of the Buddhists are subdued: perhaps they were not skilled memorialists?

Reading the statements in the documents reveals a very complex narrative of opposing views, which cannot be related here. The important information is, however, that although the majority of Karen agreed on the basic notions supporting their national identity versus Burmese identity, they were not united politically above the local or district levels. The local associations flooded the British with contradictory statements and ideas. Interestingly, the relatively wealthy Karen from the Irrawaddy Delta (many leaders came from this region) and the poor Karen in the eastern mountains had mutual interests at one level: local control of resources; the Delta Karens wanted to keep their fertile land while the mountain Karen wanted teak concessions and economic aid.

In 1947 the Karen name of the state appeared for the first time in the documents as Kaw Thu Lay (Kawthoolei). The term has been translated as 'Flowering country'; however, the meaning is symbolic: 'the old land', according to Saw Tha Din. Importantly, it does not refer to any exact geographical area but to a symbolic space. And looking at the political landscape in 1947 as it appears from the documents and publications, it is clear that Kawthoolei was not an interconnected land. This lack of interconnectedness can be illustrated by the list of delegates to the Karen meetings. They represented local KNA associations and districts, with a few delegates from the Buddhist organizations, and they often presented contradictory views. A list from the mass meeting in July 1945 showed not only differences in class and status, but delineated the political geography and its centres: Bassein (Sir San C. Po), Rangoon (Sidney Loo Nee and U Punna Wuntha), Pegu (Saw Hunter Tha Hmwe) – but with the Karen Club in Rangoon as a separate delegation (Saw Tha Din and Saw Ba U Gyi, who followed Saw Tha Din as president of the KNU in 1947) – all belonging to the Karen elite. When the Japanese surrendered, the Karen leaders from Papun joined. However, this area was the most divided in opinions about the status of a future state. In particular, the Buddhist Karen in the KYO wanted to join Burma and even some of the heroes from Force 136 in Papun – Saw Di Gay among others – who signed the constitution and was later executed by the KNU. The Karen around Papun had formed the United Karen Organization with the purpose of securing their own representation although formally related to the KNU. They did not want the interference of Karen leaders from the plains. Initially, the leader of the Loyal Karen Organization in Toungoo, Saw Johnson Po Min, demanded a separate state instantly, then later he supported the AFPFL and a unitary state.[42] In many cases the local relations and identities overruled the religious differences and organizational affiliations although religious and political identity dominated the overall picture.

Kawthoolei remained a symbolic ethnic space with deep opposite lines of identification in terms of class, education, custom, religion – in fact all the criteria often listed in the memoranda as general elements for a Karen identity. This contradictory character of the process of identification is crucial in order to understand the complexity.

Another line of division was the generation gap. According to Saw Tha Din, the young leaders were much more militant and when the British failed to reply to the Karen proposal – in late 1947 including the Delta and Insein – the rebellion was unavoidable. The Karen National Defence Organization (KNDO) was formed in 1948 in order to protect Karen against atrocities similar to the wartime killings. Yet, the arming of a Christian defence force invited attack from a Burmese defence organization formed by the Peoples Volunteer Organization (PVO) and supposedly controlled by Ne Win and the army. In Palaw in Tenasserim, in the place where Mason commenced his work as missionary, 80 Christian Karen were killed in their church on Christmas Eve 1948. Loaded with symbolic matter, this was the start of 54 years of devastating civil war. Looking back in history, that event was inevitably going to take place within this conjuncture – it was already symbolically inscribed in history.

Saw Tha Din insisted that had the British told them that an independent state was not realistic and would not win British and Commonwealth support after Burma's independence, then they would have changed their strategy. The feeling of not getting the exact information and of being deserted by their white brother became an ingrained part of future political legend in the KNU. They firmly believed that they would obtain support from Britain and other Western countries. Saw Tha Din formulated the Karen expectations in the Memorandum in 1946: 'An intuitive feeling born of tradition and prophecy that their White Brother would come to help them had long taken root in them, and this prophecy has to a large degree been fulfilled.' [43] Thus, Karen nationalism largely relied on support from the younger, white brother. However, by boycotting the elections, the KNU probably alienated many Karen as well as British supporters, to whom democracy was as important as nationalism.

The following years saw Kawthoolei marred by internal factions of left and right, of local warlords such as the KNU leader and former headmaster, Saw Hunter Tha-Hmwe, who styled himself *kau ga cha* – 'lord of the land' in Papun. This trend seemed to have its roots back in Karen rebellions and struggles in the nineteenth century, more than in modern nationalism. In 1955 Papun fell and Kawthoolei shrank drastically over the following years.[44] Bo Mya reintroduced patriotism and nationalism in a Christian version when he became president of the KNU in 1976 after out-manoeuvring the leftist Karen National Unity Party led by Mahn Ba Zahn. Inside Burma, the KNDO/KNU had competition from several parties. The United Karen League (UKL), mainly Delta Karen, was the largest. Under the leadership of Ba Maung Chain, Minister of the Karen State and daughter of San C. Po, the UKL tried to mediate between the KNU and the government. Union Karen Organization (UKO) was Buddhist and based in the Karen State. This party worked closely with the government and fiercely opposed the KNU. Karen from the UKO disclosed the hiding place of KNU president Saw Ba U Gyi, who was ambushed north of Kawkareik and killed by the army. A smaller party, the Karen Congress, was also Buddhist. These parties all supported the Karen State within the Union.

As shown above, the imagination of a Karen nation became very complex when the diversity and local segmentation within the ethnic unity entered the process, and within this complexity. I suggest that the religions divide was decisive, yet somehow not made explicit, because it is a structure embedded and partly concealed in the local communal divide. The British pointed to poor Karen leadership, no sense of community and the old Karen weakness of following prophetic types of leaders. The Karen leaders replied that it suited the British well to act confused, thus avoiding clarification of their position and thus contributing to the confusion. The White Paper of 1945 mentioned a Karen State – a reward for loyalty – but the problem in the proposal was that representation of the Karen nation was based on the assumption of a culturally homogeneous entity in contradiction to the realities. During the negotiations, the imagination of a Karen nation had become too blurred and the boundaries to fuzzy to all parties. However, this is not to say that the Karen nation was and is an illusory construction but was an entity with huge inner contradictions. The greatest suffering hit all those Karen, Buddhists, Animists, or Christian, to whom no neutral position was, or has been, available in this long conflict, not even in the refugee camps in Thailand. Thus, all are likely to be drawn into the conflict as victims.

1994: CONJUNCTURE OF RELIGIOUS DIVIDE

After more than 40 years of struggle, sufferings and displacement it is perhaps not surprising that many Karen looked to a the establishment of a space with peace, a place without weapons and violence. That is perhaps the reason why many Buddhist Karen in 1994 had joined the Buddhist movements led by the monk U Thuzana and inspired by the venerable U Thamanya and his vegetarian-meditative Buddhists who are very much in line with Karen traditions. The two monks formed zones of peace around their monasteries, sanctuaries and sacred spaces in the landscape, with pagodas in the centre, where displaced Karen could take refuge and get free food. U Thuzana had a prophecy: when 50 white pagodas have been built, peace will come and spread among the Karen. Several thousands of poor and displaced Karen gathered at his and Thamanya's monasteries with their families. This is very much in line with the Buddhist movements in previous centuries. His movement criticized the KNU for not paying attention to the poor Buddhist Karen and their religion and demanded the construction of a pagoda in Manerplaw, the KNU headquarters until 1995. He himself organized the construction of a white pagoda on a hill overlooking Manerplaw at Thu Mwe Tha. Some KNLA officers and many subaltern Karen – Pwo in particular – supported him. When the armed wing, DKBA, began to use violent tactics similar to the Burmese army in the name of the DKBO and U Thuzana, he withdrew to meditate and is said to have continued building pagodas. Most of the population living around his Myang Gyi Ngu monastery left when food supplies dwindled. The DKBA is a dwindling force surviving on looting and drug sales. DKBA soldiers led by a monk attacked a Muslim village in the Karen State and torched it. Other Muslim villages were attacked previously, a development possibly part of a country-wide campaign. Meanwhile, his teacher, the late Hsayadaw U Thamanya, became the spiritual adviser of Daw Aung San Suu Kyi and an estimated 20.000 Pa-o, Karen and others have settled in a well-organized community in search for protection, peace and a livelihood. Interestingly, the monk had supporters among both the Rangoon business community and among poor hill villagers.[45] Significantly, Bo Mya, former president of the KNU, was in charge of the reopened negotiations with the SPDC. The negotiations have become difficult after Khin Nyunt's dismissal and because the KNU did not dare to give up armed protection of the villages they still control. Violence, displacement and violence seem to have increased. The DKBA lost their patron, Khin Nyunt, and there have been reports of clashes with the army. As of late 2005, the situation is still uncertain, though violence seems to have decreased somewhat.

Figure 9.3. Mae La refugee camp, Thailand. (Photo: M. Gravers)

Minor Karen groups who have entered an agreement with the regime, such as the Karen Peace Army, control some areas. In 2000 a small KNU faction called God's Army attracted the media with its mixture of Christianity and supernatural beliefs (see Gravers 2001a). The zone of peace and Buddhist merit is probably still a model, that can attract Karen across denominations and inter-ethnic boundaries. Although not a totally neutral position, it is a model, that at least promotes the idea of non-violence, which is so badly needed if peace and reconciliation are going to succeed.

In this conjuncture the KNU has maintained its position towards the military regime and is reluctant to enter an agreement forcing the Karen National Liberation Army to give up its weapons.[46] However, the KNU now supports a federal constitution and is not going to demand an independent state. The problem, though, is how to base a new constitution on ethnic criteria, which are often disputed internally as well as externally by the various groups and categories. The KNU still has to address the internal diversity among the Karen, including the generation gap. The Karen National League (KNL), founded in 1997 by relatively young, educated Karen in diaspora seems to support the present KNU political line. Although they support the KNU they also look to the global situation and the change in views of ethnic liberation movements in this 'era of terrorism'. Yet they are conscious of the generational differences in experience, knowledge and opinion: 'Are we dominated by younger people, at the expense of alienating older people?'[47] The young advocate new strategies for reconciliation relevant in the present world order and will not accept a future as permanent poor refugees, who are obliged to serve a futile struggle and risk health and life. In fact, they continue the long Karen tradition in search of peace and prosperity as the basis for Karen identity.

An equally important task is to assess and research the different experiences and knowledge generated among the various Karen communities inside Burma, in the refugee camps as well as in the Karen diaspora around the world. A pan-Karen global and cosmomopolitan identity is under construction: cf. the slogan on the Karen/org website: 'Karen around the world unite'. The majority of the Karen diaspora, however, linger in refugee camps and struggle for an identity that maintains the 'homely' and 'traditional' they left involuntarily (see Dudley, this volume). I am sure these experiences, outside as well as inside Burma, have developed far beyond the ideas and values of 1947 on which the present elder generation still seems to conduct the struggle. A committee, the Karen Development Committee, which is preparing for peace and reconciliation, has been formed in Yangon consisting of respected Karen elder leaders, doctors, clerics and scholars. In 2002, a convention arranged by this committee drew a large gathering of Karen in Hpa-an.[48] However, the Karen Peace Committee, based in Hpa-an, and consisting of Christian leaders and Buddhist monks, are offended by the activities of the Development Committee and by their intervention locally. It seems as though the old pattern of split repeats itself but the situation is perhaps seen in a very different perspective inside the Karen communities in Burma.[49] Initiatives for reconciliation have to come from organizations, that can encompass the diversity and control the centrifugal powers.

CONCLUDING ANALYSIS

At the most general level, religious conversion among the non-Burman ethnic groups created a serious contradiction between a new, imagined homogeneous pan ethnic (pan-Karen) identity and the previous communitarian identities based on local moral and ritual communities. Beneath this simple opposition, however, is a vast complexity, which we have to consider. The following is but a very incomplete attempt at a huge task.

Conversion to Christianity (and Buddhism) created new social and cultural distinctions based on knowledge traditions which included elements of traditional Karen cosmology and myths and a specific validity *vis-à-vis* Buddhism – a moral superiority in particular. It created new boundaries within Karen communities and resulted in violent confrontations in specific conjunctures. These conjunctures form a historical genealogy which is an important part of the national imagination of pan-Karen identity as well as of the literature on the Karen; in other words, a crucial ingredient of Karen identification. Moreover, Christianity became part of an external categorization of the Karen (Kayin) by the Burmans as synonymous with the foreigners who colonized Burma – and in recent years with the external neo-colonial forces, as defined by the military regime. These were viewed as disruptive forces in 1852, 1886, 1947, endangering the Burmese state. It is also a category confronted by a process of 'Burmanization' such as demolishing Christian crosses and churches. For example, the army have replaced Christian crosses on hilltops in the Chin division with Buddhist pagodas as part of an intensified symbolic power struggle.[50]

At one extreme of this process of difference and opposition, conversion (Christian and Buddhist) has thus created a common identification beyond the local communities. It has empowered individuals and communities with knowledge, organization and economically. During my recent fieldwork in Thailand, Karen often mentioned the hope for an improved livelihood as the reason for giving up animism and converting to Christianity or following charismatic monks. This may also have been the case in Burma. Last, but not least, liberation from evil spirits and their demands of animal sacrifices in complicated rituals is important – a liberation also emphasized today by animist Karen who adopt Buddhism in order to stop the costly and difficult rituals. Thus, conversion is both a communal and an individual experience.

At the other extreme of the process of religious change, the Karen have maintained their customs and strict moral order in the local communities. Conversion thus was not seen as merely a conversion to modernity, but a retrieval of their old religious order.[51] Thus, Buddhism and Christianity as two different traditions of knowledge were integrated in Karen custom within the same process of transformation and crisis as expressed in the chain of conjunctures. Each conjuncture refers to previous ones and carries the prediction of future conjunctures. Furthermore, religion formed the basis for political organization. Christian associations were the foundation of the KNA/KNU as a political movement. Unfortunately, we know very little about the foundation of the Buddhist Karen organizations.

The cognitive model of Kawthoolei has continued to be an important element in the Karen nationalist struggle. However, the social bonds and political cohesion necessary to maintain the reality of this model has been undermined by internal diversity, as I have tried to demonstrate. An autonomous symbolic and almost sanctified space, like Kawthoolei, is increasingly difficult to maintain and define geo-politically, and a future Karen definition of a nation will have to include the diversity of 'all the clans'. It will have to address the problem of internal boundaries and local differences in order to create a realistic strategy that is less focused on boundary making. Christianity and national unity have been symbolically enlarged beyond realities while local diversity and concerns have been ignored.

Moreover, the violent conflicts involving Buddhism and Christianity have created boundaries defined by a mixture of religion and violence. Violence produces a unique form of embodied knowledge and experience, forever stored in the social memory as extreme physical and symbolic losses. These losses enter the ethnic boundaries signifying an eternal opposition. Such identity boundaries, based on widespread suffering and deep mistrust, are perhaps the most difficult to reconcile and eliminate in the future – unless a new cognitive model with other modalities of mutual identification is established. The new model must, I suggest, initiate co-operation in a demilitarized, civil society, dealing with practical matters such as the resettlement of displaced persons, housing, supplies, education and work in order to re-establish local communities of trust. Local identities can be used as a source of plurality in democracy provided that they are not the objects of a politics of difference. Self-identification within local communities does not exclude a sense of belonging to a wider Karen community. On the other hand, if the focus is on the incompatibilities of differences, internally as well as externally, and the sense of eternal victimhood is emphasized, it will be extremely difficult to dismantle the symbolic minefields of the ethnic-religious boundaries. Ethnic (religious) autonomy has become synonymous with a modern existential right and, at the same time, a source of conflict and fear in the sense of individual and collective loss and destruction. Only by a careful analysis of the historical ingredients are we able to envisage new social bonds and practices beyond conflict-ridden boundaries.

Religion can unite and support a universal Karen-ness; at the same time it can generate division and struggles for legitimacy, inclusive as well as exclusive. Thus, religion is a crucial medium of political representation and it often sanctifies a specific social order, its classifications and identifications. In spite of the struggle between religious representations of Karen identity, the Karen knowledge tradition (*ta a lu a la*) remains an alternative mode of identification to those subsumed under the politics of difference. In this respect, it is crucial to understand that conversion rarely, if ever, has implied discarding custom among the Karen (Gravers 2004b).

Is it then possible to imagine an alternative scenario with emphasis on a pan-Karen identity? Perhaps, provided that the Karen knowledge tradition is liberated from the political discourse of nationalism and ethnicism; and provided that religion does not imply a total conversion of socio-cultural and political identification. *Ta a lu a la* is basically democratic as long as it recognizes local customs (*mo a lu pha a la*). In its core it contains a discourse on ethics and morality, that has been included in all religious denominations. This discourse focuses on peace, prosperity and non-violence in a community of trust– these constitute important elements in a democratic discourse and generate a new conjuncture of expectations and of reconciliation.

In concluding this chapter, the complexity of the problems of ethnic and religious diversity has only been analysed superficially, and many voices, Burmese and Karen, have not been included in this presentation. However, I hope to have demonstrated the importance of analysing the process of identification in its historical complexity and to have outlined a consistent pattern within a chain of conjunctures.

A NOTE ON THE ETYMOLOGY OF THE TERM 'KAREN'

The term 'Karen' is derived from Mon *Kareang* and Burman *Kayin*. Mon however, differentiated between Kareang Bamar (Sgaw) and Kareang Mon (Pwo). In Tavoy, missionaries recorded the term *Mie'so* (*Miattho*) for Sgaw and *Mie'kin* (*Miatkhyin*) for Pwo. (*Miatkhyin* implying 'river-Chin' is probably a typical confusion of ethnic terms before the modern idea of ethnicity as static and firm categories.)

Mason (1860: 71) translated *ayin* as 'pristine', 'bottom' and *ka* is a primitive particle meaning 'aboriginal'. However he emphasized that the Karen are not the aboriginals of Burma. This is significant because there was no obvious negative connotation implied at that time and Mason was a keen linguist. The category Kayin seems to have included the Karen-ni ('red Karen') as they were called in the colonial time and who use the term 'Kayah' (sometimes with *liy* = red). The Pa-o are often classified as a 'Karen' group but maintain a separate identity, though related to the large Karennic speaking category. They argue that the Pa-o had their own history and lost their kingdom to the Burmans. They also emphasize that they differ in appearance.[52] In Kayah State there are several minor groups related to Kayah/Karen (see F.K.L. Chit Hlaing chapter 4 and Dudley chapter 3 this volume).

Sgaw use the term *'Pgha G' Nyau'* and add *Sghau* as an ethnic classifier to differentiate from *Pgho*. These two terms became 'Sgaw' and 'Pwo' in English. Likewise some Pwo use the ethnic classifiers *Sho* for Pwo and *Shaung* for Sgaw as ethnic classifiers but use the term *'Ga Phloung'*. Further, people will refer to area and place of origin: 'Karen' from Toungoo meeting cousins from Bassein or Papun will use a long register of identifications, including language, customs, place/village names, relatives and so forth, in order to establish both common identity and diversity.

Mason (1860) and *BMM* (1833: 115) recorded these differences, but in the mass volume of missionary and colonial publications the diversity was subsumed under the term 'Karen', thus concealing the differences. This mode of homogenizing categorization caused many problems during the independence negotiations in 1947 – a lesson to be learned!

AUTHOR'S NOTE

I am indebted to many helpful persons during my stays at the OIOC, British Library, in particular Patricia Herbert and Daw San San May. The initial inspiration came from Saw Tha Din in his lectures in Sangkhlaburi, Thailand in 1971. He taught my two colleagues Kirsten Ewers Andersen and Anders Baltzer Jørgensen and myself the essence of Karen conversion and nationalism and how they are historically intertwined. The friendly discussions in Gothenburg 2002 further stimulated the work. Thanks to a grant from the Carlsberg Fund, I was able to collect additional information during fieldwork in Thailand in 2003. I am grateful for the valuable comments and suggestions from the two anonymous readers of the manuscripts.

NOTES

[1] Memorandum entitled *Historical Background* attached to a pamphlet entitled *The Case for the Karens* 1946. Oriental and India Office Collections (OIOC): Mss. Eur.E.252/22. For further details see Gravers 1996a.

[2] The KNU website www. Karen.Org gives the figure 3o per cent Christians. It is very difficult to assess the figures; more Sgaw than Pwo are Christians.

[3] It is very difficult to reconstruct pre-colonial use of ethnic terms. The 'Karen-ness' of today certainly did not exist; as Pwo Karen informants said to the author in 1970: 'Pwo, Sgaw and Pa-o are like siblings and cousins' – related but of different lines.

[4] This description builds on general information obtained from Karen refugees and missionaries since my first fieldwork in Thailand in 1970–72 and not on exact data on the correlation between religion, status and ethnicity. In a recent interview with *Mizzima News*, Bo Mya, vice-president of the KNU, called U Thuzana, the Pwo Karen founder of the DKBO, 'the treacherous monk, [who] doesn't know any politics and doesn't know what religion truly means', 15 March 2004, www.karen.org/news/wwwboard//messages.

[5] See Jenkins (2001), Sökefeld (2001); Barth (2002b) on differences and categorization; see Lehman (1967a: 102) on categorization in Burma; and Wilmsen and McAllister (1996) on the politics of difference. On the politics of ethnicity in Burma, see R. Taylor (1982).

[6] See Karin Dean's discussion of space and boundary in this volume.

[7] Some scholars consider a common Karen identity to be an invention (Raja 1990: 121), or problematic, 'as peoples known as "Karen" do not share a common language, culture, religion or material characteristics' (Cheesman 2002: 199). However, what is indeed problematic is to deny the Karen a common, authentic identity, primordial or not, and a denial based on academic deconstruction of Karen historical narratives, (see further Gravers 1996a on authenticity). The category 'Karen' and the various sub-groups are segments within the same process of identification. The history of politicization of Karen identity and ethnicity is related in details in Harriden (2002).

[8] Saw Po Chit: 'Karens and Karen State', booklet published in 1946, *Karens Political Future*, pp.167–174.

[9] KNU (1992: 6; 1998: 1). In the last document it is said that the Karen 'having all the essentials of a nation'. In a 1992Grenada documentary in the series 'Disappearing Worlds', a Sgaw Karen teacher characterizes the Karen as meek, humble and honest; and the Burmans as violent.

[10] While conducting fieldwork in the 1970s, during the struggle between the Thai Communist Party and the army, I was often asked: 'Are we going to fight, like in Burma in the past and the present?'

[11] On the concept of knowledge versus culture see Barth (2002a).

[12] The local differences, for example in rituals, are also manifest among the Buddhist Pwo in Uthaithani and Kanchanaburi I have visited since 1970.

[13] The Baptist Missionary Magazine (BMM), (1844: 230–232).

[14] For a discussion of Karen ideas of change, see Gravers (2004b).

[15] BMM (1845: 85).

[16] Francis Mason, who was a member of the Royal Asiatic Society and a great ethnographer, was a driving force in promoting the unitary depiction of a Karen culture and assisted by the second Karen convert, Saw Quala, who collected myths and traditions among the Karen (see BMM 1834; 1856). But not all missionaries adopted the idea of the lost tribe.

[17] See Mason (1833: 354): 'War, fighting and quarrelling will be unknown', when Ariya arrives. See furtherGravers (2001c). It is not difficult to imagine, that some Karen confused Jesus and Ariya. Even today, some Karen in Sangkhlaburi believe that it may be the same figure.

[18] F. Mason (1884: 155).

[19] Missionary Vinton was asked by Karen near Moulmein: 'Are you God?' (BMM 1836: 295). Those who converted were probably Karen with no relations to patrons among monks and Burmese officials.

[20] 'Wherever the power of the Holy Spirit has been manifest, church growth and development have always resulted' (Saw Doh Say 1990: 132); '... the Holy Spirit is the Supreme Strategist...' (ibid. 168–169). See Harding (1987) on the role of the Holy Spirit in Baptist conversion.

[21] The late president of the KNU, Saw Tha Din, emphasized this in his lectures to my two colleagues and me in Sangkhlaburi, Thailand 1971.

[22] See BMM (1840: 216;1833: 43; 1853: 176). Women often resisted conversion fiercely because they were responsible for the household rituals, and thus for the well being of its members. The *au hrae* ritual of sacrificing chickens and pigs has mainly a function of healing in the family and relates to births and marriages. See Hyami (2004) for a detailed description. Among the Buddhist Pwo Karen of the Lu Baung movement, a woman who converts risks her health and that of her family as well.

[23] See Hefner (1993: 13) for an anthropological discussion of this perspective.

[24] During my fieldwork in Thailand, Karen always complained that *kho la* [the foreigner] never reveals all his knowledge! When the Telakhon movement rejected the Bible offered by Baptist missionaries, the reason they gave was that it did not reveal scientific knowledge (Stern 1968: 324).

[25] For details and the historical sources on the rebellion, see Gravers (1999; 2001c).

[26] Interview 15 January 1971. Than Bya published several books in Sgaw on Karen history: *The Karens and their Sufferings 1824–54*, Rangoon, 1904; and *The Karens and Their Progress A.D. 1854–1914*, Rangoon, 1913.

[27] More research is needed on the origin and structure of the KNA. In New York in 1860, Ellen B. Mason presented a Karen flag, blue with a sword across the

Bible and these words: 'The Word of God, which is the Sword of the Spirit', created by Saw Quala, who wanted a national banner *'as other book nations'* (E. B. Mason 1862: 265, my emphasis).

[28] Bunker (1902: 237); Cady (1958: 99, 138).

[29] One of the most recent is Falla (1991). Other titles combining Karen custom, religion and nationalism, since E. B. Mason (1862), are McMahon (1876); Smeaton (1887); Bunker (1902); San C. Po (1928); Morrison (1947).

[30] See further Gravers (1999). A more detailed analysis of the social stratification among the Karen is needed in order to ascertain this trend. However, in general the Karen prospered in 'Plural Society'. The club was a cover for resistance against the Japanese.

[31] Buddhism and monks became a crucial factor in Burmese nationalism and resistance against colonialism (see U Maung Maung 1980). In recent years they have been part of the struggle for democracy as well as in the military regime's nationalistic hegemony. More details and references are found in Gravers (1996b; 1999).

[32] Burma Round Table Conference 1931–32, OIOC, Md 4004 vi, 233.

[33] For a recent source see the pamphlet published by the KNU (1992). According to this source, the Karen arrived in Yunnan in 1385 BC and in Burma 739 BC. See also KNU (1998). The year 739 is now presented as a historical fact, like in the New Year Speech of KNU President, Saw Ba Thin Sein in 2005, Karen Era 2744 (www. karen. Org/New Year 2005/). Saw Tha Din argued in the memorandum of 1946 that Toungoo was founded by the Karen 600 years ago and cited Ellen B. Mason (1862); see also the *Case for the Karens*, p. 9.

[34] *The Case for the Karens* p. 7.

[35] *Karen's Political Future* OIOC M/4/3023 1947: 351.

[36] During the war many Karen joined the British Force 136 to fight the Japanese and in 1945, about 12,000 Karen were armed!

[37] *Karen's Political Future*, pp. 22–28.

[38] Saw Hanson Thadaw (1961) provides interesting demographic data. The British urged the Karen to settle in the lowlands and a considerable movement took place. After the insurrection in 1949, many moved uphill to avoid violence.

[39] *The Case for the Karens* p. 4. Sir John Clague calculated the Karen population to be 1,514,142; 250,000 of these Christians; 70 per cent of all Karen lived in the Delta around 1947, as wealthy as their Burman neighbours; 86 per cent of the population in Salween were Karen (OIOC, M-4-30-24).

[40] See the file FO/643/71 in the Public Record Office, Kew. See also Maung Maung (1989: 346) who says that the BBKA was equally strong as the KNA.

[41] British Memorandum 1933, OIOC M/120: 4

[42] Actually, there were several independent, local Karen organizations with affiliations to the main organizations. The complexity of this political geography

is described in the document *'The Karen's Political Future'* M/4/3023; Tinker (1983–84) published several of the documents.

43 *The Case for the Karens*, Memorandum p. 2 OIOC.

44 On the complex developments and the factions, see Tinker (1983–1984); M. Smith (1991: 214) writes that Saw Hunter Tha Hmwe was a fundamentalist Christian, a strong nationalist and racialist who believed that the Old Testament had shown the way to the Karen national revolution. He opposed the left-leaning Karen National United Party (KNUP) and signed a peace accord with Ne Win resulting in fighting between his forces and supporters of KNUP near Papun.

45 Keiko Tosa (2002). On the attacks on Muslims, see Irrawaddy 30 April, 2003. U Thamanya died in November 2003 and was followed by a Pa-o monk.

46 The older generation in the KNU leadership may find it hard to give up the armed struggle. The young are looking for new strategies and want to co-operate with Karen organizations inside Burma (Saw Kwe Htoo *et al.* 2004). All have worried that the army will not respect an agreement.

47 Cited from a speech by Karen National League president, Naw May Oo, in 1999, www.Karen.org/news/www/board//messages/380.html. See also freeburmacoalition.org/_The younger generation seem to have abandoned most of the traditional KNU nationalistic rhetoric.

48 Personal communication; the meeting was reported in *the Myanmar Times*, 5–11 May, 2003: 6.

49 Oh Yoon Ah (personal communication) in an interesting study among the Karen of Insein has shown that the younger generation of Baptist Karen do not share the KNU vision of a nation and identify more with a broader Burmese community and even with a Myanmar identity.

50 On the situation in the Chin State, see Za Uk Ling and Bawi Lian Mang (2004). Churches have been demolished and Christian Chin beaten by soldiers.

51 For a discussion of conversion, modernity and globalization of Christianity, see van der Veer (1996). He emphasizes the ambivalence about the past. However, Baptist Karen seem to reconcile the past and the present. Christianity reinstated the moral order, God controls the supernatural forces, and Christian rituals have replaced the traditional ones, as it was explained to me in a Sgaw Karen Baptist community in 2000, Mae Chaem district, Thailand (Gravers 2004b). They also 'convert' or inscribe Christianity into their customs.

52 Khun Okker, chairman of Pa-o Peoples Liberation Organization, personal communication, December 2004.

REFERENCES

Agnew, John and Corbridge, Stuart 1987. *Place and Politics: The Geographical Mediation of State and Society.* Boston: Allen & Unwin.

—— 1995. *Mastering Space: Hegemony, Territory and International Political Economy.* London and New York, Routledge.

Amnesty International 1988. *Burma. Extrajudicial Execution and Torture of Members of Ethnic Minorities.* London.

—— 1990. *Myanmar. 'In the National Interest'. Prisoners of Conscience, Torture, Summary Trial under Martial Law.* London.

Amyodha Yinkheihmu Sazaung [Magazine of national culture] 1962, vol. 1. (in Bamar).

Anderson, Benedict 1983. *Imagined Communities: Reflections on the Origin and Spread of Nationalism,* London: Verso.

Anderson, James 1996. 'The Shifting Stages of Politics: New Medieval and Postmodern Territorialities'. *Enviroment and Planning D: Society and Space,* Vol. 14.

Appadurai, A. (ed.). 1986. *The Social Life of Things. Commodities in Cultural Perspective.* Cambridge: Cambridge University Press.

Appadurai, Arjun 1996. 'Life after primordialism.' In Appadurai (ed.); *Modernity at Large. Cultural Dimensions of Globalizations.* Minneapolis: University of Minnesota Press, pp. 139–157.

Appleby, Joyce 1998. 'The power of history', *The American Historical Review,* Vol. 103, No. 1. February.

Atran, Scott 1990. *Cognitive Foundation of Natural History.* Cambridge: Cambridge University Press.

Aung-Thwin, Michael 1983. 'Divinity, spirit, and human: Conceptions of classical Burmese kingship'. In Lorraine Gesick (ed), *Centres, Symbols, and Hierarchies: Essays on the Classical States of Southeast Asia.* Monograph Series no. 26. New Haven: Yale University Southeast Asia Studies, pp. 45–86.

—— 1998. *Myth and History in the Historiography of Early Burma: Paradigms, Primary Sources, and Prejudices.* Ohio University Center of International Studies.

Aye Naing B.A., U 1980. *Hsenhit Yadhi Myanma Yoya Yadhi Pwe Daw Mya*, [The twelve months of traditional festivals in Myanmar], Department of Religious Affairs Printing. (In Bamar).

Banks, M. 1996. *Ethnicity: Anthropological Constructions*. London: Routledge.

Baptist Missionary Magazine (BMM), vols.11–17, 1831–1837;vols 19–21, 1839–1841; vols. 24–25; 1844–1845; vol. 29, 1849; vols. 31–33, 1851–1853; vol. 36, 1856; vol. 48, 1868; vol. 60, 1880; vols. 65–66, 1885–1886.

Barnes, R. H. 1995. 'Introduction'. In R. H. Barnes, A. Gray and B. Kingsbury (eds); *Indigenous Peoples of Asia*. Ann Arbor: Association for Asian Studies.

Barth, Fredrik 1969. *Ethnic Groups and Boundaries. The Social Organization of Culture Difference*. Oslo: Universitetsforlaget.

—— 2000. 'Boundaries and connections'. In A. P. Cohen (ed.), *Signifying Identities. Anthropological Perspectives on Boundaries and Contested Values*. London: Routledge.

—— 2002a. 'Anthropology of knowledge', *Current Anthropology*, Vol. 43, No.1: pp. 1–11.

—— 2002b. 'Boundaries and connections'. In Anthony P. Cohen (ed.), *Signifying Identities. Anthropological Perspectives on Boundaries and Contested Values*. London: Routledge, pp. 17–35.

Bauman, Zygmunt 2001. *Community. Seeking Safety in an Insecure World*: Malden, Polity Press.

Bigandet, Paul Ambroise 1887. *An Outline of the History of the Catholic Burmese Mission from the Year 1720 to 1887*. Rangoon: Hanthawaddy Press.

Bloul, Rachel A.D. 1999. 'Beyond ethnic identity: Resisting exclusionary identification', *Social Identities* Vol. 5, No. 1.

Bourdieu, P. 1977. *Algérie 1960: Structures Économiques et Structures Temporelles*. Paris: Les Éditions de Minuit.

—— 1984. *Distinction*. London: Routledge & Kegan Paul.

—— 1992. *Language and Symbolic Power*: Cambridge, Polity Press.

Bourdieu, P. and Passeron J.C. 1977. *Reproduction in Education, Society & Culture*. London: Sage.

Brac de la Perrier, Bénédicte 2003. 'Sibling relationships in the Nat stories of the Burmese cult to the "Thirty-seven"'. *Moussons* 5, pp. 31–48.

Brown, David 1994. *The State and Ethnic Politics in Southeast Asia*.New York: Routledge Curzon.

Bunker, Alonso 1902. *Soo Thah. A Tale of the Karens*. New York: Flemming H. Revell Company.

Burma Centre Netherlands and Transnational Institute (eds.) 1999. *Strengthening Civil Society: Possibilities and Dilemmas for International NGOs*. Silkworm Books.

Burma Citizenship Law (Pyithu Hluttaw Law of No. 4 of 1982).

Burma Gazette, part 1, 13 July 1895. Rangoon: Authority.

Burma Roundtable Conference. House of Commons 1931–1932, MD 404vi.

Burma Socialist Lanzin Party (BSLP) (ed.) 1968. *Tainyindha Yinkheihmu hnin Yoya Dalei Htonsan Mya, Shan*, [Culture and Customs of National Race of the Shan], Yangon: Central Office of Burma Socialist Lanzin Party. (In Bamar).

The Burma Socialist Programme Party 1963. 'The system of correlation of man and his environment'. Rangoon.

Cady, John F. 1958. *A History of Modern Burma*. Ithaca: Cornell University Press.

Calhoun, Craig 1994. *Neither Gods Nor Emperors: Students and the Struggle for Democracy in China*. Berkeley: University of California Press.

Callahan, Mary 1996. The Origins of Military Rule in Burma. PhD Thesis, Cornell University.

Carey, B. S. and Tuck H.N. 1983 [1896]. *Chin Hills: A History of the People, British Dealing with them, their Customs and Manners, and a Gazetteer of their Country*. Rangoon: Government Printing. Reprinted in New Delhi: Cultural Publishing House.

Carson, Laura 1927. *Pioneer Trails, Trails and Triumph*. New York: Baptist Board Publication.

The Case for the Karens 1946. Pamphlet entitled:'After India ...Burma?' London, and a memorandum entitled 'Historical Background', Mss.Eur.252/22, Sir John Clague Collection.

CCSDPT (Co-ordinating Committee for Services to Displaced Persons in Thailand). 1995. *Educational Assessment of Mon and Karenni Refugee Camps on the Thai/Burmese Border*. Bangkok: CCSDPT.

Census of India 1931, 1933 Vol.11 Burma Pt1, 1933, Rangoon: Office of the Superintendent., Government Printing and Stationery.

Cheesman, Nick 2002. 'Seeing "Karn" in the Union of Myanmar',. *Asian Ethnicity*, Vol. 3, no. 2, pp. 199–220.

The Chin Human Rights Organization (CHRO) 2004. *Religious Persecution: A Campaign of Ethnocide against Chin Christians in Burma*. Ottawa: CHRO.

Chit Hlaing, F. K. L. 2004a. 'On the "globality hypothesis" about social/cultural structure: An algebraic solution'. Paper for the Mathematical Anthropology Panel, chaired by Dwigth Read (UCLA) and M. Fischer (University of Kent at Canterbury), at the 2004 European Meetings on Cybernetic Systems Research (EMCSR) at Vienna.

—— 2004b. 'Cultural models, schemata, and generative knowledge domains: How are they related?' Paper for a Conference on Cultural Models. DeKalb: Northern Illinois University.

Christie, Clive J. 1996. *A Modern Histiry of Southeast Asia: Decolonization, Nationalism and Separatism*. Singapore: Institute of Southeast Asian Studies.

Cit Phumisak 1992. *Tai-zoku no Rekishi* [History of the Tais, Khwam Pen Khong Kham Sayam Thai Lao Le Khom Le Laksana Thaung Sangkhom Chu Chonchat], Tokyo: Keiso-Shobou. (In Japanese).

Cohen, A. P. 2000. 'Introduction'. In A. P. Cohen (ed.), *Signifying Identities. Anthropological Perspectives on Boundaries and Contested Values.* London: Routledge.

Comaroff, Jean and John Comaroff 1992. 'Of totemism and ethnicity'. In J.and J. Comaroff: *Ethnography and the Historical Imagination.* Boulder: Westview Press.

Connor, Walker 1978. 'A nation is a nation, is a state, is an ethnic group, is a...', *Ethnic and Racial Studies*, Vol. 1, No. 4.

Cooper, T. T 1978. 'Entry of missionaries into the Kahkyen Hills'. Oriental and India Office Collection, British Library [OIOC] L/PS/7/18.

Cross, E.B. 1854. 'The Karens', *Journal of the American Oriental Society* Vol. 4: pp. 291–315.

Curach, Liz 2002. 'From riches to rags: an examination of library provision in Burma'. Paper delivered at Burma-Myanma(r) Research and its Future: Implications for Scholars and Policymakers, Gothenburg University, 21–25 September, 2002.

Daniel, E. V. and Knudsen J. C.. 1995. 'Introduction.' In E. V. Daniel and J. C.Knudsen (eds), *Mistrusting Refugees.* Berkeley: University of California Press.

De Vos, G. A. 1995. 'Ethnic pluralism: conflict and accommodation. The role of ethnicity in social history.' In L. Romanucci-Ross and G. A. De Vos (eds), *Ethnic Identity: Creation, Conflict, and Accommodation.* London: Sage.

Downs, Frederick 1992. *History of Christianity in India: North East India in the Nineteenth and Twentieth Centuries*, Vol. V, Part 5. Bangalore: The Church History Association of India.

—— 1994. *Essays on Christianity in North-East India.* New Delhi: Indus Publishing Co.

Dudley, S. 1997. 'Recent arrivals in Karenni Camp 2. An ethnographic report.' Unpublished report for the International Rescue Committee, Mae Hong Son, Thailand.

—— 1999. '"Traditional" culture and refugee welfare in north-west Thailand.' *Forced Migration Review*, Vol. 6, pp. 5–8.

—— 2000. Displacement and identity: Karenni refugees in Thailand. Unpublished D.Phil. thesis, University of Oxford.

—— 2002. 'Diversity, identity and modernity in exile: "traditional" Karenni clothing', in A. and R. Blurton (eds), *Burma: Art and Archaeology.* London: British Museum Press

—— 2006. '"External" aspects of self-determination movements in Burma.' To be published in F. Stewart & V. Fitzgerald (eds), *Global and Local Economic and Cultural Aspects of Self-determination Movements*, Routledge, pp. 203–224.

—— Forthcoming. *Political Systems of Exiled Burma: Ethnicity, Culture and Nationalism amongst Karenni Refugees in Thailand.*

Elias, N. 1876. *Introductory Sketch of the History of the Shans in Upper Burma and Western Yunnan*, Calucutta: The Foreign Department Press.

Enriquez, Major C. M. (undated). 'Kachin Recruiting Lecture 1'. In *Races of Burma: A Note on the Races and Recruiting Areas of Burma* . Undated lecture notes, Green Centre Archive, Green Centre for World Art, Brighton Pavilion & Museums, p. 1.

—— (undated) 'Kachin Recruiting Lecture IV'. In *Races of Burma: A Note on the Races and Recruiting Areas of Burma.* undated lecture notes, Green Centre Archive, Green Centre for World Art, Brighton Pavilion & Museums, p. 35.

ENSCC 2002. 'The New Panglong Initiative: Re-Building the Union of Burma'. *Policy Papers*, The Ethnic Nationalities Solidarity and Cooperation Committee, Chiangmai: The UNLD Press. (Revised and expanded in 2004).

Eriksen, T. H. 1993. *Ethnicity and Nationalism: Anthropological Perspectives.* London: Pluto Press.

Evans, P. ,D. Rueschemeyer and T. Skocpol (eds) 1985. *Bringing the State Back In.* Cambridge University Press.

Falla, Jonathan 1991. *True Love and Bartholomew. Rebels on the Burmese Border.* Cambridge: Cambridge University Press.

Ferguson, James and Gupta Akhil 2002. 'Spatializing states: Toward an anthroplogy of neoliberal governmentality', *American Ethnologist* Vol. 29, No. 4, pp. 981– 1002.

Fink, Christina 2001. *Living in Silence: Burma Under Military Rule.* Zed Books.

Firth, Raymond 1996. *Religion: A Humanist Interpretation.* London: Routledge.

Fiskesjoe, Nils Magnus Geir 2000. 'The Fate of Sacrifice: The Making of Wa History'. Unpublished PhD dissertation, Chicago: University of Chicago.

Foley, William 2003. 'Texts and genre in fieldwork in literate and pre-literate societies'. Presentation made at workshop on endangered languages and language documentation, SOAS, University of London, 1 March 2003.

Friedman, Jonathan (ed.) 2002. *Globalization, the State, and Violence.* Walnut Creek: Altamira Press.

Frontier Areas Committee of Enquiry (FACE) 1947. *PART 1(REPORT), PART 2 (APPENDICES)*, Superintendent Government, Printing and Stationery, Burma.

Furnivall, John S. 1939. 'The Fashioning of Leviathan: The beginnings of British rule in Burma', *Journal of the Burma Research Society* Vol. XXIX, No. II ; Reprinted Occasional Paper, Department of Anthropology, Australian National University, 1991.

—— 1956 [1948]. *Colonial Policy and Practice. A Comparative Study of Burma and Netherlands India.* New York: New York University Press.

Gangte, T.S. 1993. *The Kukis of Manipur.* New Delhi: Gyan Publishing.

Geertz, Clifford 1963. 'The integrative revolution'. In C. Geertz (ed.) *Old Societies and New States: The Quest for Modernity in Asia and Africa.* New York: The Free Press.

Gellner, E. 1983. *Nations and Nationalism.* Oxford: Blackwell.

—— 1994. *Encounters with Nationalism.* Oxford: Blackwell.

Glazer, N. and Moynihan D. P. (eds)1975. *Ethnicity: Theory and Experience.* Cambridge, MA: Harvard University Press.

Gravers, Mikael 1996a. 'The Karen making of a nation'. In Tønnesson, Stein and Hans Antlöv (eds), *Asian Forms of the Nation.* Richmond: Curzon Press, pp. 237–269.

—— 1996b. 'Questioning authocracy in Burma. Buddhism between Traditionalism and modernism'. In David Westerlund (ed.), *Questioning the Secular State. The Worldwide Resurgence of Religion in Politics.* London: Hurst & Company, pp. 297–322.

—— 1999. *Nationalism as Political Paranoia in Burma. An Essay on the Historical Practice of Power.* Richmond: Curzon Press.

—— 2001a. 'God's army – The Karen twins, the invisible army and the media' *NIASnytt. Nordic Newsletter of Asian Studies*, No. 2, pp. 12–16.

—— 2001b. 'Karen notions of environment – space, place and power in a political landscape'. In Poulsen, Ebbe, F. Skov et al. (eds). *Forest in Culture – Culture in Forest. Perspectives from Northern Thailand.* Bangkok: Research Centre on Forests and People in Thailand. (Thai–Danish Research Project).

—— 2001c. 'Cosmology, prophets, and rebellion among the Buddhist Karen in Burma and Thailand'. *Moussons* Vol. 4 pp. 3–31,(Institut de Recerche sur le Sud-Est Asiatique, Université de Provence).

—— 2004a. 'Moving from the edge – Modernizing Karen traditions'. Paper prepared for the International Conference on the Impact of Globalization, Regionalism and Nationalism on Minority People in Southeast Asia, Chiang Mai, Thailand 15–17 November 2004, p. 35.

—— 2004b. 'Ethnic violence, reconciliation and Panglong visited'. For the Danish–Burma Committee: Seminar on Democracy, Constitution and Reconciliation, Chiangmai 23–28 May 2004. Chiangmai, pp. 7–19, 133–145.

Green, A. and R. Blurton (eds), *Burma: Art & Archaeology.* British Museum Press.

Green, J. H. 1934. 'The Tribes of Upper Burma north of 26° Degrees Latitude and their Classification'. Unpublished dissertation for Cambridge University. p. 254.

Grierson, G. A 1967. *Linguistic Survey of India, Vol. 111: Tibeto-Burman Family,* Part 111, (Calcutta: Government Printing, 1904). Reprinted Delhi: Motilal Banarsdass.

Grundy-Warr, Andy 1998. 'Turning the political map inside out: A view of mainland Southeast Asia' In Victor R. Savage, Lily Kong and Warwick Neville (eds), *The Naga Awakens: Growth and Change in Southeast Asia*. Singapore: Time Academics Press.

Guibernau, Montserrat 1999. *Nations Without States: Political Communities in the Global Age*. MA, USA: Polity Press in association with Blackwell Publishers Ltd.

Guillon, Emmanuel 1999. *The Mons: A Civilization in Southeast Asia*. The Siam Society. Bangkok.

Gupta, A. and J. Ferguson (eds) 1997. *Culture, Power, Place. Explorations in Critical Anthropology*. Durham: Duke University Press.

Handler, R. and J. Linnekin 1984. 'Tradition, genuine or spurious?' *Journal of American Folklore*, Vol. 97, pp. 273–90.

Hannay, Simon Fraser 1847. Sketch of the Singphos or the Kakhyens of Burma: the position of this tribe as regards Baumo, and the inland trade of the Valley of the Irrawaddy with Yunnan and their connection with the north-eastern frontier of Assam. Calcutta: Missionary Orphan Press, p. 3.

Hanson, O. 1954a. *Kachin*. Rangoon: Baptist Board of Publications.

—— 1954b. *Dictionary of the Kachin Language*. 2nd imprint. Rangoon: Baptist Board of Publications.

Harding Susan 1987. 'Convicted by the Holy Spirit: The rhetoric of fundamental Baptist conversion', *American Ethnologist*, Vol. 14, No. 1,167–188.

Harrell, Stevan 2001. *Ways of Being Ethnic in Southwest China*. Seattle: University of Washington Press.

Harriden, Jessica 2002. 'Making a name for themselves: Karen identity and the politicization of ethnicity in Burma', *The Journal of Burma Studies*, Vol. 7, pp. 84–144.

Hasegawa, Kiyoshi 1996. 'Jozabu-Bukkyo-Bunkaken ni okeru "Chiiki" to "Minzoku" no Seisei: Unnan-sho Tokko-Tai-zoku no Jirei kara [Making of a "Region" and an "Ethnic Group" in Therawada Buddhist Cultural Area: Cases of the Tai-Nue in the Dehong of Yunnan, China]' In Hayashi (ed.), *Inter-ethnic Relations in the Making of Mainland Southeast Asia*, pp. 79–107, Center for Southeast Asian Studies, Kyoto University. (In Japanese).

Hau, Vum Kho 1963. *Profile of Burma Frontier Man*. Bundung: Published by the author.

—— 2004. *Between Hills and Plains. Power and Practice in Socio-Religious Dynamics among the Karen*. Kyoto Area Studies on Asia. Center for Southeast Asian Studies, Kyoto University. Volume 7. Melbourne: Kyoto University Press and Trans Pacific Press.

Hefner, Robert W. (ed.) 1993. *Conversion to Christianity. Historical and Anthropological Perspectives on a Great Transformation*. Berkeley: University of California Press.

Herzfeld, Michael 2001. *Anthropology. Theoretical Practice in Culture and Society*. Oxford, Blackwell.

Hill, Ann Maxwell 2004. 'Provocative behavior: Agency and feuds in Southwestern China'. *American Anthropologist*, Vol. 106, No.4, pp. 675–686.

Hinton, Peter 1979. 'The Karen, millenarianism, and the politics of accomodation to lowland states' In: Keyes (ed.) *Ethnic Adaption and Identity: The Karen on the Thai Frontier with Burma*. Philadelphia: ISHI.

Hmannan Maha Yazawin Dawgyi (5th edition) 1993. vol.1. (in Bamar), Ministry of Information, Myanmar.

Ho Ts'ui-p'ing 1996a. 'The numerical force of the Jingpo Manau festival'. Paper presented to the 97th Annual Meeting of the American Anthropological Association, Philadelphia.

—— 1996b. 'The business of the Jingpo Manau'. Paper Presented at the Association for Asian Studies Annual Meeting, Honolulu, Hawai'i.

—— 2004. 'Rethinking Kachin wealth ownership'. Paper for the EUROSEAS panel on Reconsidering Political Systems of Highland Burma. A Study of Kachin Social Structure-Comparative approaches 50 years on from Leach. EUROSEAS Conference, Paris, Sorbonne.

Hobsbawm, Eric 1983. 'Introduction: Inventing Traditions', in Hobsbawm, E. and T. Ranger (eds), *The Invention of Tradition*, Cambridge University Press, pp. 1–14.

—— 1990. *Nations and Nationalism since 1780: Programme, Myth, reality*. 2nd ed. Cambridge University Press.

Horowitz, D. L. 1985. *Ethnic Groups in Conflict*. Berkeley: University of California Press.

Houtman, Gustaaf 1999a. *Mental Culture in Burmese Crisis politics: Aung San Suu Kyi and the National League for Democracy*. Monograph 33, Institute for the Study of Languages and Cultures of Asia and Africa, Tokyo University of Foreign Studies.

—— 1999b. 'Remaking Myanmar and human origins'. *Anthropology Today*, Vol. 15, No. 4, pp. 13–19.

Hup, Cung Lian 1993. *Innocent Pioneers and Their Triumphs in a Foreign Land*. Chicago: Lutheran School of Theology.

HURFOM (Human Rights Foundation of Monland), 2003. *No Land to Farm: A Comprehensive Report on Land, Real Estate and Properties Confiscation in Mon's Area, Burma (1998–2003)* (October).

Hutchinson J. and Smith, A. D. 1996. *Ethnicity*. Oxford and New York: Oxford University Press.

Hutton, E. H. 1921. *The Angami Nagas*. London: Macmillian.

Images of Asia 1996. *'No Childhood at all'. Report on Child Soldiers in Burma*. Chiangmai.

Immigration and Manpower Department 1986. *1983 Population Census*, Rangoon: Ministry of Home and Religious Affairs, Socialist Republic of the Union of Burma.

International Crisis Group 2000. Burma/Myanmar: How strong is the military regime? *ICG Asia Report 11*; December 2000.

Ja Li, Pungga 1995. 'Bandu La (sh) Dumdu La', *Hparat Ninghkawng Meggazin.* Yangon, pp. 61—64.

Jenkins, Richard 1994. 'Rethinking ethnicity: Identity, categorization and power' *Ethnic and Racial Studies*, Vol. 17, No. 2.

—— 1996. 'Ethnicity *etcetera*: social anthropological points of view.' *Ethnic and Racial Studies*, Vol.19, No. 4, pp. 807–822.

—— 2000. 'Categorization: Identity, Social Process and Epistemeology.' *Current Sociology*, Vol. 48, No. 3, pp. 7–25.

Jin Liyan 1995. 'Leaf-letters and straw-bridges' In *The JingPos, Women's Culture Series: Nationalities in Yunnan.* Compiled by Yunnan Publicity Centre for Foreign Countries, Kunming, China: Yunnan Education Publishing House.

Johnson, Robert 1988. *History of American Baptist Chin Mission,* Vol. 1–2. Valley Forge: Published by the author.

Kammere, Cornelia Ann 1986. 'Gateway to the Akha World'. Unpublished PhD dissertation. University of Chicago.

Kapferer, Bruce 1988. *Legends of People, Myth of State.* Washington DC: Smithsonian Institution Press.

Karen Women's Organization 2004. 'Shattering silences. Karen women speak out about the Burmese military regime's use of rape as a strategy of war in Karen State'. Mae Sot: KNU.

Karenni Government. N.d. 'Karenni seek justice and legitimacy.' Unpublished policy document.

—— 1996. 'Forced relocation in Karenni.' Press Release. 24 July 1996.

Keyes, Charles F. (ed.) 1979 *Ethnic Adaption and Identity: The Karen on the Thai Frontier with Burma.* Philadelphia: Institute for the Study of Human Issues (ISHI).

Khä Sën 1996. *Pün Khä Tai lë Pün Möng Tai* [House of Tai race and origin of Tai State]. (In Shan).

Kipgen, Mangkhosat 1996. *Christianity and Mizo Culture,* (Jorhat, Assam and Aizawl: Mizo Theological Conference.

Kleinman, Arthur, Veena Das and Margaret Lock (eds) 1997: *Social Suffering.* Berkeley; University of California Press.

KNU (Karen National Union) 1992. *The Karens and their Struggle for Freedom.* Kawthoolei.

—— 1998. *History of the Karens and KNU.* www.karen org./knu/KNU-His.htm

Korom, F. J. (ed.). 1997. *Tibetan Culture in the Diaspora.* Vienna: Verlag der Österreichischen Akademie der Wissenschaften.

KRNRC (Karenni Resistant National Revolutionary Council).1974/1997. *Inde-*

pendence and Self-Determination of the Karenni States. Place unknown: KRNRC. Re-published Mae Hong Son, Thailand: Karenni Government.

Kyaw Zwa Moe 2005. 'Farewell to the "liberated Aaea".' The Irrawaddy On-Line Edition, February 2005, www.irrawaddy.org

Lacrampe, M. and Plaisant, M. 1849. 'Les Karian du Pegu'. *Nouvelle Annales de Voyages*, Vol. CXII, Paris, pp. 170–185.

La Raw, Maran 1967. 'Towards a basis for understanding the minorities in Burma: the Kachin example'. In Peter Kunstadter (ed.) *Southeast Asian Tribes, Minorities and Nations*. Princeton:

Lang, Hazel 2002. *Fear and Sanctuary: Burmese Refugees in Thailand*. Cornell Southeast Asia Program, Ithaca.

Leach, E. R. 1954. *Political Systems of Highland Burma*. Cambridge, MA: Harvard University Press.

—— 1960. 'The frontiers of "Burma"', *Comparative Studies in History and Societies*, Vol. 3, pp. 49–73.

Lebar Frank M. et al. 1964. *Ethnic Groups of Mainland Southeast Asia*, HRAF Press.

Lehman, F. K. 1963. *The Structure of Chin Society*. Urbana: University of Illinois Press.

—— 1967a. 'Ethnic categories in Burma and the theory of social systems'. In: P. Kunstadter (ed.). *Southeast Asian Tribes, Minorities and Nations*. Vol. 1. Princeton: Princeton University Press.

—— 1967b. 'Kayah society as a function of the Shah-Burma-Karen context'. In J. H. Steward (ed.). *Contemporary Change in Traditional Societies*.Vol. 1. Urbana: University of Illinois Press.

—— 1975. 'Formal approaches to ethnicity'. In R. L. Merrit and S. J. Brzensinski (eds), *Comparative International Studies*. Urbana: Department of Political Science, University of Illinois.

—— 1979. 'Who are the Karen, and if so, why?' In: Charles F. Keyes (ed.) *Ethnic Adaption and Identity: The Karen on the Thai Frontier with Burma*. Philadelphia: ISHI.

Lewis, James Lee 1924. 'The Burmanization of the Karen People: A Study in Racial Adaptability', University of Chicago, Ph.D. dissertation, n.p.

Lieberman, Victor 1978. 'Ethnic Politics in Nineteenth Century Burma'. In *Modern Asian Studies* Vol. 12, No. 3, pp. 455–82.

—— 1984. *Burmese Administrative Cycles*. Princeton: Princeton University Press.

Lintner, Bertil 1997. *The Kachin: Lords of Burmas Nothern Frontier*. Chiang Mai: Teak House publication.

Litzinger, Ralph A. 2000. *Other Chinas: The Yao and the Politics of National Belonging*. Durham and London: Duke University Press.

Liu Xiaoxing 1998. 'Change and Continuity of Yi Medical Culture in Southwest China'. Unpublished PhD dissertation. Urbana: University of Illinois at Urbana Champaign.

Low, James 1850. 'The Karean tribes or aborigines of Martaban and Tavoy'. *Journal of the Indian Achipelago and Eastern Asia*, Vol. 4.

Luce, G. H. 1959. 'Old Kyaukse and the coming of the Burmans', *Journal of The Burma Research Society*, Vol. XLII, June.

Malkki, L. H. 1995. *Purity and Exile. Violence, Memory, and National Cosmology among Hutu Refugees in Tanzania.* Chicago: University of Chicago Press.

Marlowe, David H. 1979. 'In the Mposaic: The cognitive and structural aspects of Karen–other relationships'. In Keyes (ed.) *Ethnic Adaption and Identity: The Karen on the Thai Frontier with Burma.* Philadelphia: ISHI.

Marshall, Harry I. 1922. *The Karen People of Burma.* Columbus: Ohio State University Press.

Mason, Ellen B. 1862. *Civilizing Mountain Men.* London: James Nisbet & Co.

Mason, Francis. 1860. *Burmah. Its People and Natural Productions, or Notes on the Nations' Fauna, Flora, and Minerals.* Rangoon: Thos. S. Ranney.

—— 1884. *The Karen Apostle or Memoir of Ko Thah Byu*, the First Karen Convert, with Notices Concerning His Nation. Bassein, Burma: Sgau Karen Press.

Matisoff, James A. 2003 *Handbook of Proto-Burman. System and Philosophy of Sino-Tibetan Reconstruction.* Berkeley: University of California Press.

Maung Aung Myoe 1999 'Military doctrine and strategy in Myanmar: A historical perspective' ANU Strategic and Defense Studies Center, Working Paper 339.

—— 1998. 'The organisational development of the Burmese army'. ANU Stratetic and Defense Studies Center, Working Paper 327.

Maung Maung, U 1980. *From Sangha to Laity.Nationalist Movements of Burma 1920–1948.* ANU Monographs on South Asia no. 4. New Delhi: Manohar Publications.

—— 1989. *Burmese Nationalist Movements 1940–1948.* Edinburgh: Kiscadale.

McKay, J. 1982. 'An exploratory synthesis of primordial and mobilizationist approaches to ethnic phenomena', In *Ethnic and Racial Studies*, Vol. 5, No. 4, October, p. 396.

Mclean, Ian (ed.) 1996. *The Concise Oxford Dictinary of Politics.* Oxford University Press.

McMahon, A.R., 1876. *The Karens of the Golden Chersonese.* London: Harrison.

Mi Mi Lwin 1992 'Koloni Hkit Shanpyi Outchotyei Thamaing' [History of administration of Shan States in the colonial period] (1923–1937), M.A.Thesis, University of Yangon, n.p. (In Burmese).

Miller, D. 1995. 'Introduction: anthropology, modernity and consumption.' In D. Miller (ed.), *Worlds Apart: Modernity through the Prism of the Local.* London: Routledge.

Ministry of Home and Religious Affairs 1987. *Kachin State 1983 Population Census*, Rangoon: Ministry of Home and Religious Affairs, Socialist Republic of the Union of Burma.

Mon National Education Committee 2002. 'Statistics of schools and teachers (2002–03).

Morrison, Ian 1947. *Grandfather Longlegs. The Life and the Galant Death of Major H.P. Seagrim.* London: Faber & Faber.

Muir, Richard 1997. *Political Geography: A New Introduction.* London: Macmillan Press.

Naw Mong 1997. 'Looking back at the past', *Golden Jubilee Shan State Magazine*, edited by Taunggyi Association, Yangon, pp. 168–173.

New Mon State Party. 'Fundamental political policy and fundamental constitution of administration'. Department of Party Procedure 15 December 1994; unofficial translation from Mon language document.

—— 1967. 'NBC News interview' (Reprinted Mon National University 1985).

—— 2002. 'Mon Revolution Day statement'.

Newland, Arthur George Edward 1894. *The Image of War: Service on the Chin Hills.* Calcutta: Thacker & Sprink.

Newman, David 2003. 'Boundary geopolitics: Towards a theory of territorial lines?' In Eiki Berg and Henk van Houtum (eds), *Routing Borders Between Territories, Discourse and Practices.* Aldershot: Ashgate..

Newman, David and Anssi Paasi 1998. 'Fences and neighbours in the postmodern world: Boundary narratives in political geography', *Progress in Human Geography*, Vol. 22, No. 2.

Oh Yoon Ah 2002. 'State, Christian Church and generation gap in ethnic identity formation: A case study of Insein Karen community.' Paper presented at the Burma Studies Conference on Burma-Myanmar Research and its Future in Gothenburg, Sweden, 21–25 September 2002.

Østergaard-Nielsen, E. K. 2001. 'The politics of migrants' transnational political practices.' Paper presented at Transnational Migration: Comparative Perspectives conference, Princeton University, July. http://www.transcomm. ox.ac.uk/working%20papers/Levitt.pdf

Paasi, Anssi 1996. *Boundaries and Consciousness: The Changing Geographies of the Finnish–Russian Border.* Chichester: John Wiley.

Parry, N. E. 1932. *The Lakher.* Calcutta. Reprinted in Aizawl: Tribal Research Institute, 1976.

Pedersen, M, E. Rudland and R. May (eds) 2000. *Burma-Myanmar: Strong Regime, Weak state?Adelaide:* Crawford house Publishing

Phayre, Arthur 1967. *History of Burma,* (London: Trubner, 1883). Reprinted New York: Augustus M. Kelly.

—— 1959. 'Relationship with Burma, Part I. Burmese invasions of Siam', Translated from the Hmannan Yazawin Dawgyi, *The Siam Society Journal*, Vol. V. Bangkok: The Siam Society.

Pigou, Piers 2001. Interviews with SPDC, NLD & ALD. *Burma Debate* Vol. 8, Nos. 2 and 3:19—25.

Pum Suan Pau 1998. *Growth of Baptist Churches in Chin State: The Chins for Christ in One Century Experience.* Manila: Union Theological Seminar.

Raja, Ananda 1990. 'Ethnicity, nationalism, and the nation-state: The Karen in Burma and Thailand'. In Gehan Wijeyewardene (ed.): *Ethnic Groups across National Boundaries in Mainland Southeast Asia.* Singapore: ISEAS. pp. 102–133.

Reid, S. 1983. *Chin-Lushai Land* (Calcutta: Government Printing 1893). Reprinted Aizawl: Tribal Society.

Renard, Ronald D. 1987. 'Minorities in Burmese history', *Sojourn* Vol. 2, No.2, pp. 255–271.

Renard, Ronald D. 1997 'For the fair name of Myanmar: They are being blotted out of Burma's history'. In John J. Brandon, (ed.) *Burma/Myanmar in the Twenty-First Century: Dynamics of Continuity and Change.* Bangkok: Open Society Institute, pp. 169–206.

Ringmar, Eric 1996. *Identity, Interest and Action: A Cultural Explanation of Sweden's Intervention in the Thirty Years War.* Cambridge: Cambridge University Press.

Rotberg, R.I. (ed.) 1998. *Burma: Prospects For a Democratic Future.*World Peace Foundation and Harvard Institute for International Development. Washington D.C.: Brookings Institution Press.

Rothermund, Dietmar 1997. 'Nationalism and the reconstruction of traditions in Asia'. In Sri Kuhnt-Saptodewo et al. (eds) *Nationalism and Cultural Revival In Southeast Asia: Perspectives from the Center and the Region.* Wiesbaden: Harrassowitz Verlag, pp. 13–28.

Rujaya Abhakorn, M. R. 2000. 'The fabrication of ethnicity and colonial polity east of the Thanlwin'.In *Myanmar Two Millennia* Vol. 4, pp. 186–200, Universities Historical Research Centre, Myanmar.

Sachensroder, W and U. Frings 1998. *Political Party Systems and Democratic Development in East and Southeast Asia; Volume 1; Southeast Asia.* Aldenshot: Ashgate.

Sack, Robert 1986. *Human Territoriality: Its Theory and History.* UK, USA, Australia: Cambridge University Press.

Sadan, Mandy. 2000. 'The Kachin photographs in the J. H. Green collection: a Contemporary Context'. In *Burma Frontier Photographs*, E. Dell (ed.) Merrell.

—— 2002a. 'The Kachin Manau and Manau Shadung: the development of an ethno-cultural symbol'. In Alexandra Green and T. Richard Blurton (eds): *Burma Art & Archaeology.* London: British Museum Press.

—— 2002b. 'Environmental imagination and the emergence of 'Kachin' in early 19th century colonial archives'. Paper delivered at Burma-Myanma(r) Research and its Future: Implications for Scholars and Policymakers, Gothenburg University, 21–25 September.

—— 2003 'Kachin textile contexts' In E. Dell & S. Dudley *Textiles from Burma*, London: Philip Wilson Publishers.

—— 2004. 'Reconsidering political systems of Highland Burma. A study of Kachin social structure–comparative approaches 50 years on from Leach'. EUROSEAS Conference, Paris, Sorbonne.

—— Forthcoming. 'History and ethnicity: Cultural contexts of the category Kachin in the colonial and postcolonial state, 1824–2004'. PhD thesis in the History Department, SOAS, London University.

—— Forthcoming b 'Kachin regeneration scheme'. Report of Proceedings of a conference held in Maymyo on 23, 25 and 26 October 2004.

Sai Kham Mong 2001. 'Buddhism and the Shans',*Myanmar Historical Research Journal*, Vol. 7, pp. 27–39, Universities Historical Research Centre.

Saimong Mangrai, Sao 1965. The Shan States and the British annexation, Data Paper No. 57, Ithaca: Cornell University.

Sakhong, Lian H. 2001. 'A two-fold path. The transition to federalism in Burma.' *Burma Debate* Vol. 8, Nos. 2 and 3, pp. 26–30.

—— 2000a. *Religion and Politics among the Chin People in Burma, 1896–1949.* (PhD dissertation). Uppsala University: *Studia Missionalia Upsaliensia LXXX.*

—— 2003. *In Search of Chin Identity: A Study in Religion, Politics and Ethnic Identity in Burma.* Copenhagen: Nordic Institute of Asian Studies.

Sakhong, Pu 1971. 'Kan Pupa Thawhkehnak Kong'. Aibur: Manuscript.

Sakhong, Za Peng 1983. 'Lai History'. M.A. thesis: Mandalay University.

Sahlins, Marshall 1985. *Islands of History.* Chicago: The University of Chicago Press.

San Aung 1973. *Nyinyutyei Ayeidawpon* [Unity revolution], Ministry of Information. Yangon (In Burmese).

San C. Po 1928. *Burma and the Karens.* London: Elliot Stock.

San Shwe 1992. 'Konbaung Hkit Hnaung Shan Myanmar Hsethsanyei' [Shan-Bamar Relationship in the Late period of the Konbaung Dynasty] (1819–1885), M.A.Thesis, University of Yangon, n.p. (In Burmese).

Sangermano, Father Vincenzo 1995. *The Burmese Empire* (Westminster: Archibald and Co., 1833). Reprinted, Bangkok: White Orchid Press.

Sao King Tung 1954. *Khü Tai – Möng Tai* [Tai race–Tai state]). (In Shan).

Sar Desai, D.R. 1994. *Southeast Asia: Past and Present*, 3rd edition. Boulder: Westview Press.

Saw Doh Say 1990. *A Brief History and Development Factors of the Karen Baptist Church of Burma (Myanma).* Ann Arbor: University Microfilm International.

Saw Hanson Tadaw 1961. 'The Karens of Burma: A study in human Geography'. In G.A. Theodorson (ed.), *Studies in Human Ecology.* New York, pp. 496–506.

Saw Kwe Htoo, Naw May Oo,Saw Htoo Htoo Lay, Brigd. Matu Say Poe 2004. 'From political aspiration to national consensus: The need for a national consultative conference in the Karen context'. www. karen.org/news2/messages.

Schmidt, Bettina E. and Ingo W. Schröder (eds) 2001. *Anthropology of Violence and Conflict*. London, Routledge.

Scott, James 2002. 'Hill and valley in Southeast Asia or why civilizations can't climb hills'. Key Note Address at the Conference Burma Research and its Future, Gothenburg, Sweden 21–25 September 2002, p. 13.

Scott, J. G. and Hardiman , J. P. (comp.) 1900–1901. *Gazetteers of Upper Burma and Shan States* (GUBSS), 5 vols, Rangoon, Superintendent Government. Printing, Burma.

Scribner, Sylvia and Cole, Michael 1999. *The Psychology of Literacy*. Harvard University Press.

Selth, Andrew 1999. 'The Burmese armed forces next century: Continuity or change?' Canberra: ANU Strategic and Defence Studies Centre, Working paper 338.

Shakespeare, J. 1912. *The Lushai Kuki Clan.* London: Macmillan & Co.

Shan Human Right Foundation and Shan Womens's Action Network 2002. 'Licence to rape. The Burmese military regime's use of sexual violence in the ongoing war in Shan State'. Chiang Mai: The Shan Human Rights Foundation and The Shan Women's Action Network.

Shan Pyine Yinkheihmu Sazaung (SPYS) [Periodical of culture in Shan State], 1966, Taunggyi. (In Bamar and Shan).

Shintani, Tadahiko and Caw Caay Hän Maü 2000. *Shan (Tay) go Oninron to Moji ho* [Phonemics and writing system of Shan (Tay) Language], ILCAA, Tokyo University of Foreign Studies. (In Japanese).

Shorto, H.L. 1967. 'The Dewatau Sotapan: A Mon prototype of the 37 Nats'. *Bulletin of the School of Oriental and African Studies*, Vol. 30, No.1, pp. 127–141.

Silverstein, Josef 1980. *Burmese politics. The Dilemma of National Unity*, New Brunswick: Rutger University Press.

—— 1987. 'Ethnic protest in Burma: Its clauses and solutions.' In Rajeshwari Ghose (ed.): *Protest Movements in South and South-East Asia. Traditional and Modern Idioms of Expression.* Centre of Asian Studies, University of Hongkong, pp. 81–94.

—— 1993 *The Political Legacy of Aung San.* Revised Edition. Ithaca: Southeast Asian Program, Cornell University.

—— 1997. 'Fifty years of failure in Burma'. In Michael Brown and Sumit Ganguly (eds). *Government Policies and Ethnic Relations in Asia and the Pacific. CSIA Studies in International Security.* Cambridge, MA; The MIT Press, pp. 167–196.

Singer, Noel 1995. *Old Rangoon.* Gartmore: Kiscadale.

Smeaton, Donald M. 1887. *The Loyal Karens of Burma*. London: Kegan Paul, Trech & Co.

Smith, A. D. 1986. *The Ethnic Origins of Nations*. Oxford, UK: Basil Blackwell Ltd.

—— 1991. *National Identity*. Harmondsworth: Penguin Books.

—— 1994. 'Ethnic nationalism and the plight of minorities', *Journal of Refugee Studies*. Vol. 7, Nos. 2–3, pp. 186–198.

Smith, Alan 1997. 'Ethnic conflict and federalism. The case of Burma'. In Günther Bächler (ed.); *Federalism against Ethnicity? Institutional, Legal and Democratic Instruments to Prevent Violent Minority Conflicts*. Zürich, Verlag Rüegger, pp. 231–259.

Smith, Linda Tuhiwai 2001. *Decolonizing Methodologies – Research and Indigenous Peoples*, 3rd edn. London and New York: Zed Books.

Smith, Martin. 1991. *Insurgency and the Politics of Ethnicity*. London: Zed books.

—— 1994. *Ethnic Groups in Burma. Development, Democracy and Human Rights. Report by Anti-Slavery International*. London.

—— 1999. *Burma: Insurgency and the politics of Ethnicity*. Dhaka: The University Press; Bangkok: White Lotus; London, New York: Zed Books Ltd.

—— 2001. 'Burmese politics after 1988: an era of new and uncertain change.' In R. H. Taylor (ed.), *Burma: Political Economy under Military Rule*. London: C. Hurst & Co.

—— 2002. *Burma (Myanmar): The Time for Change*. London: Minority Rights Group.

Smith, William Robertson 1996. "Sacrifice: Preliminary survey" in *Lectures on the Religion of the Semites: The Fundamental Institutions* (2d ed.; London: Black, 1894). Reprinted in C. E. Carter and C. L. Meyers (eds), *Community, Identity, and Ideology: Social Science Approaches to the Hebrew Bible*. Winona Lake, Indiana: Eisenbrauns.

Snodgrass, Major 1827. *The Burmese War, 1824–1826*. London: John Murray & Co.

Sökefeld, Martin 2001. 'Reconsidering ethnicity', *Anthropos*, Vol. 96, pp. 527–544.

Solnit, David 1997. *Eastern Kayah Li: Grammar, Texts, Glossary*. Honolulu: University of Hawai'i Press.

Soongul, Ro 2002. 'The genesis of ethnic category: British colonial expansion and ethnic categorisation in Burma'. ASEASUK conference paper.

South, Asley 2003. *Mon Nationalism and Civil War in Burma: The Golden Sheldrake*. London: Routledge Curzon.

—— 2004a. 'Political transition in Myanmar: A new model for democratisation' *Contemporary Southeast Asia*. Vol. 26, No. 2.

—— 2004b. 'Ceasefire group strategy: Beyond the national convention', *The Irrawaddy*, Vol.12. No. 8, pp. 16–17.

Spiro, Melford E. 1982. *Buddism and Society.* 2nd edition. Berkeley and Los Angeles: University of California Press.

Steinberg, David 1992. Myanmar 1991. 'Military Intransigence',In *Southeast Asian Affairs.* Singapore, ISEAS, the Institute of Southeast Asian Affairs, pp. 221–237.

—— 2001. 'Myanmar's minority conundrum. Issues of ethnicity and authority'. *Burma Debate*, Vol. VIII, Nos.2—3, pp. 31–35.

—— 2002a. *Burma: The State of Myanmar.* Georgetown University Press.

—— 2002b. 'Help is needed and should go ahead'. *International Herald Tribune*, 28 August.

Stern, Theodore 1968. 'Ariya and the Golden Book: A Millenarian Buddhist Sect among the Karen'. *Journal of Asian Studies*, Vol. 27, No. 2,pp. 297–328.

—— 1979. 'A People between: The Pwo Karen of Western Thailand'. In: Charles Keyes (ed.) *Ethnic Adaption and Identity: The Karen on the Thai Frontier with Burma.* Philadelphia: ISHI.

Stevenson, HCN 1945. 'The case for applied anthropology in reconstructing Burma'. *Man* Vol. xiv, No. 2, pp. 2–5.

Sundkler, Bengt 1980. *Bara Bukoba: Church and Community in Tanzania.* London: Hurst & Company.

Svensson, Palle 2004. 'Democratization and federalism'. The Danish–Burma Committee: Seminar on Democracy, Constitution and National Reconciliation, 23–28 May. Chiangmai, pp. 20–37, 146–157.

Takatani, Michio 1996. '"Shan" Sekai to sono Myakuraku' [Shan Pyi and Its Context]. In Y. Hayashi, (ed.) *Inter-ethnic Relations in the Making of Mainland Southeast Asia*, Center for Southeast Asian Studies, Kyoto University, pp. 12–29. (In Japanese).

—— 1998a. 'Shan no Yukue' [Who are the Shan ? An ethnological perspective], *Tonan Ajia Kenkyu* [Southeast Asian Studies], Center for Southeast Asian Studies, Kyoto University, Vol. 35 No. 4, pp. 38–56. (In Japanese).

—— 1998b 'An anthropological analysis of burmanization of the Shan', In Y. Hayashi (comp.) *Inter-Ethnic Relations in the Making of Mainland Southeast Asia* 1: pp. 115–130, Center for Southeast Asian Studies, Kyoto University, n.p.

—— 2003 'Shan Construction of Knowledge'. In *Texts and Contexts in Southeast Asia*, Universities Historical Research Centre, Myanmar, pp. 52–66.

Tambiah, S. J. 1989. 'Ethnic conflict in the world today', *American Ethnologist*, Vol.16, pp. 335–349.

—— 1996. *Leveling Crowds: Ethnonationalist Conflicts and Collective Violence in South Asia.* Berkeley: University of California Press.

Taylor, Peter J. 1995. 'Beyond containers: Internationality, interstatedness, interterritoriality', *Progress in Human* Geography, Vol. 19, No.1.

—— 1999. 'Places, spaces and Macy´s: Place-pace tensions in the political geography of modernities', *Progress in Human* Geography Vol. 23, No.1.

Taylor, Robert 1982. 'Perceptions of ethnicity in the politics of Burma', *Southeast Asian Journal of Social Science*, Vol. 10, No. 1.

—— 1987. *The State in Burma*. London: Hurst.

Tegenfeldt, Herman G. 1974. *A Century of Growth: The Kachin Baptist Church of Burma*. South Pasadena, California: William Carey Library

Than Tun 1990. 'The Royal Orders of Burma, A.D. 1598–1885', *Part Ten, Epilogue, Glossary and Index*, Center for Southeast Asian Studies, Kyoto University.

Thant Myint-U 2001. *The Making of Modern Burma*. Cambridge: Cambridge University Press.

Thant Sin, U 1935. *Tatiya-Thathana Pyu Sadan*, [Record of the third great Buddhist propagation and donation ceremony], Yadana Thiha Journal Press. (In Burmese).

Thein Lwin 2000. 'The teaching of ethnic language and the role of education in the context of Mon ethnic nationalism in Burma – Initial report of the first phase of the study on the Thai-Burma Border (November 1999 – February 2000)' (mss 3-3-2000).

Thongchai Winichakul 1995. *Siam Mapped: A History of the Geo-Body of a Nation*. Chaing Mai: Silkworm Books.

Thurgod, Graham and LaPolla, Randy J. (eds) 2003. *The Sino-Tibetan Languages*. London and NY: Routledge.

Tin, Pe Maung and G. H. Luce (translated) 1923. *The Glass Palace Chronicle of the Kings of Burma*. London: Oxford University Press.

Tinker, Hugh 1983–1984. *Burma. The Struggle for Independence 1944–1948*, 2 vols. London: Her Majesty's Stationery Office.

Toe Hla 1982. 'Hnit 200 kyaw ga Lashio Myo hnin Hnin 80 Pyi Lashio', *Shan Pyine Deitha Koleit Lashio 1980–81 Magazin*, Lashio: Lashio College, pp. 13–16. (In Bamar).

Tongchai Winichakul 1994. *Siam Mapped: A History of the Geo-body of a Nation*. Honolulu:University of Hawaii Press.

Tønnesson, Stein and Hans Antlöv (eds) *Asian Forms of the Nation*. Richmond, Surrey: Curzon Press.

Tosa, Keiko 2002. 'Analysis of the formation of Thathana Mye. Complementary relationship between pilgrims and residents of Thmamanya Taun.' Paper presented at the Burma Studies Conference on Burma–Myanmar Research and its Future in Gothenburg , Sweden, 21–25 September 2002.

Tun Thein 1999. *Mon Political History*. Mon Unity League, Bangkok 1999; (unofficial translation from the Burmese).

Turton, A. (ed.) 2000. *Civility and Savagery: Social identity in Tai States*. Richmond, Surrey: Curzon.

Tzang Yawnghwe, Chao 1987. *The Shan of Burma: Memories of a Shan Exile,* Singapore: Institute of Southeast Asian Studies.

Uk, Lian 1968. The Chin Customary Law of Inheritance and Succession as Practiced Among the Chins of Haka Area. Ll.B. thesis: Law Department of Rangoon University.

United Nations Commission on Human Rights 1998. *Special Briefing: The Human Rights Situation of Women in Burma.* Geneva.

University History Research Centre (Rangoon) 1999. *The 1947 Constitution and the Nationalities,* Vol 1. Yangon: Innwa Publishing House.

Van der Veer, Peter (ed.) 1996. *Conversion to Modernity. The Globalization of Christianity.* London: Routledge.

Van Driem, George 2001. *Languages of the Himalayas.* Leiden: Brill.

Vumson, Sunatak 1986. *Zo History.* Aizawl: Published by the Author.

Wang, Zhusheng 1997. *The Jingpo : Kachin of the Yunnan Plateau.* Tempe, Arizona: Program for Southeast Asian Studies.

White, Geoffrey M. 1995. *Identity Through History* Cambridge: Cambridge University Press.

Wilmsen, Edwin N. and Patrick McAllister (eds) 1996. *The Politics of Difference. Ethnic Premises in a World of Power.* Chicago: University of Chicago Press.

Wyatt,David K. 1984. *Thailand. A Short History.* New Haven: Yale University Press.

Yawnghwe, Chao Tzang 2004. 'State constitutions and the challenges facing the ethnic nationalities', *Ethnic Nationalities Journal (Burma)* Vol. 2, No.1, pp. 38–46.

Za Uk Ling, Salai and Salai Bawi Lian Mang (eds) 2004. *Religious Persecution. A Campaign of Ethnocide Against Chin Christians in Burma.* Ottawa:Chin Human Rights Organization.

Zawla, K. 1976. *Mizo Pi Pu te leh Anthlahte Chanchin* [History of the Mizo Forefathers and their Descendents].Aizawl: Mizoram.

Zhang, Wenyi 2004. 'The Circulatory Marriage: Kinship Systems of Jingpo in Jinzhuzhai', MA thesis, Peking University. Yunnan, China.

Zhao, Suisheng 2000. '"We are patriots first and democrats second": The rise of Chinese nationalism in the 1990s'. In Edward Friedman and Barrett McCormick (eds) *What if China Doesn't Democratize? Implications for War and Peace.* Armonk, New York: M.E. Sharpe/An East Gate Book.

Newspapers and Websites

Human Rights Foundation of Monland

The Mon Forum (monthly newsletter)

New Light of Myanmar

Times Online

The Sunday times

www.karen.org

www.myanmar.com/nlm/art/mar14.html

www.karen.org/knu/KNU_His.html

Documents

Oriental and India Office Collections (OIOC), British Library

    M/1/33 (Excluded Areas)

    M/4/2811 (Panglong)

    M/4/2854 (Frontier Area Commission Enquiry Report)

    M/4/2832 (Anthropology)

    L/Pj/6/264 (Pacification of Upper Burma, 1889)

    British Memorandum 1933, M/120.

    Karen's Political Future 1945–1947, M/4/3023.

INDEX